Citroën Owners Workshop Manual

by J H Haynes
Member of the Guild of Motoring Writers
and Bruce Gilmour

Models covered
All Citroën GS & GSA Saloon and Estate models, including special editions
1015 cc, 1129 cc, 1222 cc & 1299 cc

ISBN 1 85010 163 9

© Haynes Publishing Group 1977, 1980, 1983, 1986

All rights reserved. No part of this book may be reproduced or transmitted in any form or by
any means, electronic or mechanical, including photocopying, recording or by any information
storage or retrieval system, without permission in writing from the copyright holder.

Printed in England (290–6M4)

ABC

THE BOOK

Haynes Publishing Group
Sparkford Nr Yeovil
Somerset BA22 7JJ England

Haynes Publications, Inc
861 Lawrence Drive
Newbury Park
California 91320 USA

British Library Cataloguing in Publication Data
Gilmour, Bruce
Citroën GS & GSA owners workshop manual.
1. Citroën automobile
I. Title
629.28'722   TL215.C56
ISBN 1-85010-163-9

Acknowledgements

Thanks are due to Citroen Cars Ltd for the supply of technical information and the use of certain illustrations. Castrol Limited provided lubrication data, and the Champion Sparking Plug Company supplied the illustrations showing the various spark plug conditions. Sykes-Pickavant provided some of the workshop tools. Thanks are also due to all those people at Sparkford who helped in the production of this manual.

About this manual

Its aim

The aim of this manual is to help you get the best value from your car. It can do so in several ways. It can help you decide what work must be done (even should you choose to get it done by a garage), provide information on routine maintenance and servicing, and give a logical course of action and diagnosis when random faults occur. However, it is hoped that you will make full use of the manual by tackling the work yourself. On simpler jobs it may even be quicker than booking the car into a garage, and having to go there twice, to leave and collect it. Perhaps most important, a lot of money can be saved by avoiding the costs the garage must charge to cover its labour and overheads.

The manual has drawings and descriptions to show the function of the various components so that their layout can be understood. Then the tasks are described and photographed in a step-by-step sequence so that even a novice can do the work.

Its arrangement

The manual is divided into thirteen Chapters, each covering a logical sub-division of the vehicle. The Chapters are each divided into consecutively numbered Sections and the Sections into paragraphs (or sub-sections), with decimal numbers following on from the Section they are in, eg 5.1, 5.2, 5.3 etc.

It is freely illustrated, especially in those parts where there is a detailed sequence of operations to be carried out. There are two forms of illustration: figures and photographs. The figures are numbered in sequence with decimal numbers, according to their position in the Chapter: eg, Fig. 6.4 is the 4th drawing/illustration in Chapter 6. Photographs are numbered (either individually or in related groups) the same as the Section or sub-section of the text where the operation they show is described.

There is an alphabetical index at the back of the manual as well as a contents list at the front.

References to the 'left' or 'right' of the vehicle are in the sense of a person in a seat facing towards the front of the vehicle. Unless otherwise stated, nuts and bolts are removed by turning anti-clockwise, and tightened by turning clockwise.

Vehicle manufacturers continually make changes to specifications and recommendations, and these, when notified, are incorporated into our manuals at the earliest opportunity.

Whilst every care is taken to ensure that the information in this manual is correct no liability can be accepted by the authors or publishers for loss, damage or injury caused by any errors in, or omissions from, the information given.

Introduction to the Citroen GS and GSA

The Citroen GS was first introduced to the UK market in 1971 with the GS Confort model which was powered by a 1015 cc engine. Since then, additional models have been introduced and the engine size increased to 1130 cc (1977 to 1980), 1222 cc (1972 to 1980) and 1299 cc (from 1979 on).

The design gives maximum space and safety in conjunction with good appearance and smooth aerodynamics, always a feature of Citroen design.

From the outside it has the looks of a medium sized (rather than small) car.

A feature of the car is the use of the well established Citroen self-levelling hydro-pneumatic independent suspension system whereby the vehicle height adjustment control can be manually set through three positions according to ground clearance requirements, (normal, intermediate and maximum). The intermediate setting provides additional clearance when driving over poor roads or in snow whilst the maximum setting is primarily designed for wheel changing or for driving short distances over extremely difficult conditions.

Originally fitted with a four-speed manual gearbox as standard, some later models are fitted with a five-speed manual gearbox. A three-speed semi-automatic transmission is also available as an optional fitting.

Contents

Citroen GS Saloon

Citroen GS Estate

Quick reference data

Capacities and settings

Engine crankcase	... 4 litre (7 Imp pints) engine dry
Gearbox (manual):	
4-speed	... 1.4 litre (2.5 Imp pints)
5-speed	... 1.5 litre (2.6 Imp pints)
Gearbox (semi-automatic):	
Dry	... 4 litre (7 Imp pints) converter included
Oil change	... 1.4 litre (2.5 Imp pints)
Hydraulic reservoir	... 3.3 litre (5.8 Imp pints)
Spark plug gap	... 0.65 to 0.80 mm (0.026 to 0.032 in)
Contact breaker gap	... 0.35 to 0.45 mm (0.014 to 0.018 in)
Rocker clearance (cold)	... 0.20 mm (0.008 in)
Petrol tank	... 43 litres (9.75 Imp gall)
Tyre pressures:	
Front	... 1.8 kg/sq cm (26 psi)
Rear	... 1.9 kg/sq cm (28 psi)

Wheel alignment

Front	... 0 to 2 mm (0 to 0.8 in) toe-in
Rear:	
To September 1973	... 4 mm (0.16 in) toe-in to 4 mm toe-out
From September 1973	... 0 to 2 mm (0 to 0.08 in) toe-in

Vehicle height (normal driving position)

Saloon and Estate	... 1.349 m (53.1 in)

Voltage ... ... 12 volts

Dimensions

Overall length:	
Early models (Saloon and Estate)	... 4.120 m (13 ft 6¼ in)
Late model Saloons	... 4.195 m (13 ft 9¼ in)
Late model Estate	... 4.156 m (13 ft 7 5/8 in)
Overall width:	
Early models	... 1.608 m (5 ft 3¼ in)
Late models	... 1.626 m (5 ft 4 in)
Ground clearance (normal setting):	
Early models	... 146.6 mm (5.7 in)
Late models	... 154.0 mm (6 in)
Wheelbase	... 2550 mm (8 ft 4 3/8 in)
Track (front)	... 1378 mm (4 ft 6¼ in)
Track (rear)	... 1328 mm (4 ft 4 in)

Kerb weights

Saloons (early types):	
G Special	... 925 kg (2039 lb)
Club/Pallas	... 930 kg (2050 lb)
Semi-automatic variants	... 942 kg (2077 lb)
Saloons (late types):	
GSA Club/Pallas	... 920 kg (2028 lb)
Semi-automatic variants	... 940 kg (2072 lb)
Estates (early types):	
G Special	... 935 kg (2061 lb)
GS Club/Pallas	... 940 kg (2072 lb)
Semi-automatic variants	... 925 kg (2039 lb)
Estates (late types):	
GSA Club/Pallas	... 964 kg (2127 lb)
GSA Club Special	... 920 kg (2028 lb)
Semi-automatic variants	... 974 kg (2149 lb)

Buying spare parts and vehicle identification numbers

Buying spare parts

Spare parts are available from many sources, for example: Citroen garages, other garages and accessory shops, and motor factors. Our advice regarding spare parts is as follows:

Officially appointed Citroen garages - This is the best source of parts which are peculiar to your car and otherwise not generally available (eg, complete cylinder heads, internal gearbox components, badges, interior trim etc). It is also the only place at which you should buy parts if your car is still under warranty; non-Citroen parts may invalidate the warranty. To be sure of obtaining the correct parts it will always be necessary to give the storeman your car's engine and chassis number, and if possible, to take the old part along for positive identification. Many parts are available under a factory exchange scheme - and parts returned should always be clean. It obviously makes good sense to go straight to the specialists on your car for this type of part for they are best equipped to supply you.

Other garages and accessory shops   These are often very good places to buy material and components needed for the maintenance of your car (eg, oil filters, spark plugs, bulbs, fan belts, oils and grease, touch-up paint, filler paste etc). They also sell general accessories, usually have convenient opening hours, charge lower prices and can often be found not far from home.

Motor factors - Good factors stock all of the more important components which wear out relatively quickly (eg, clutch components, pistons and cylinders, valves, exhaust systems, brake pipes/seals and pads, etc). Motor factors will often provide new or reconditioned components on a part exchange basis - this can save a considerable amount of money.

Vehicle identification numbers

Modifications are a continuing and unpublished process in vehicle manufacture quite apart from major model changes. Spare parts manuals and lists are compiled upon a numerical basis, the individual vehicle numbers being essential to correct indentification of the component required.

There are considerable specification differences between the models covered by this manual. Always use the correct Citroen model number when describing your car to a storeman.

The *vehicle manufacturer's plate* is located under the bonnet, on the right-hand side behind the L.H.M fluid reservoir. This plate has the following information on it:

Type of vehicle
Series
Chassis number
Gross vehicle weight (PTC)
Gross train weight (with trailer) (PTR)
The *engine plate*, just to the right of the oil filter cartridge, carries the make, engine type and engine number.

Manufacturer's plate

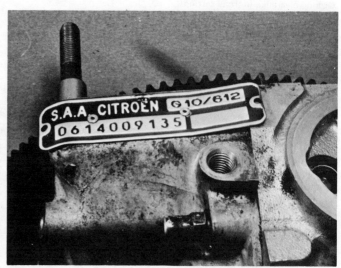

Engine plate location

Tools and working facilities

Introduction

A selection of good tools is a fundamental requirement for anyone contemplating the maintenance and repair of a motor vehicle. For the owner who does not possess any, their purchase will prove a considerable expense, offsetting some of the savings made by doing-it-yourself. However, provided that the tools purchased are of good quality, they will last for many years and prove an extremely worthwhile investment.

To help the average owner to decide which tools are needed to carry out the various tasks detailed in this manual, we have compiled three lists of tools under the following headings: Maintenance and minor repair, Repair and overhaul, and Special. The newcomer to practical mechanics should start off with the 'Maintenance and minor repair' tool kit and confine himself to the simpler jobs around the vehicle. Then, as his confidence and experience grows, he can undertake more difficult tasks, buying extra tools as, and when, they are needed. In this way, a 'Maintenance and minor repair' tool kit can be built-up into a 'Repair and overhaul' tool kit over a considerable period of time without any major cash outlays. The experienced do-it-yourselfer will have a tool kit good enough for most repair and overhaul procedures and will add tools from the 'Special' category when he feels the expense is justified by the amount of use these tools will be put to.

It is obviously not possible to cover the subject of tools fully here. For those who wish to learn more about tools and their use there is a book entitled 'How to Choose and Use Car Tools' available from the publishers of this manual.

Maintenance and minor repair tool kit

The tools given in this list should be considered as a minimum requirement if routine maintenance, servicing and minor repair operations are to be undertaken. We recommend the purchase of combination spanners (ring one end, open-ended the other); although more expensive than open-ended ones, they do give the advantages of both types of spanner.

Combination spanners - 8, 10, 11, 12, 13, 14, 16, 17, 19 mm
Adjustable spanner - 9 inch
Engine sump drain plug socket (21 mm)
Engine starter dog/fan securing nut socket (42 mm)
Gearbox drain and filler plug socket (21 mm)
Spark plug spanner (with rubber insert)
Spark plug gap adjustment tool
Set of feeler gauges
Brake adjuster spanner (where applicable)
Brake bleed nipple spanner
Screwdriver - 4 in. long x ¼ in. dia. (plain)
Screwdriver - 4 in. long x ¼ in. dia. (crosshead)
Combination pliers - 6 inch
Hacksaw, junior
Tyre pump
Tyre pressure gauge
Oil can
Fine emery cloth (1 sheet)
Wire brush (small)
Funnel (medium size)

Repair and overhaul tool kit

These tools are virtually essential for anyone undertaking any major repairs to a motor vehicle, and are additional to those given in the Basic list. Included in this list is a comprehensive set of sockets. Although these are expensive they will be found invaluable as they are so versatile - particularly if various drives are included in the set. We recommend the ½in. square-drive type, as this can be used with most proprietary torque wrenches. If you cannot afford a socket set, even bought piecemeal, then inexpensive tubular box spanners are a useful alternative.

The tools in this list will occasionally need to be supplemented by tools from the Special list.

Sockets (or box spanners) to cover range 6 to 27 mm
Reversible ratchet drive (for use with sockets)
Extension piece, 10 inch (for use with sockets)
Universal joint (for use with sockets)
Torque wrench (for use with sockets)
'Mole' wrench - 8 inch
Ball pein hammer
Soft-faced hammer, plastic or rubber
Screwdriver - 6 in. long x 5/16 in. dia. (plain)
Screwdriver - 2 in. long x 5/16 in. square (plain)
Screwdriver - 1½ in. long x ¼ in. dia. (crosshead)
Screwdriver - 3 in. long x 1/8 in. dia. (electricians)
Pliers - electricians side cutters
Pliers - needle nosed
Pliers - circlip (internal and external)
Cold chisel - ½ inch
Scriber (this can be made by grinding the end of a broken hacksaw blade)
Scraper (this can be made by flattening and sharpening one end of a piece of copper pipe)
Centre punch
Pin punch
Hacksaw
Valve grinding tool
Steel rule/straight edge
Allen keys
Selection of files
Wire brush (large)
Axle stands
Jack (strong scissor or hydraulic type)

Special tools

The tools in this list are those which are not used regularly, are expensive to buy, or which need to be used in accordance with their manufacturers instructions. Unless relatively difficult mechanical jobs are undertaken frequently, it will not be economic to buy many of these tools. Where this is the case, you could consider clubbing together with friends (or a motorists club) to make a joint purchase, or borrowing the tools against a deposit from a local garage or tool hire specialist.

The following list contains only those tools and instruments freely available to the public, and not those special tools produced by the vehicle manufacturer specifically for its dealer network. You will find occasional references to these manufacturers special tools in the text of this manual. Generally, an alternative method of doing the job without the vehicle manufacturers special is given. However, sometimes, there is no alternative to using them. Where this is the case and the relevant tool cannot be bought or borrowed you will have to entrust the work to a franchised garage.

Valve spring compressor
Piston ring compressor
Ball joint separator
Universal hub/bearing puller
Impact screwdriver
Micrometer and/or vernier gauge
Dial gauge
Stroboscopic timing light
Dwell angle meter/tachometer
Universal electrical multi-meter
Cylinder compression gauge
Lifting tackle
Trolley jack
Light with extension lead

Buying tools

For practically all tools, a tool factor is the best source since he will have a very comprehensive range compared with the average garage or accessory shop. Having said that, accessory shops often offer excellent quality tools at discount prices, so it pays to shop around.

Remember, you don't have to buy the most expensive items on the shelf, but it is always advisable to steer clear of the very cheap tools. There are plenty of good tools around, at reasonable prices, so ask the proprietor or manager of the shop for advice before making a purchase.

Care and maintenance of tools

Having purchased a reasonable tool kit, it is necessary to keep the tools in a clean and serviceable condition. After use, always wipe off any dirt, grease and metal particles using a clean, dry cloth, before putting the tools away. Never leave them lying around after they have been used. A simple tool rack on the garage or workshop wall, for items such as screwdrivers and pliers is a good idea. Store all normal spanners and sockets in a metal box. Any measuring instruments, gauges, meters, etc., must be carefully stored where they cannot be damaged or become rusty.

Take a little care when the tools are used. Hammer heads inevitably become marked and screwdrivers lose the keen edge on their blades from time-to-time. A little attention with emery cloth or a file will soon restore items like this to a good serviceable finish.

Working facilities

Not to be forgotten when discussing tools, is the workshop itself. If anything more than routine maintenance is to be carried out, some form of suitable working area becomes essential.

It is appreciated that many an owner mechanic is forced by circumstances to remove an engine or similar item, without the benefit of garage or workshop. Having done this, any repairs should always be done under the cover of a roof.

Wherever possible, any dismantling should be done on a clean flat workbench or table at a suitable working height.

Any workbench needs a vice: one with a jaw opening of 4 in. (100 mm) is suitable for most jobs. As mentioned previously, some clean dry storage space is also required for tools, as well as the lubricants, cleaning fluids, touch-up paints and so on which soon become necessary.

Another item which may be required, and which has a much more general usage, is an electric drill with a chuck capacity of at least 5/16 in. (8 mm). This, together with a good range of twist drills, is virtually essential for fitting accessories such as wing mirrors and reversing lights.

Last, but not least, always keep a supply of old newspapers and clean, lint-free rags available, and try to keep any working area as clean as possible.

Spanner jaw gap comparison table

Jaw gap (in)	Spanner size
0.250	$\frac{1}{4}$ in AF
0.276	7 mm
0.313	$\frac{5}{16}$ in AF
0.315	8 mm
0.344	$\frac{11}{32}$ in AF; $\frac{1}{8}$ in Whitworth
0.354	9 mm
0.375	$\frac{3}{8}$ in AF
0.394	10 mm
0.433	11 mm
0.438	$\frac{7}{16}$ in AF
0.445	$\frac{3}{16}$ in Whitworth; $\frac{1}{4}$ in BSF
0.472	12 mm
0.500	$\frac{1}{2}$ in AF
0.512	13 mm
0.525	$\frac{1}{4}$ in Whitworth; $\frac{5}{16}$ in BSF
0.551	14 mm
0.563	$\frac{9}{16}$ in AF
0.591	15 mm
0.600	$\frac{5}{16}$ in Whitworth; $\frac{3}{8}$ in BSF
0.625	$\frac{5}{8}$ in AF
0.630	16 mm
0.669	17 mm
0.686	$\frac{11}{16}$ in AF
0.709	18 mm
0.710	$\frac{3}{8}$ in Whitworth; $\frac{7}{16}$ in BSF
0.748	19 mm
0.750	$\frac{3}{4}$ in AF
0.813	$\frac{13}{16}$ in AF
0.820	$\frac{7}{16}$ in Whitworth; $\frac{1}{2}$ in BSF
0.827	21 mm AF
0.866	22 mm
0.875	$\frac{7}{8}$ in AF
0.920	$\frac{1}{2}$ in Whitworth; $\frac{9}{16}$ in BSF
0.938	$\frac{15}{16}$ in AF
0.945	24 mm
1.000	1 in AF
1.010	$\frac{9}{16}$ in Whitworth; $\frac{5}{8}$ in BSF
1.024	26 mm
1.063	$1\frac{1}{16}$ in AF; 27 mm
1.100	$\frac{5}{8}$ in Whitworth; $\frac{11}{16}$ in BSF
1.125	$1\frac{1}{8}$ in AF
1.181	30 mm
1.200	$\frac{11}{16}$ in Whitworth; $\frac{3}{4}$ in BSF
1.250	$1\frac{1}{4}$ in AF
1.260	32 mm
1.300	$\frac{3}{4}$ in Whitworth; $\frac{7}{8}$ in BSF
1.313	$1\frac{5}{16}$ in AF
1.390	$\frac{13}{16}$ in Whitworth; $\frac{15}{16}$ in BSF
1.417	36 mm
1.438	$1\frac{7}{16}$ in AF
1.480	$\frac{7}{8}$ in Whitworth; 1 in BSF
1.500	$1\frac{1}{2}$ in AF
1.575	40 mm; $\frac{15}{16}$ in Whitworth
1.614	41 mm
1.625	$1\frac{5}{8}$ in AF
1.654	42 mm AF
1.670	1 in Whitworth; $1\frac{1}{8}$ in BSF
1.688	$1\frac{11}{16}$ in AF
1.811	46 mm
1.813	$1\frac{13}{16}$ in AF
1.860	$1\frac{1}{8}$ in Whitworth; $1\frac{1}{4}$ in BSF
1.875	$1\frac{7}{8}$ in AF
1.969	50 mm
2.000	2 in AF
2.050	$1\frac{1}{4}$ in Whitworth; $1\frac{3}{8}$ in BSF
2.165	55 mm
2.362	60 mm

Recommended lubricants and fluids

Component or system	Lubricant type or specification
1 Engine oil	Multigrade engine oil, viscosity 15W/40, 15W/50 or 20W/50
2A Manual gearbox	Hypoid gear oil, viscosity 80W/90W
2B Semi-automatic gearbox	Total 'Fluid T'
3 Hydraulic system	LHM hydraulic fluid

These are general recommendations for a temperate climate. If in doubt consult a Citroen dealer, or refer to the owner's handbook supplied with the vehicle.

Routine maintenance

For modifications, and information applicable to later models, see Supplement at end of manual

Maintenance is essential for ensuring safety and desirable for the purpose of getting the best in terms of performance and economy from the car. Over the years the need for periodic lubrication has been greatly reduced if not totally eliminated. This has unfortunately tended to lead some owners to think that because no such action is required the items either no longer exist or will last forever. This is certainly not the case, it is essential to carry out regular visual examination as comprehensively as possible in order to spot any possible defects at an early stage before they develop into major and expensive repairs.

The maintenance information given in this Section is not of a detailed nature as the information required to carry out the necessary task is to be found in the appropriate Chapters throughout this manual.

Every 250 miles (400 km) or weekly - whichever comes first

Steering
Check the tyre pressures
Examine the tyres for wear or damage

Hydraulic system
Check the fluid level in the reservoir

Lights, wipers and horns
Do all the lights work at the front and rear?
Are the headlamp beams aligned properly?
Check the windscreen washer fluid level

Engine
Check the level of the oil, top-up if necessary
Check the level of the electrolyte in the battery and top-up the level as necessary

Every 3,000 miles (4,800 km)

Engine
Change the oil

Engine sump drain plug (arrowed)

Gearbox
Check the oil level and top-up if necessary

Doors, bonnet and boot lid
Lubricate hinges and locks

Handbrake
Check the operation and efficiency

Every 6,000 miles (10,000 km)

Engine
Clean the spark plugs and check the gap. Renew if necessary.
Renew the oil filter cartridge
Air filter cartridge - pre May 1980 models - clean and oil dip referring to Section 2 in Chapter 2
Check operation of carburettor choke
Clean the oil cooler fins
Drain and renew the engine oil

Alternator
Check belt tension
Check terminals for tightness

Clutch
Check free-movement, adjust if necessary.

Hydraulic system
Clean the filter. Check the system visually for leaks.

Car height
Check the operation of the manual control

Gearbox filler/level plug and drain plug (arrowed)

Brakes
 Check the pad thickness of the front and rear brakes
 Adjust the handbrake

Roadwheels
 Tighten the wheel nuts

Lights and accessories
 Check the operation of all front and rear lights including the indicators and brake lights
 Check condition of wiper blades and wiper/washer operation
 Check the horn(s) for satisfactory operation
 Check seat belts for condition and security at their anchorage points

---

Every 12,000 miles (20,000 km)

Engine
 Tighten the cylinder heads
 Adjust the rocker clearances (cold)
 Clean and adjust the carburettor
 Renew the in-line fuel filter
 Contact breaker - renew (where applicable)
 Check the ignition timing
 Check tightness of inlet manifold clamp (early 1015cc engines)
 Adjust the tension of the timing belts
 Clean the battery terminals and smear them with petroleum jelly

Suspension
 Lubricate the front and rear suspension ball joints
 Check and adjust the car heights

Steering
 Examine steering linkage for wear
 Check wheel alignment

Gearbox
 Change the oil
 Renew the oil strainer (automatic transmission)

Every 24,000 miles (40,000 km)

Hydraulic system
 Drain and refill with L.H.M fluid
 Check all unions for tightness
 Main accumulator - check the pressure rise

Engine
 Renew the timing belts

Other aspects of Routine Maintenance

1 *Cleaning:* The best way to examine a car and know its general condition, is to clean it thoroughly, inside and out. One of the main results of this, not covered by other maintenance operations, is the finding of any traces of rust in the body panels. If rust is allowed to go unchecked it could affect some panels which may make the car unsafe and keep it off the road.
2 *Exhaust systems:* Although no periodic maintenance is prescribed for the exhaust system it must be checked regularly. The system must be secure and leakproof to keep the noise level to the minimum. Leaks can result in dangerous fumes entering the car interior and affecting the driver and passengers with disastrous consequences. Faults in the exhaust system can result in the vehicle being declared unfit for use.
3 *Safety;* When jacking-up the car always select a suitable strong point, chock a wheel on the opposite side, in front and behind. Never work under a car supported by the jack only, use axle stands or other reliable supports. See Chapter 13 for further information.
 When towing the car use the two holes provided in the ends of the front frame crossmember. From the rear, do not attach hooks to the axle, but to the two holes provided on the bumper support, after opening the boot door.

Torque wrench settings

For modifications, and information applicable to later models, see Supplement at end of manual

Engine	lbf ft	kgf m
Crankshaft main bearing nuts	30	4.1
Crankcase mating nuts	11	1.5
Camshaft bearing nuts	13	1.8
Starting handle dog locknut	130	17.9
Camshaft sprocket nut	59	8.1
Anti-emulsion shield bolts	10	1.4
Engine mounting bolts to crankcase	40	5.5
Oilway plugs	28	3.9
Cylinder head nuts:		
First stage (all nuts)	6	0.8
Final stage (12 mm nuts)	12	1.6
Final stage (13 mm nuts)	16	2.2
Oil bypass valve plug in cooler	36	5.0
Cylinder head oil pipe union (banjo) hollow bolt	13	1.8
Flywheel bolts	50	6.9
Driveplate (auto trans) bolts to crankshaft	80	11.0
Driveplate bolts to torque converter	20	2.7
Oil temperature switch	18	2.5
Oil pressure switch	16	2.2
Oil cooler bolts	13	1.8
Engine oil drain plug	30	4.1
Carburettor mounting bolts	13	1.8
Oil pump nuts	13	1.8
Timing belt tensioner nuts	13	1.8
Oil strainer mounting screw	10	1.4
Rocker cover nuts	7	1.0
Rocker shaft end plugs	13	1.8
Exhaust flange nuts	11	1.5
Spark plugs	14 to 18	1.9 to 2.5

Clutch and manual gearbox

	lbf ft	kgf m
Clutch pressure plate cover bolts	13	1.8
Differential shaft nut	115	15.9
Speedometer drive nut on pinion shaft	86	11.9
Primary shaft bearing nut	62	8.6
Gearbox half casing bolts	11	1.5
Gearbox rear cover bolts	21	2.9
Clutch housing nuts	13	1.8
Differential shaft ring nuts	72	9.9
Reverse lamp switch	10	1.4
Rear flexible mounting bolts	29	4.0

Semi-automatic transmission

	lbf ft	kgf m
Oil strainer	11	1.5
Drain plug	33	4.6
Oil level plug	11	1.5
Filler plug	32	4.4
Speedometer drive nut to pinion shaft	86	11.9
Primary shaft bearing nut	62	8.6
Converter housing oil pump bolts	13	1.8
Pressure distributor mounting bolts	12	1.6
Rear cover bolts	20	2.7
Half casing bolts	11	1.5

Hydraulic system

	lbf ft	kgf m
Pipe union nuts:		
3.5 mm dia pipe	6	0.8
4.5 mm dia pipe	6	0.8
6.0 mm dia pipe	8	1.1
Pressure switch	9	1.2
Automatic control rod clamps	6	0.8
Anti-roll bar clamps	10	1.4

Front axle and suspension

	lbf ft	kgf m
Upper suspension arm pivot pin	46	6.4
Upper suspension arm castellated nut	22	3.0
Upper suspension arm balljoint	22	3.0
Lower suspension arm pivot pin	84	11.6
Lower suspension arm balljoint	22	3.0
Anti-roll bar connecting rod balljoints	22	3.0
Anti-roll bar connecting rod balljoints to upper suspension arms ...	22	3.0
Anti-roll bar bearing nuts	15	2.1
Anti-roll bar clamp bolt	8	1.1
Hub-to-driveshaft nut	275	38
Hub ring nut	350	48.4
Front axle unit mounting bolts (Fig. 7.11):		
Bolt No. 1	70	9.7
Bolt No. 2 (initial)	14	1.9
Bolt No. 2 (final)	35	4.8
Bolt No. 3	35	4.8
Bolt No. 4	35	4.8

Braking system

	lbf ft	kgf m
Caliper (old type) mounting bolts	35	4.8
Caliper (new type) mounting bolts	43	5.9
Caliper pipe unions	6	0.8
Rear caliper bolts	28	3.8
Control valve retaining bolts	12	1.6
Handbrake eccentric lock-screws	29	3.9
Handbrake cable adjuster locknuts	11	1.5

Steering and wheels

	lbf ft	kgf m
Track-rod end locknuts	28	3.8
Rack housing to front axle assembly	28	3.8
Rack end fitting	28	3.8
Pinion cover plate setscrews	10	1.4
Steering column clamp bolts	10	1.4
Universal joint clamp bolts	10	1.4
Track-rod end balljoint stud nut	14	1.9

Rear axle and suspension

	lbf ft	kgf m
Suspension arm retaining bolt	14	1.9
Hub ring nut	275	38
Hub end nut	275	38
Rear axle unit (subframe) mounting nuts	25	3.4

Chapter 1 Engine

For modifications, and information applicable to later models, see Supplement at end of manual

Contents

Specifications

Engine (general)

	1015cc	1222cc
Type		
Number of cylinders	4 (flat)	
Bore	74 mm	77 mm
Stroke	59 mm	65.6 mm
Cubic capacity	1015cc	1220cc
Maximum power (DIN)	55.5 hp at 6500 rpm	60 hp at 5750 rpm
Maximum torque	7.2 mkg (52 lb f ft) at 3500 rpm	8.9 mkg (64.4 lb f ft) at 3250 rpm
Maximum engine speed	6500 rpm	6250 rpm
Location of No. 1 cylinder	Left-hand - rear	
Firing order	1 - 4 - 3 - 2	

Camshafts

	1015cc	1222cc
Drive	Toothed belt	
Number of belt teeth:		
RH belt	91 teeth	93 teeth
LH belt	103 teeth	105 teeth
Endfloat	0.05 to 0.15 mm (not adjustable)	

Crankshaft and connecting rod assembly

	1015cc	1222cc
Endfloat of connecting rods	0.13 to 0.18 mm	
Bore of small-end bushes	$20.005 ^{+0.011}_{-0.006}$ mm	$22.005 ^{+0.011}_{-0.006}$ mm
Endfloat of crankshaft	0.09 to 0.20 mm (not adjustable)	
Number of crankshaft bearings	3	
Type of bearings	Split shell	
Diameter of bearings:		
No mark	57.5 mm	
Red mark	57.4 mm	

Crankcase

Type	Light alloy, split in two halves

Cylinder heads

Type	Light alloy, 1 to each pair of cylinders

Cylinders

	1015cc	1222cc
Type	Single barrel - finned	
Height:		
Red mark	75.78 to 75.80 mm	86.88 to 86.90 mm
Green mark	75.80 to 75.82 mm	86.89 to 86.92 mm

Pistons

Type	Light alloy
Width of ring groove:	
Compression ring	1.5 mm
Scraper ring	2 mm
Oil control ring	4 mm

Piston rings

Gap	0.30 to 0.45 mm

Gudgeon pins

Type	Fully-floating
Length	69.9 mm
Diameter	20 mm

Rockers

Rocker shaft diameter	$16.975 \, {}^{+0.01}_{-0.0}$ mm
Rocker arm bore diameter	$17.02 \, {}^{+0.25}_{-0.0}$ mm

Valves

Inlet:	
Head diameter	39 mm
Stem diameter	8 mm
Face angle	120°
Length	97.4 mm
Exhaust:	
Head diameter	34 mm
Stem diameter	8.5 mm
Face angle	90°
Length	96.3 mm

Valve springs

Length under load	32 mm at 25.4 kg $\pm$ 2.5 kg
	24 mm at 59.6 kg $\pm$ 2 kg

Rocker clearance (cold) - between rocker and cam

Inlet	0.20 mm
Exhaust	0.20 mm

Note: Rocker arm to valve stem clearance is set at 1 mm (0.040 in) for checking valve timing only.

Valve timing	G10 engine (1015cc)	G12/611 and G12/612 engine (1220cc)	G12/619 engine (1220cc)
Inlet valve opens (BTDC)	2° ± 1° 30′	4° 10′ ± 1° 30′	5° 30′
Inlet valve closes (ABDC)	34° ± 1° 30′	31° 50′ ± 1° 30′	34° 30′
Exhaust valve opens (BBDC)	34° ± 1° 30′	36° 10′ ± 1° 30′	32°
Exhaust valve closes (ATDC)	2° 30′ ± 1° 30′	0° 20′ ± 1° 30′	4° 30′

Fan

External diameter	290 mm
Number of blades	9 (offset)
Drive	Direct from crankshaft

Lubrication system

Type	Pressure feed
Oil pump type	Twin gear
Oil pressure at 80°C:	
2000 rpm	4.7 bar (68 psi) minimum
6000 rpm	6.2 to 7 bar (90 to 102 psi)
Pressure switch setting	0.5 to 0.8 bar (7 to 11.6 psi)
Thermal switch setting	135 ± 3°C
Relief valve spring:	
Free-length	51.6 mm
Length under load	33 mm
Bypass valves setting:	
Filter (white marking)	0.9 to 1.15 bar (13 to 16.6 psi)
Cooler (green marking)	1.8 to 2.5 bar (26 to 36 psi)
Oil cooler	Pressure fed tube type
Oil capacity:	
Engine dry	4 litre (7 Imp. pints)
Oil change (without new filter)	3.5 litre (6.25 Imp. pints)

1   General description

Two engines of different capacity are fitted in Citroen GS models: 1015cc and a 1220cc.

Both engines are very similar in design although quite different in terms of parts used. The operations described in this Chapter apply to both engines unless special mention is made to the contrary.

The engine is of an air-cooled, horizontally opposed flat four cylinder design. In both engines the bore diameter is greater than the stroke. The crankcase and cylinder heads are of light alloy. The crankshaft and connecting rod assembly runs in three split shell bearings between the two halves of the crankcase. The crankshaft and connecting rod assembly is a factory assembled part and cannot be dismantled. Crankshaft or big-end bearing failure necessitates renewal of the complete assembly. Oil seals are fitted at the front and rear ends of the crankshaft. There is no separate sump, the crankcase acts as an oil reservoir.

The four, finned cylinder barrels are separately mounted and each pair has a common cylinder head. The two camshafts, one in each cylinder head are driven by toothed-belts from the driving pinions on the front of the crankshaft. The right-hand camshaft operates the fuel pump and the distributor is driven by the left-hand shaft. The overhead valve mechanism has two rocker shafts to each cylinder head and the rockers are operated directly by the camshafts. The valves are fitted with single coil springs and split collets retain the valve caps. (On early G10 engines two springs were fitted to each valve).

The lubrication system is pressurized by an oil pump driven at half crankshaft speed by the left-hand toothed-belt. A connecting rod, operated by an eccentric on the oil pump shaft, drives the hydraulic high pressure pump. Incorporated in the lubrication system is a light alloy cooler, relief valve, bypass valves and filter. The cooler bypass valve allows the oil, when cold, to pass directly to the filter. The filter bypass valve allows the oil to bypass the filter in the event of the filter becoming blocked (due to lack of maintenance) and the relief valve passes oil back to the sump when the pressure is in excess of 7 bar (102 psi).

The cooling fan is fitted directly on the front of the crankshaft and is secured with the hand starting dog. Ducting directs air from the fan shroud round the cylinders and cylinder heads, and over the oil cooler. The alternator, which is belt driven from the fan, is mounted on top of the engine at the front.

A conventional flywheel, having a ring gear with which the starter motor pinion engages, is bolted to the rear end of the crankshaft. On engines with a semi-automatic transmission the torque converter driveplate is bolted to the crankshaft.

The engine and gearbox assembly is mounted at three points in the car, two flexible mountings at the rear of the crankcase and one at the rear of the gearbox.

Fig. 1.1. Cross-section of 1015 cc engine until August 1972

Fig. 1.2. Cross-section of 1015 cc and 1222 cc engine since August 1972

Fig. 1.3. Horizontal cross-section of engine

Fig. 1.4. Schematic diagram of lubrication system

1 Oil pump	3 Oil cooler	5 Bypass for oil filter	8 Crankshaft
2 Bypass for cooler	4 Oil pressure control valve	6 Oil filter	9 RH cylinder head
		7 Oil pressure switch	10 LH cylinder head

Fig. 1.5. Lubrication system (1972 on)

2 Major operations possible with the engine in the car

1   Removal and replacement of a rocker shaft or rocker arm.
Note: When removing the exhaust valve rocker shaft it is necessary to remove the bolts from the front flexible engine mountings and raise the engine gearbox assembly.
2   Removal and replacement of a driving belt, tensioner or timing gear.
3   Removal and replacement of a camshaft.
4   Removal and replacement of a pump drive (or seal) or an oil pump.
5   Removal and replacement of a hydraulic high pressure pump.

3 Major operations requiring removal of the engine

Before the following work can be carried out it is necessary to remove the engine from the car.
1   Removal and replacement of main bearings.
2   Removal and replacement of crankshaft and connecting rod assembly.
3   Removal and replacement of crankshaft front and rear seals.
4   Removal and replacement of flywheel or torque converter.
5   Removal and replacement of cylinder heads, cylinders and pistons.

4 Engine removal - method (general)

There are two methods of engine removal: as an engine and gearbox assembly or the engine only, as a separate unit (if removal of the gearbox is not required). Both methods are described in this Chapter.

5 Engine and gearbox assembly - removal procedure

1   For removal of the engine and gearbox assembly, a hoist, engine sling or strong rope, and four axle stands or solid wooden blocks are required.
2   Jack-up and support the front of the car with the wheels off the ground.
3   Place the vehicle height control lever in the 'normal' position and then slacken the pressure regulator bleed screw to release the pressure in the suspension circuits (photo).
4   Place the height control lever in the 'high' position and wait until the rear suspension has completely settled. Check that there is no pressure in the front suspension system (cylinders free); if not, operate the front height corrector (refer to Chapter 7). Jack-up and support the rear of the car.
5   Prop up the bonnet on its stay and mark the position of the hinges, this will help when replacing the bonnet. Remove the nut holding the stay on the bonnet and the four bolts securing the bonnet to the hinges. Lift away the bonnet, it helps to have an assistant for this, and place it safely out of the immediate work area (photo).
6   Disconnect the battery leads, negative terminal first.
7   Remove the spare wheel and front wheels.
8   Slacken the securing bolts and remove the grille by pulling it upwards (photos).
9   Remove the indicator lights, pull out the connectors from the headlights and free the electrical harness from its brackets on the fan panel. Disconnect the leads from the alternator (or generator) and the horn. Remove the rubber collar from the inlet tube to the air filter.
10 Rotate the locks while holding the headlights. Release the spring clip holding the sidelights, and remove the head and sidelights (photo).
11 Disconnect the control cable from the bonnet lock. Remove the bolts holding the fan panel on each side. Remove the horn with its bracket and the fan panel (photos).
12 From each side of the lower finishing panel remove the nut and bolts holding the lateral parts of the bumper, the bolts holding the front of the plates protecting the anti-roll bar bearings and the bolts holding the panel. Remove the finishing panel (photos).
13 Uncouple the driveshafts by removing the two nuts and four bolts securing the driveshafts to the differential shafts and the two bolts holding the ball joints of the lower suspension arms. Drop the lower suspension arm and pull the driveshafts from the studs on the differential shafts (photos).

14 Disconnect the leads from the:

Distributor
Engine oil pressure warning lamp
Coil to distributor (HT lead)
Starter motor
Engine oil thermal switch
Reversing light switch

and for cars fitted with automatic transmission disconnect the following additional leads:

The leads from the electro-valve (on the clutch housing)
The leads from the starter inhibitor switch (on the rear cover of the gearbox).

15 Remove the spare wheel support.
16 Remove the fixing bolts from the heater distribution box, uncouple the control cable and remove the box with its hose (photos).
17 Remove the speedometer flexible drive by removing the spring clip and withdrawing the drive.
18 Uncouple the handbrake cable by removing the locknuts, and the adjusting nuts and releasing the cable ends from the brake units (photo).
19 Slacken the clutch cable adjusting nuts and release the cable from the clutch fork. If an assistant is available have him depress the clutch pedal whilst, from underneath the car, you chock the clutch fork. Have the assistant release the pedal and the cable end can easily be released from the clutch fork (photo).
20 Remove the retainer from the gearlever link pin. Remove the pin and uncouple the gearlever.
21 Disconnect the accelerator and choke cables from the carburettor. Remove the bolts holding the cable sleeve bracket on the clutch housing.
22 Disconnect the flexible feed pipe from the fuel pump (blank the orifice with a 7mm diameter bolt).
23 On cars fitted with automatic transmission disconnect the flexible pipes from the converter oil cooler.
24 Disconnect the hydraulic pipes:

a) *Disconnect the main feed pipe from the two way union.*
b) *Remove the bolt holding the pipe bracket.*
c) *Unscrew the feed pipe for the front brakes and release it from the appropriate brake unit.*
d) *Remove the bleed screw (where fitted) to avoid it being damaged when the engine-gearbox assembly is being removed (blank off the orifice).*
e) *Disconnect the return pipe from the pressure regulator and remove the rubber collar which holds the pipe.*
f) *Disconnect the intake pipe from the high pressure pump. Release the pipe from the bracket on the right-hand wheel arch (photo).*

25 Fit a sling around the engine, positioned so that it will not damage any accessories when taking the weight of the engine and gearbox assembly. Place the hoist in position and take up the tension on the sling until the weight of the engine and gearbox assembly is supported without lifting it.
26 Remove the clamps from the exhaust pipe, the bolt holding the central exhaust pipe support on the gearbox housing and the 'Y' shaped connecting pipe. Remove the bolt holding the rear flexible mounting at the rear of the gearbox and the bolts from the flexible mountings at the rear of the engine crankcase, from underneath the car (photos).
27 Pull the engine and gearbox assembly carefully forward and remove the clip holding the dust cover on top of the gearbox. Pull up the dust cover and, using a pin punch, remove the roll pin holding the fork operating lever to the ball joint. Remove the operating lever (photos).
28 Make a final check that there are no more items to disconnect and that there is nothing likely to get caught-up when the engine and gearbox assembly is removed.
29 Pull the engine and gearbox assembly forward, clear of the car, taking care that the distributor does not foul the left-hand wheel arch and that the pipe linking the brake units does not come in contact with the crossmember of the axle unit.
30 Remove the crankcase drain plug, drain the oil into a container and replace the drain plug. Place the engine on a bench or wooden platform.
31 Remove the left and right-hand exhaust connecting pipes (photo).

Fig. 1.6. Removing the fan panel

1 Securing bolts   2 Bonnet catch

Fig. 1.9. Hydraulic piping (lhd models shown)

1 Two-way union   4 Pressure regulator return
2 Bolt   pipe
3 Bleed screw   5 Pipe clip

Fig. 1.7. Uncoupling the driveshafts

1 Lower suspension arm ball joint bolts

Fig. 1.10. Front engine mountings and exhaust pipe support

1 Exhaust pipe clamps   3 Engine front mounting bolts
2 Exhaust pipe bracket   4 Exhaust pipe

Fig. 1.8. Removing the heater distribution box

1 Distribution box   2 Hose
                           3 Bolts

Fig. 1.11. Gearchange linkage

1 Dust cover   2 Fork operating lever

Fig. 1.12. Removing the gearchange fork
operating lever
1 Pin punch

5.3 Slackening the pressure regulator bleed
screw to release the pressure from the hydraulic
system

5.5 The bonnet hinge bolts

5.8a Front grille securing bolt

5.8b Removing the front grille

5.10 Removing the side and headlights

5.11a Bonnet lock and control cable

5.11b Fan panel and front bumper with end
pieces removed

5.12a Removing the front bolts of the anti-
roll bar bearing guard plate

5.12b The end securing bolts of the lower
finishing panel

5.12c Removing the lower finishing panel
and front bumper

5.13a Uncoupling the driveshaft from the
differential shaft

5.13b Removing the bolts securing the ball joints of the lower suspension arm

5.16a The heater distribution box

5.16b Heater box control cable attachment

5.18 Handbrake cable to brake unit connection

5.19 Releasing the clutch cable from the operating fork

5.24 Disconnecting the hydraulic pipes

5.26a The exhaust pipe support bolted to the gearbox housing

5.26b Exhaust clamps of 'Y' shaped connecting pipe

5.26c Gearbox rear flexible mounting

5.27a Gear lever roll pin

5.27b Pulling the engine/gearbox assembly forward

5.31 Removing the right-hand exhaust connecting pipe

6 Engine (only) - removal procedure

1 Carry out the operations described in Section 5, paragraphs 1 to 12, inclusive.

2 Disconnect the leads from the:

Distributor
Oil pressure warning lamp
Coil to the distributor (HT lead)
Starter motor
Oil thermal switch.

Release the electrical harness and lay it on the left-hand extension arm. Remove the distributor cap and rotor to prevent possible damage to these components when removing the engine.

3 Carry out the operations described in Section 5, paragraphs 15, 16, 21 and 22.

4 Disconnect the hydraulic circuits:

a) *Disconnect the pump inlet flexible pipe from the hydraulic reservoir. Release it from the clip on the wheel arch and remove the rubber collar.*

b) *Disconnect the pipe from the pressure regulator, remove the nuts securing the clips holding the pipe, free the clips and remove the pipe from the pressure regulator. Blank-off the ends of the pipes.*

5 On cars fitted with automatic transmission remove the following

a) *Disconnect the pipe from the pressure regulator to the two-way union. Remove the bolt holding the pipe clip to the crossmember.*

b) *Disconnect the leads from the electro-valve.*

c) *Remove the bolts securing the pressure regulator and place the regulator on the right-hand extension.*

d) *Remove the starter motor.*

e) *Disconnect the flexible hose which supplies air to the torque converter oil cooler.*

f) *Remove the three bolts, accessible through the starter motor aperture in the casing, holding the torque converter driveplate. Mark the relative position of the converter to the driveplate, so that it can be refitted in the same location.*

Note: To hold the torque converter in position while the engine is being removed it is necessary to fit a retaining bracket on the pressure regulator mounting. The Citroen bracket (Part No. 3186-T) is illustrated, but a suitable bracket can be made from sheet metal.
Caution: The electro-valve must **never** be disconnected from the control distributor of the converter.

6 Disconnect the exhaust pipes, by removing the plates from the lower heater ducts, the front connection collars and slackening the bolt of the central exhaust pipe support on the gearbox.

7 Fit a sling around the engine, positioned so that it will not damage any accessories, and using a hoist take the weight of the engine.

8 Remove the bolts from the flexible mounting at the rear of the crankcase and raise the engine and gearbox assembly until the clutch housing comes into contact with the upper crossmember of the suspension frame. Support the gearbox from underneath, taking care not to damage the clutch cable.

9 Make a final check to ensure that everything is disconnected and that cables and pipes are tucked to one side where they will not get caught up as the engine is removed.

10 Remove the four nuts securing the gearbox to the engine and carefully pull the engine forward, ensuring that the distributor does not foul the wheel arch and avoiding putting any strain on the gearbox input shaft.

11 Drain the engine oil and place the engine on a bench or wooden platform.

7 Engine and gearbox assembly - separating

1 Remove the four nuts securing the gearbox to the engine.

2 Withdraw the gearbox from the engine taking care not to strain the gearbox input shaft.

3 If a torque-converter is fitted, refer to Section 6, paragraph 5, for method of disconnecting the convertor-drive plate.

4 When removing the gearbox from the engine support the torque-converter so that it is retained with the gearbox.

Fig. 1.13. Hydraulic pipe connections

1 Pipe from pressure regulator   3 Clip securing nut
2 Pressure regulator securing bolt   4 Collar

Fig. 1.14. Hydraulic pipe connections

1 Pressure regulator securing bolts   3 Clip retaining bolt
2 Electro-valve leads   4 Supply pipe to two-way union

Fig. 1.15. Torque converter retaining bracket

1 Electro-valve

8 Engine - dismantling (general)

1   When the engine is removed from the car it, and particularly its accessories, are more vulnerable to damage. If possible mount the engine on a stand, or failing this, make sure it is supported in such a manner that it will not topple over whilst undoing tight nuts and bolts.
2   Cleanliness is important when dismantling the engine to prevent exposed parts from contamination. Before starting the dismantling operations clean the outside of the engine with paraffin, or a good grease solvent if it is particularly dirty. Carry out this cleaning away from the area in which the dismantling is to take place.
3   If a stand is not available carry out the work on a bench or wooden platform. Avoid working with the engine directly on a concrete floor, as grit presents a real source of trouble.
4   As parts are removed clean them in a paraffin bath. However, do not immerse parts with internal oilways in paraffin as it is difficult to remove, usually requiring a high pressure air line. Clean oilways with wire.
5   It is advisable to have suitable containers to hold small items by their groups as this will help when reassembling the engine and also prevents possible losses.
6   Always obtain complete sets of gaskets when the engine is being dismantled. It is always a good policy to fit new gaskets in view of the relatively small cost involved. Retain the old gaskets when dismantling the engine with a view to using them as a pattern to make a replacement if a new one is not available.
7   When possible replace nuts, bolts and washers in their location as this helps to protect the threads and will also be helpful when the engine is being reassembled as it establishes their location.
8   Retain unserviceable items until the replacement parts are obtained so that the replacement parts can be checked against the old part to ensure that the correct item has been supplied.

9 Engine ancillaries - removal

Although the items listed may be removed separately with the engine installed (as described in the relevant Chapters) it is more appropriate to take them off after the engine has been removed from the car when extensive dismantling is being carried out.

Fuel system
   Carburettor
   Fuel pump

Ignition
   Distributor
   Spark plugs

Electrical components
   Starter motor
   Alternator.

10 Engine - dismantling procedure

1   Remove the clutch assembly, referring to Chapter 4. Remove the six flywheel retaining bolts and remove the flywheel.
2   Remove the upper duct covers.
3   Remove the hand starter dog, the fan and the alternator drivebelt. Remove the nuts securing the fan cowl to the three mounting studs and remove the cowl washers and spacers.
4   Remove the under cylinder ducts (1015 cc engines) by releasing the spring clip to free them from the oil return tubes of the cylinder heads.
5   Undo the union screws on the right and left-hand cylinder heads and on the carburettor heater box and remove the cylinder head lubricating pipe.
6   Remove the oil cooler and seals, the oil temperature thermal switch and the oil pressure switch.
7   Remove the inlet pipes, exhaust manifold pipes and the heating ducts.
8   Remove the nut and bolts securing the carburettor heater box and remove the box. Collect the O-ring between the heater box and the engine casing (early engines) or the pipe-intake manifold and carburettor assembly (later engines).

9   Remove the oil filter. As the oil filter is unscrewed oil will run over the top of the engine, have a cloth ready to mop up the oil.
10   Loosen the nuts holding the left-hand tension roller, compress the roller and remove the outer flange from the crankshaft outer drive pinion and the left-hand toothed belt. Slacken the nut holding the right-hand tension roller, compress the roller and remove the intermediate flange of the drive pinion and the right-hand toothed belt. Remove the inner drive pinion, protection plate and key from the crankshaft. Remove the tension rollers and thrust plates.
11   Restrain the camshaft sprockets from turning, undo the securing nuts and remove the sprockets.
12   Remove the cylinder head covers. Undo the eight cylinder head retaining nuts on each cylinder head and lift off the heads. Remove the oil return tubes, and the ducts beneath the cylinders (where fitted).
13   Remove the four cylinders and mark them so that they will be refitted in the same positions. To avoid scoring of the pistons fit a piece of rubber tubing over the studs.
14   Remove the gudgeon pin retaining circlips situated towards the outside of the engine, ('a' and 'b' in Fig. 1.19) and push out the gudgeon pins using a suitable mandrel. Remove the pistons and place them and the gudgeon pins with their respective cylinders. Remove the piston rings. **Note:** It is important that the respective pistons and cylinders are kept together if they are to be refitted as they are a matched set.
15   Remove the five bolts securing the oil pump drive gear and remove the gear by levering it on two diametrically opposed points, taking care to avoid damaging the pump bearing. Collect the O-ring and remove the high pressure pump connecting rod, the oil pump cover plate and the oil pump pinions.
16   Place the crankcase with the left-hand half of the casing downwards and remove the assembly nuts. Separate the two halves of the casing, remove the front and rear crankshaft seals and lift out the crankshaft-connecting rod assembly. Remove the half bearings shells from each half of the casing. Remove the bolts securing the oil strainer. To assist the removal of the strainer, heat the casing around the strainer pipe at 'A' in Fig. 1.20. Remove the oil system relief valve by removing the retaining circlip and collecting the washer, spring washers, the piston, the spring, the sleeve and the spring cap. Remove the filter and oil cooler bypass valves.

11 Cylinder heads - dismantling

1   Loosen the locknuts and back-off the rocker adjusting screws under load. From each end of the rocker shafts remove the blanking bolts and copper seals, the spacers and the 'O' ring seals. Remove the rocker cover stud and with a 3 mm Allen key remove the grubscrew which holds the rocker shaft. Remove the rocker shafts, rocker arms and springs.
2   Remove the nuts securing the camshaft rear bearing, free the bearing by tapping lightly with a mallet on the end of the camshaft and remove the camshaft and bearing assembly. The camshaft and the rear bearing form an assembly which cannot be dismantled. Remove the front seal.
3   Position a 16 mm diameter rod, 'A' in Fig. 1.25, successively in place of each rocker arm shaft successively. And then a valve spring compression tool (Citroen tool Pt. No. 1652-T, is illustrated) compress the valve spring, using a block of wood under the valve head to prevent the valve opening. Remove the split cotters, cups, springs, thrust washers and seals. Remove the valve and the rod 'A'. Mark the valves so that if they are to be refitted they can be located in the same positions.

12 Cylinder heads - cleaning and renovation

1   After the cylinder heads have been dismantled they should be thoroughly cleaned to remove all carbon deposits in the combustion chambers. Avoid damaging the valve seats when removing the carbon. Examine the heads for cracks or other damage. If there are any visible cracks the head should be scrapped. Pay particular attention to the area around the valve seats and spark plug holes as these are where cracks are most likely to occur.
2   Slight pitting of the valves and valve seats can usually be rectified by lapping with carborundum paste. If the seats are badly pitted or burned they will require grinding. Valve seat angles and diameters are given in Fig. 1.27, but as machining requires special equipment you may decide to have it done by your local agent.

Fig. 1.16. Cooling and heating ducts - 1015 cc engines

A   Cooling ducts
B   Heating ducts
C   Duct covers

D   Deflector
E   RH mounting plate

F   LH mounting plate
G   Screen

H   Deflector fitted towards fan cowl
J   Ducts under cylinders

Fig. 1.17. Cooling and heating ducts - 1222 cc engines

A   Cooling ducts   B   Heating ducts   C   Duct covers   D   Ducts under cylinders

Fig. 1.18. Removing the camshaft drivebelts

1 LH camshaft sprocket   4 RH camshaft sprocket
2 Crankshaft outer flange   5 LH tension roller
3 RH tension roller   6 Cylinder head lubrication pipe

Fig. 1.19. Removing the gudgeon pins
A Rubber tubing a and b Circlips

Fig. 1.20. Removing the oil strainer

1 Bolts   2 Strainer

Fig. 1.21. Removing the oil pressure relief valve

2 Circlip

Fig. 1.22. Oil pressure relief valve

1 Spring   5 Spring washer
2 Spring cap   6 Piston
3 Circlip   7 Sleeve
4 Washer

Fig. 1.23. Dismantling a cylinder head

1 Adjusting screw   5 Grubscrew
2 Spacer   6 Stud
3 Blanking bolt   7 Rear bearing
4 Cap (early engines)

Fig. 1.24. Rocker arm shaft

1 Rocker shaft   2 Spacer   4 Copper seals   6 Spacer
                    3 Blanking bolts   5 'O' ring seals

1652-T

Fig. 1.25. Removing the valves

Fig. 1.26. Valve assemblies

1 Seal   5 Thrust washer
2 Split cotters   6 Thrust washer
3 Cup   7 Spring
4 Spring

3   If the valves require grinding on a valve grinding machine, the chamfer of the valve heads is:
   a) Intake valves = 120°
   b) Exhaust valves = 90°
Make a slight chamfer at 'a' (Fig. 1.27) on the valve head to smooth the edge.
4   When lapping-in slightly pitted valves and valve seats with carborundum paste proceed as follows: Apply a little coarse grinding paste to the valve seat and using a suction valve grinding tool, lap the valve into its seat with a semi-rotary movement, lifting the valve from time-to-time. A light spring under the valve head will assist in this operation. When a dull matt even surface finish appears on both the valve and the valve seat, clean off the coarse paste and repeat the operation with a fine grinding paste until a continuous ring of light grey matt finish appears on both valve and valve seat. Carefully clean off all traces of grinding paste. Blow through the gas passages with compressed air.
5   Check the valve springs against the following load/dimensions.

Specifications:
1015 cc engine (early models)

2 Springs	Loaded length mm (in)	Load kg (lb)
Outer	32 (1.260)	23,5 ± 2 (51.7 ± 2)
	24,5 (0.965)	50 ± 3 (110 ± 6.6)
Inner	26,8 (1.055)	9,9 ± 0,9 (21.8 ± 2)
	19,3 (0.760)	21,1 ± 1,0 (46.5 ± 2.2)

1015 cc and 1222 cc engines

1 Spring	Loaded length mm (in)	Load kg (lb)
	32 (1.260)	25,4 ± 2,5 (55.9 ± 5.5)
	24 (0.945)	59,6 ± 2 (131 ± 4.4)

6   Examine the rocker shafts, rockers and camshafts for wear or damage. If the camshaft rear bearing is defective the complete camshaft and bearing assembly must be renewed. Fit a new rear bearing seal. If necessary, replace the rollpin '1' (Fig. 1.28) and fit it positioned with the slot 'a' towards the outside of the camshaft. The fixing stud for the camshaft sprocket must be smeared with Loctite and tightened to 2.5 to 3 kg f m (18 to 22 lb f ft).

Fig. 1.27. Valve seat angles

Fig. 1.28. Fitting a camshaft wheel stud

1 Pin   a Slot in rollpin   2 Stud

13 Cylinder heads - reassembly

Note: It is not possible to fit the single valve spring on cylinder heads equipped for two springs for valve.

1 Fitting of the valves is the reverse of the removal sequence. Always fit new valve seals on assembly. Ensure that the split cotters are seated correctly (photos).

2 When fitting the joint between the rear bearing housing of the camshaft and the cylinder head, line-up the notch in the joint with the groove in the casing for the oil return of the cylinder head. Fit the joint dry. Oil the camshaft front seal bearing surface and fit the camshaft in the cylinder head. Fit the front seal. The seal must be fitted when the camshaft is in place, otherwise it will be damaged when fitting the camshaft. Tighten the camshaft securing nuts to 1,5 to 1,8 kg f m (11 to 13 lb f ft) (photos).

3 Fitting of the rocker shafts and arms is the reverse of the removal sequence. Note the markings on the rocker shafts for identification. The left-hand intake and right-hand exhaust shafts are identical and have no markings. The right-hand intake and the left-hand exhaust shafts are identical and are marked with an indentation 'd' (Fig. 1.29). This marking is very important for the correct fitting of the shafts in relation to the lubrication holes.

4 Oil the shafts and fit them in the cylinder heads with the shouldered ends 'c' towards the front of the camshaft. Temporarily fit a blanking screw on the end of the shaft, to allow the positioning of the shaft so that the grubscrew hole lines-up with the blend hold. Fit the grubscrew with the threads smeared with Loctite. Remove the blanking screw. When fitting the rocker cover fixing stud, fit the shortest length of thread in the cylinder head.

14 Crankshaft and connecting rods - general

1 The crankshaft and connecting rod assembly is a factory built unit and cannot be dismantled by the owner. A big-end bearing failure and damaged or worn main bearing journals necessitate the renewal of the complete assembly. Small-end bushes can be replaced but this requires special equipment and should be left to your Citroen agent.

2 The pilot bearing and oil seal in the rear of the crankshaft can be replaced as follows: Remove and discard the seal and bearing bush. Soak the new bush, for one hour, in clean engine oil before fitting it. Press the bush into the crankshaft to the dimensions shown in Fig. 1.30 and fit a new seal with the face bearing the manufacturers mark facing outwards.

15 Cylinders and pistons - cleaning and reassembly

1 It is not possible to renew cylinders and pistons separately as replacements are only sold in sets of four cylinder/piston assemblies. All four of which must be fitted to the same engine, as the difference in weight between two pistons must not exceed a few grams.

2 If the cylinder bores are worn this will result in excessive oil consumption and loss of power. A preliminary check for wear can be made by feeling the inside walls of the cylinder about ½ inch (12.7 mm) down from the top edge. If a ridge can be felt at any point, then the bores should be measured with an internal micrometer to ascertain

actual amount of wear. Take measurements at different positions in the bore to get a complete picture of wear and ovality.

3 If the same pistons are being refitted with only the rings being renewed, carefully clean the piston ring grooves with the aid of a broken piece of used ring. If there is excessive vertical clearance of the rings in the piston ring grooves the pistons require renewal.

4 Before fitting the new rings to the pistons check the ring gap by placing each ring in the cylinder in which it will be fitted, and using a piston, make sure they rest square in the bore near the bottom of the cylinder. Measure the gap between the ring ends with a feeler gauge: it should be between 0,30 to 0,45 mm (0.012 - 0.018 in).

5 When fitting the rings, note that they have a marking, 'HAUT', 'H' or 'TOP' on one of the faces near the gap, this marking must be positioned facing the top of the piston. Fig. 1.31 shows the location of the rings on the piston. The U-FLEX rings in their free state have an inside diameter greater than that of the piston and it is necessary to use a piston ring clamp when fitting the pistons into the cylinders (photo).

6 There are two classes of cylinder (having different heights) marked by touches of green or red paint. Both cylinders fitted to one side of the engine must be of the same colour. Before fitting the pistons in the cylinders insert the gudgeon pin circlip on the same side 'b' (Fig. 1.32) as the fins 'c'. Position the piston ring gap at 120° spacing and fit the piston ring clamp. Fit the piston part way into the lower end of the corresponding cylinder, as marked at dismantling. Position the pistons in such a way that after fitting the connecting rod the figure at 'a' (compression ratio 9) is legible as illustrated and the fins 'c' are positioned as shown. Oil the gudgeon pin and insert it in the piston boss so as to leave a gap to enable the connecting rod small end to be fitted (photos).

16 Flywheel starter ring gear - removal and replacement

1 Remove the flywheel starter ring by driving it off with a hammer.
2 Clean the contact areas of the replacement ring and the flywheel and ensure the surface is smooth and even.
3 Heat the ring with a blow torch, moving it round the ring all the time to ensure even expansion. Heat the ring to between 200 to 250° C (straw yellow colour) and fit the ring to the flywheel with the teeth lead-in (chamfer) towards the gearbox.
4 Check that the run-out on the starter ring does not exceed 0.3 mm (0.012 in).

17 Engine - reassembly (general)

1 To ensure maximum life with minimum trouble from a rebuilt engine, not only must everything be correctly assembled, but also must be spotlessly clean. All oilways must be clear, locking washers and spring washers must be fitted where indicated. Oil all bearings and other working surfaces thoroughly with engine oil during assembly.
2 Before assembly, renew any bolts, studs or screws with damaged threads and use of new spring washers is advisable.
3 Apart from having a supply of normal tools, a supply of clean rags and an oil can should be available.
4 Before starting work, clear the work area of any unwanted parts and arrange all the components nearby, prepared for reassembly.

Fig. 1.29. Rocker shaft identification

Fig. 1.30. Pilot bearing and oil seal

1 Bearing 2 Seal

Fig. 1.31. Fitting the piston rings

1 Compression ring
2 Scraper ring
3 Scraper-collector ring

Fig. 1.32. Fitting the pistons

13.1a Fitting a valve in the cylinder head

13.1b Fitting the valve stem oil seal

13.1c Valve spring and cup in position on the valve ready for fitting of the split cotters

13.1d Compressing the valve spring and fitting the split cotters

13.2a Fitting the left-hand camshaft

13.2b Fitting the right-hand camshaft

15.5 Fitting the piston in the cylinder using a piston ring clamp

15.6a Piston with gudgeon pin partly fitted in bore

15.6b Fit the piston in the cylinder with the figure '9' the right way up

18 Engine - reassembly procedure

1 Fit the seal on the intake pipe of the oil strainer, smear the end of the pipe with Loctite and insert it in its housing on the engine casing. Insert the anti-emulsion shield between the engine casing and the strainer. Tighten the securing bolts to 1,4 kg f m (10 lb f ft) (photo).
2 Fit the oil filter bypass valve (white mark) as follows: Fit the valve, the washer and then the cup, secure the cup in the housing by tapping it in lightly. Fit the oil cooler bypass valve (green mark) in the same way. Smear the threads of the retaining plug with Loctite, fit with a copper washer and tighten to 4,5 to 5 kg f m (32 to 36 lb f ft) (photos).
3 Fit the lubrication system plugs with a copper washer, smear the threads with Loctite and tighten to 3,5 to 4 kg f m (25 to 29 lb f ft).
4 Make sure that the main bearing bores of the engine casings are clean and fit the bearing shells into the right and left-hand casings. Check that the bearing shells are properly engaged in the locating dowels and oil the bearing shells and journals of the crankshaft. Fit the crankshaft and connecting rod assembly in the left-hand casing and with a set of feeler gauges check that the endfloat of the crankshaft, measured at the centre bearing, is between 0,09 and 0,20 mm (0.0035 and 0.0078 in) (photos).
5 Smear the mating faces of the half casings with jointing compound and place the right-hand casing on the left-hand one. Fit the copper washers and nuts to the crankshaft main bearing studs, and the plain washers and nuts to the studs which hold the half casings together. Tighten all nuts to the specified torque.
6 Oil the lip of the front and rear crankshaft seals and fit both seals carefully over each end of the crankshaft (both seals are identical). Always fit new seals after each engine dismantling. Never fit the seals before assembling the half engine casings as this would crush the seals and cause oil leakage (photo).
7 Refer to Fig. 1.22 and fit the oil pressure relief valve. Fit the cap with the lugs 'b' towards the bottom of the housing, the sleeve and the spring. Oil the piston and fit it, with the guide 'c' on the spring side, the spring washer, plain washer and circlip.
8 Oil and fit the oil pump rotors. Fit the cover plate so that the cavities 'b' (Fig. 1.35) are placed towards the inside of the engine casing and the small hole 'c' opposite cavity 'a' (Fig. 1.34). Place the hydraulic high pressure pump connecting rod in position. Temporarily fit a guide stud to assist assembly (photo).
9 Fit the 'O'-ring seal, oil the shaft and eccentric. Place a shim between the sprocket and the bearings at 'g' (Fig. 1.36) to prevent damaging the seal. Offer up the pump drive gear, to the guide stud with the groove 'd' of the connecting rod passage, positioned towards the high pressure pump, and engage the shaft in the central pinion. Turn the shaft in order to engage the flat part 'e' into the oil pump pinion. Guide the high pressure pump connecting rod to engage it on the eccentric 'f' of the drive gear. Remove the guide stud and fit the five washers and retaining bolts, tighten to 1,5 to 1,8 kg f m (11 to 13 lb f ft). Remove the shim from between the sprocket and the bearing. Check that the pump turns freely (photo).
10 Oil the small-ends of the connecting rods, offer up the cylinder piston assemblies to the connecting rods, as shown in Fig. 1.32 and complete the fitting of the gudgeon pins in the pistons. Fit the gudgeon pin circlips, ensure that they are fully engaged in their grooves. Oil the pistons and inside of the cylinders and completely engage the cylinder. Where applicable fit the under cylinder cooling ducts.
11 Fit and lubricate the 'O' rings on the oil return tubes and engage the longest ends into their engine casing housings. Turn the crankshaft to bring the pistons to their mid-stroke position and fit the cylinder heads while guiding the oil return tubes into position. Fit the washers and nuts, screw them up finger tight then torque tighten them initially, in the sequence shown in Fig. 1.37 to 0,8 to 1 kg f m (5.8 to 7.2 lb f ft). Before tightening the right-hand cylinder head, position the cylinders to allow for the fitting of the brake unit (early 1015 cc engines). Finally tighten the cylinder head nuts, in the same sequence to 1,6 to 1,8 kg f m (12 to 13 lb f ft) for the 12 mm nuts and 2 to 2,5 kg f m (15 to 17 lb f ft) for the 13 mm nuts (photos).
12 The two camshaft wheels are identical. Fit a sprocket on the end of each camshaft, and engage it on the locating pin. Fit the washer and securing nut, restrain the wheel from turning and tighten the nut to 8,2 kg f m (59 lb f ft) (photos).
13 The two tensioner rollers are identical. Fit the rollers, engaged with the locating pins, on the roller shafts, fit the support plates, washers and nuts. Do not tighten the nuts at this stage (photo).

14 Fit the protective plate, (Fig. 1.38) the key on the crankshaft and the inner drive sprocket, the intermediate flange and the outer drive sprocket. Position the sprocket so that the groove 'a' is outwards on the outer sprocket and towards the crankcase on the inner sprocket.
15 When fitting the timing belts make sure that there is no trace of oil or grease on the belts, sprockets or rollers. On a given engine always fit belts from the same manufacturer.
  Turn the engine to bring the mark 'a' (Fig. 1.39), located on the intermediate flange, towards the top of the centre-line of the engine. Position the marks 'b', 'c' and 'd' on the camshaft sprockets and the oil pump as shown in Fig. 1.39. Compress the tensioner roller in the direction of the arrows and tighten the securing nuts.
16 Fit the right-hand belt (the shorter of the two) so that the white marks on the belt coincide with the marks 'a' and 'd' in such a way that:

   a - d = 42 teeth, tensioner side (1015 cc engines)
   a - d = 43 teeth, tensioner side (1222 cc engines)

Fit the left-hand belt so that:

   The white marks coincide with marks 'a' and 'b'
   The yellow mark coincides with the mark 'e'

In this position:

   a - b = 32 teeth (1015 cc engines)
   a - b = 33 teeth (1222 cc engines)
   a - c = 25 teeth (both engine types) (photo)

Fit the outer flange on the crankshaft. Slacken the roller securing nuts to release the rollers and then retighten the nuts.
17 The rocker clearances are adjusted with the engine cold. Successively adjust each of the rocker arms as follows:

   a) *Turn the engine until the heel of the rocker to be adjusted is on the back of the corresponding cam (valve completely closed).*
   b) *Loosen the adjusting screw locknut and, using a feeler gauge and a cranked screwdriver, adjust the clearance between the heel of the rocker and the back of the cam to 0,2 mm (0.008 in). The clearance for both inlet and exhaust valves is the same.*
   c) *Tighten the locknut while holding the adjusting screw from turning. Re-check that the rocker clearance is still correct (Fig. 1.41).*

18 Tension the timing belts: With the crankshaft marking and camshaft sprockets positioned as shown in Fig. 1.39, turn the crankshaft through 90° in its normal direction of rotation. Loosen the left-hand tensioner roller securing nut and retighten it to 1,8 kg f m (13 lb f ft). Turn the crankshaft in its normal direction of rotation through one complete turn and carry out the same operation on the right-hand tensioner roller.
19 Ensure that there is no roughness on the joint faces of the rocker cover and cylinder head and that they are clean and dry. Stick the gasket on the rocker covers with Bostik 1400. Carefully oil the rocker arms, shafts and cams. The lower and upper cylinder head rocker covers are different, take care when fitting them. The rocker cover with the oil filler orifice is fitted on the left-hand side. Take care to centre the covers correctly as poor centring or insufficient tightening of the fixing nut could lead to a total loss of the engine oil. Tighten the nut to 0,8 to 1,0 kg f m (6 to 7 lb f ft).
20 Fit the cooling ducts 'a' (Figs. 1.16 and 1.17).

   a) *Left-hand side, fit the duct on the engine casing.*
   b) *Right-hand side:*
      Fit the brake unit (1015 cc engines only).
      Fit the duct on the right-hand cylinder head.
      Fit the bolt '3' in Fig. 1.40 with the rear support plate of the air filter under the duct plate.
      Fit the bolt '4' with the front support plate of the air filter under the duct plate (1015 cc engines only) (photo).

21 Fit the cylinder head lubrication pipes, tighten the union screws to 1,8 to 2 kg f m (13 to 14.5 lb f ft) and check that there is a minimum clearance of 5 mm (0.2 in) between the pipes and the camshaft sprockets. Fit the oil pressure switch with a new seal and tighten it to 2,2 kg f m (16 lb f ft) (photo).

22 Oil the seal of the oil filter cartridge. Fit the seal and screw the cartridge as tight as possible by hand, then tighten it a further ½ to ¾ of a turn with a strap wrench.

23 When refitting the flywheel always fit new securing bolts. Make sure you fit the correct bolts, they are identified by a circle marked on the centre of the head. Ensure that both contact faces of the flywheel and crankshaft are clean and the dowel properly located. Oil the bolt threads, fit the bolts and restrain the flywheel from turning while tightening the bolts to 6,4 to 6,9 kg f m (46 to 50 lb f ft). On cars with automatic transmission a driveplate is fitted in place of the flywheel and the fixing bolts must be treated with Loctite (photo).

24 Fit the exhaust pipes and tighten the nuts to 1,5 kg f m (11 lb f ft).

25 Fit a new seal on the oil temperature thermal switch and tighten it to 2,5 kg f m (18 lb f ft).

26 Fit the clutch assembly, referring to Chapter 4.

27 Fit new oil seals on each tube of the oil cooler. Fit the cooler and tighten the bolts to 1.8 kg f m (13 lb f ft) (photos).

28 Fit the starter motor, as described in Chapter 11 (photo).

29 Fit the breather tube ensuring that it does not touch the cooling duct. Fit the dipstick guide (photo).

30 Fit the heating ducts (Figs. 1.16 and 1.17).

Fit the front right-hand deflector 'H'.
Fit the rear left-hand screen 'G'.
Fit the assembly of rear right-hand mounting plate 'E' and deflector 'D'.
Couple up the heating ducts, fit washers under the heads of all screws (photo).

31 Fit the carburettor heater box or inlet pipe manifold and carburettor assembly. Tighten the bolts to 1,8 kg f m (13 lb f ft). Connect the pipe from the exhaust to the heater box.

32 Fit the hydraulic pump: During handling of the pump, hold the pump piston to prevent it coming out of its cylinder. Check that the contact faces of the pump and the engine casing are clean. Fit a new 'O' ring seal between the pump and the casing. Offer up the pump to the connecting drive rod and fit the pin. If necessary, turn the engine to bring the connecting rod to its tdc (top-dead-centre) position. Check that the piston is correctly located in the pump cylinder and that the 'O' ring is in place on the engine casing. Fit the pump over the mounting studs and bring the baseplate up to the engine casing without forcing it. Fit and tighten the securing nuts to 1,3 to 1,4 kg f m (9.5 to 10 lb f ft). Fit the cover on the pump body, connect the delivery pipe. Fit the bracket fixing the pipe onto the cylinder head (photo).

33 Fit the alternator tensioner and the alternator, do not tighten the alternator bolts at this stage. Fit the cylinder head lubrication pipe supports (photo).

34 On 1015cc engines, engage the ducts 'J' (Fig. 1.16) on the oil return tubes of the cylinder heads. The upper part of the duct must be engaged between the third and fourth cooling fin of the cylinder (photo).

35 On the fan cowl mounting studs fit a flat washer on each side of the spacer, fit the fan cowl and tighten the nuts.

36 Fit the fanbelt on the alternator pulley and engage it on the fan pulley. Fit the fan on the end of the crankshaft, the starter dog and locknut. Position the starter dog so that it is horizontal when the engine is at ignition point. Adjust by loosening the locknut and turning the threaded sleeve as necessary. Tighten the locknut to 18 kg f m (130

Fig. 1.33. Assembling the crankcase

    1 Casing studs   2 Crankshaft main bearing studs

Fig. 1.34. Fitting the oil pump

    1 Oil pump rotors   2 Guide stud

Fig. 1.35. Oil pump components

    1 Shaft   3 Cover plate
    2 Connecting rod   4 'O' ring seal
    (See text for alphabetical key)

Fig. 1.36. Cross-section of oil pump

    1 Seal (See text for alphabetical key)

lb f ft). The starter dog should have 4 to 5 mm of thread visible after tightening the nut (photo).

37 Fit the upper duct covers with the spark plug lead support fixed on the centred bolt.

38 Fit the carburettor, fuel pump, distributor, spark plugs and pressure regulator, referring if necessary to the appropriate Chapters.

39 Adjust the alternator drivebelt tension and tighten the alternator mounting bolts.

19 Engine - replacement

1 Replacement of the engine is a reversal of the removal operations. Do not forget to fit the driveshafts and connect up the exhaust pipe.

2 Carry out the following checks before starting the engine:

   a) Fuel pipes to pump and carburettor connections tightened.

Fig. 1.37. Tightening sequence of cylinder head nuts

Fig. 1.39. Fitting the timing belts

1 Tension roller nut   3 Outer flange
2 Tension roller nut

(See text for alphabetical key)

Fig. 1.38. Crankshaft timing gears

1 Nut   4 Protective plate
2 Outer sprocket   5 Inner sprocket
3 Intermediate flange   6 Tension roller

(See text for alphabetical key)

Fig. 1.40. Fitting the cooling duct

1 Brake unit (1015cc engines only)   4 Bolt
2 Seal   5 Front support plate
3 Bolt   6 Rear support plate

18.1 Fitting the oil strainer and anti-emulsion shield

18.2a The oil cooler bypass valve

18.2b Fitting the oil cooler bypass valve and retaining plug

18.4a The left-hand half-casing

18.4b Fitting the main bearing shells

18.4c Fitting the crankshaft and connecting rod assembly in the left-hand half-casing

18.4d Measuring the crankshaft endfloat with a feeler gauge

18.6 Fitting the crankshaft rear seal

18.8a Fitting the oil pump rotors

18.8b Fitting the oil pump cover plate

18.8c Placing the hydraulic pump connecting rod in position

18.9 Fitting the oil pump drive gear

18.10a Fitting the piston and cylinder assembly

18.10b Gudgeon pin fitted in position

18.11a Fitting the oil return tubes

18.11b Piston at mid-stroke position

18.11c Replacing the right-hand cylinder head

18.12 Fitting the drive sprocket on the right-hand camshaft

18.13a A timing belt tensioner roller

18.13b Fitting the right-hand tensioner roller, support plate, washer and nut

18.14a Fitting the inner protective flange plate and key on the crankshaft

18.14b Replacing the inner belt drive sprocket, the intermediate flange and the outer drive sprocket

18.16a Right-hand drivebelt fitted

18.16b Left-hand drivebelt fitted

18.16c Lining-up the marks on the belts and flanges

Figure 1.41 Rocker arm clearance - check with feeler gauge inserted between back of cam and heel of rocker arm

18.20a Replacing the left-hand cooling duct

18.20b Replacing the right-hand cooling duct

18.21 Connecting the lubricating pipe to the right-hand cylinder head

18.22 Replacing the oil filter cartridge

18.23a Flywheel bolt identification marking

18.23b Flywheel bolted in position

18.24 Fitting the right-hand exhaust manifold pipes

18.27a Fitting new seals on the oil cooler tubes

18.27b Replacing the oil cooler

18.28 Replacing the starter motor

18.29a The crankcase breather

18.29b Crankcase breather fitted in position

18.29c Fitting the dipstick guide

18.30 Assembling the left-hand heating duct

18.31a Replacing the carburettor and intake manifold pipes assembly

18.31b Connecting the pipe from the exhaust to the intake manifold

18.32a Hydraulic pump connecting rod and mounting flange

18.32b Fitting the hydraulic pump

18.33 Replacing the alternator

18.34 Engaging the under cylinder cooling duct on the oil return tubes (1015cc engines only)

18.36 Fitting the fan and the starter dog nut

19.2 Don't forget to put oil in the engine before starting-up

b) Sump drain plug tightened and oil in the engine (photo).
c) Gearbox oil level correct and plugs tightened.
d) Ignition wiring and spark plug leads connected.
e) Oil pressure and temperature sender units connected.
f) Choke and throttle cable connected.
g) Starter motor and alternator leads connected.
h) Hydraulic oil reservoir filled
j) Hydraulic pipe connections made and tightened.
k) Fully charged battery fitted and leads connected.

20 Engine - initial start-up after assembly

1   Carry out a visual examination of the engine compartment, for rags or tools which may have been overlooked, before starting the engine.
2   Prime the high pressure pump by freeing the pump suction pipe from the reservoir and filling the pump with LHM fluid through the pipe. Slacken the pressure regulator bleed screw.
3   Set the choke and start the engine. Quickly replace the suction pipe in the reservoir and tighten the pressure regulator bleed screw.
4   Run the engine at a fast idle, and check for oil leaks and leaks from the hydraulic system.
5   Select the high suspension position and top-up the hydraulic reservoir, as described in Chapter 6.
6   When the engine running temperature has been reached, adjust the idling speed, as described in Chapter 2, and road-test the car.
7   After 600 miles (1000 km) running, change the engine oil, and retighten the cylinder head bolts to the correct torque loading with the engine cold. Check the valve clearances.

21 Fault diagnosis - engine

Symptom	Reason/s	Remedy
Engine will not turn over when starter-switch is operated	Flat battery Bad battery connections Bad connections at starter motor and/or solenoid switch	Check that battery is fully charged and that all connections are clean and tight.
	Starter motor jammed	Engage a gear and rock the car back and forward. If ineffective remove the starter.
	Defective solenoid	Remove the starter and check the solenoid.
	Starter motor defective	Remove and overhaul the starter.
Engine turns over but fails to start	No spark at plug	Check ignition system in accordance with procedures given in Chapter 3.
	No fuel reaching the engine	Check fuel system in accordance with procedures given in Chapter 2.
	Too much fuel reaching the engine (flooding)	Check the fuel system as above.
Engine starts but runs unevenly and misfires	Ignition and/or fuel system faults	Check the ignition and fuel systems as though the engine had failed to start.
	Incorrect valve clearances	Check and reset clearances.
	Burnt out valves	Remove engine and overhaul as necessary.
	Worn piston rings and cylinders	Remove engine and overhaul as necessary.
Lack of power	Ignition and/or fuel system faults	Check the ignition and fuel systems for correct timing and carburettor settings.
	Incorrect valve clearances	Check and reset clearances.
	Burnt out valves	Remove engine and overhaul as necessary.
	Worn piston rings and/or cylinders	Remove engine and overhaul as necessary.
Excessive oil consumption	Oil leaks from pipe unions and gaskets of lubrication system	Identify source of leak and rectify as appropriate.
	Oil leaks from crankshaft oil seals	Remove engine and renew seals.
	Worn valve guides and/or defective valve stem seals	Remove engine and rectify as appropriate.
	Worn piston rings and cylinders (indicated by excessive blue smoke from exhaust)	Remove engine and overhaul as necessary.
Excessive mechanical noise from engine	Wrong valve clearances	Adjust valve clearance.
	Worn crankshaft bearings	Remove engine and overhaul as necessary.
Unusual vibrations	Misfiring on one or more cylinders	Check ignition system. Check for air leaks in inlet manifold.
	Loose mounting bolts	Check tightness of bolts and condition of flexible mountings.

Note: When investigating starting and uneven running faults do not be tempted into snap diagnosis. Start from the beginning and follow it through. It will take less time in the long run. Poor performance from an engine in terms of power and economy is not normally diagnosed quickly. In any event the ignition and fuel system must be checked first before assuming any further investigation needs to be made.

Chapter 2 Fuel and exhaust systems

For modifications, and information applicable to later models, see Supplement at end of manual

Contents

Specifications

Fuel pump
Type	Guiot or AC Delco mechanical
Delivery pressure	250 mb (3.5 psi)

Fuel filter
To February 1972	In fuel tank
From February 1972	Guiot G20 (disposable)

Air Cleaner ... ...
Dry element, cleanable

Fuel tank capacity ... ...
43 litres (9.75 Imp. gallons)

Carburettor - Solex 28 CIC series CIT 118

	1st choke	2nd choke
Venturi bore	21	21
Main jet	110	90
Emulsion tube	1 P 1	2 U 1
Slow running jet	50	—
Accelerator pump injector	35	—
Float	Double polyamide	

Carburettor - Solex 28 CIC series CIT 133

	1st choke	2nd choke
Venturi bore	19	19
Main jet	100	70
Emulsion tube	1 P 1	2 P 2
Slow running jet	50	—
Accelerator pump injector	45	—
Bypass jet	—	40
Econostat jet	—	140
Float	Double polyamide	

Carburettor - Solex 28 CIC^2 series CIT 137

	1st choke	2nd choke
Venturi bore	19	19
Main jet	100	75
Emulsion tube	1 P 2	2 P 3
Idling jet	45	—
Constant richness idling jet	35	—
Accelerator pump injector	50	—
Bypass jet	—	50
Econostat jet	—	160
Float	Double plastic	

Carburettor - Solex 28 CIC³ series CIT 131

	1st choke	2nd choke
Venturi bore	19	19
Main jet	100	80
Air correction jet	1 P 3	2 P 4
Idling jet	50	—
Constant richness idling jet	30	—
Accelerator pump injector	50	—
Econostat jet	—	130
Bypass jet	—	40
Float	Double plastic	

Carburettor - Weber 30 DGS (W50.00)

	1st choke	2nd choke
Venturi bore	20	20
Main jet	100	100
Air correction jet	AD 1	AD 2
Emulsion tube	F 20	F 20
Slow-running jet	45	45
Accelerator pump injector	50	—
Sprayers (mixture jets)	4, 5	4, 5
Float	Brass, weight 11 g	

Carburettor - Weber DGS 1 (W51.00)

	1st choke	2nd choke
Venturi bore	20	20
Main jet	100	107
Air correction jet	AD 2	AD 2
Emulsion tube	F 20	F 20
Idling jet	45	45
Accelerator pump injector	50	—
Sprayers (mixture jets)	4, 5	4, 5
Float	Brass, weight 11 g	
Float level setting	6.5 mm (0.25 in)	

1 General description

1 The fuel system comprises a fuel tank at the rear of the car, a mechanical fuel pump mounted on the rear right hand camshaft bearing and a Solex or Weber carburettor. Early models have a filter in the tank suction pipe, on later models an in-line filter is fitted between the tank and the pump. A dry type element is fitted in the air cleaner/silencer. Those models fitted with anti-pollution type carburettors have an air valve assembly which thermostatically controls the temperature of the intake air.

2 The fuel pump draws petrol from the fuel tank and delivers it to the carburettor. The level of the petrol in the carburettor is controlled by a float operated needle valve. Petrol flows past the needle until the float rises sufficiently to close the valve. The pump will then freewheel under slight back pressure until the petrol level drops in the float chamber. The needle valve will then open and petrol will continue to flow until the level rises again.

3 The petrol/air charge is drawn into the cylinders on the induction stroke via the heater box which is heated from the oil system on early models and by exhaust gases on the later models.

2 Air cleaner assembly - removal and replacement

1 Disconnect the breather pipe and the hot air pipe. Release the clip securing the elbow duct to the carburettor and remove the bracket retaining nuts. Remove the cleaner assembly.

2 Unclip the cover and withdraw the element. Clean the interior of the casing and casing cover. Examine the ducts and flexible pipes for damage (photo).

3 Clean the filter element by swilling it in petrol; allow it to drain and evaporate in the open air, then dip it in clean engine oil and again allow it to drain. Refit by reversing the removal operations.

3 Preheating of the air intake system - general

1 Warm air enters the control valve body from the heating duct and ambient air enters through the elbow at the side of the valve body. The temperature of the air entering the air cleaner casing is controlled by a flap valve which regulates the amount of warm air and air at ambient temperature. The flap valve is actuated by a thermostat, refer to Fig. 2.1 and the warm air enters the control valve body at 'a' and air at ambient temperature enters at 'b'.

2 During the warm up of the engine it is possible to check the movement of the flap valve by observing the mark which is on the end of the flap valve spindle. The operation of the flap valve may also be checked by inserting a thin rod into the ambient air intake and checking the flap movement.

3 Remove the control valve assembly and check the thermostat as follows:

a) *That at ambient temperature below 36ºC (97ºF) the flap valve, Fig. 2.1, closes the duct 'b'.*

b) *Immerse the thermostat element in cold water and slowly heat the water to progressively raise the temperature. Check that when the temperature reaches 39 ± 3ºC (102 ± 5ºF) the flap valve progressively closes the warm air duct (preheated air) and stays in that position.*

c) *Let the water cool and check that when the temperature falls below 39 ± 3ºC (102 ± 5ºF) the flap valve closes the ambient air intake duct.*

4 A defective control valve is not repairable by an owner and must be renewed.

2.2 Removing the air cleaner element - early type shown

Fig. 2.1. Air intake control valve assembly

1	Thermostat	(a)	Warm air duct
2	Flap valve	(b)	Ambient air duct

Fig. 2.2. Fuel tank suction pipe and sender assembly

1	Locking ring	3	Gasket
2	Flexible fuel pipe	a	Filter

4 Fuel filter - general

1 On models to February 1972 a cleanable fuel filter was fitted in the fuel tank, later models have a disposable unit fitted in the fuel line between the tank and the fuel pump. It is mounted in front of the rear axle, underneath the car on the right-hand side.

2 To remove, clean and replace the fuel tank filter proceed as follows:

   a) *Disconnect the earth lead from the battery.*
   b) *Remove the cover plate from inside the boot.*
   c) *Disconnect the two transmitter leads and uncouple the flexible suction pipe from the sender.*
   d) *Remove the transmitter locking ring from the tank, by rotating it 60° in an anti-clockwise direction, and then carefully withdraw the suction pipe and sender assembly.*
   e) *Clean the filter element in petrol and blow out with compressed air.*
   f) *First insert the float into the tank and then the suction pipe.*
   g) *Correctly locate the gasket, fit the locking ring and turn it 60° clockwise to lock.*
   h) *Connect the transmitter leads, couple up the flexible suction pipe to the sender and fit the cover plate.*
   j) *Connect the earth lead to the battery, switch on the ignition and check the operation of the fuel gauge sender.*

3 The in-line filter fitted to models from February 1972 cannot be cleaned and must be renewed every 12 000 miles (20,000 km). When fitting a replacement filter ensure that it is installed correctly with the arrow on the unit, indicating the petrol flow, pointing in the right direction (photo).

4.3 The in-line fuel filter

5 Fuel pump - general

1 The mechanical diaphragm type pump is mounted on the rear bearing housing of the right-hand camshaft and is operated by an eccentric cam ring at the end of the camshaft. An insulation spacer is fitted between the pump flange and the camshaft bearing housing to reduce heat transfer from the engine to the pump. No instructions are given for the repair of a defective pump by the owner. Test procedures are described: if the pump is found to be defective it should be renewed.

6 Fuel pump - removal and replacement

1 Disconnect the inlet pipe from the fuel tank and the delivery pipe to the carburettor. Remove the two securing nuts and washers and lift off the pump. Replacement is a straightforward reversal of the removal sequence (photo).

6.1 Fuel pump inlet and delivery pipe connections

7 Fuel pump — testing

1   To test the operation of the fuel pump, disconnect the fuel inlet pipe from the carburettor and place its open end in a container.

2   Turn the crankshaft with the starting handle, when well-defined regular spurts of fuel should be ejected from the open end of the fuel pipe.

3   If the pump is removed and a finger placed over the fuel inlet hole in the pump, a strong suction should be felt when the pump lever is actuated by a rod.

4   If either test does not prove satisfactory, renew the pump.

5   The stroke of the fuel pump is important, and a check can be carried out in the following way:

   a)   *Remove the fuel pump, as described in Section 6.*

   b)   *Using a depth gauge, Fig. 2.4, measure the distance between the upper face of the spacer and the actuating eccentric of the camshaft, first at the high and then at the low position. Turn the engine with the starting handle to facilitate this operation. The distance should be between 21.5 and 22 mm (0.846 and 0.866 in) for the high position of the eccentric and 26.5 to 27 mm (1.043 to 1.063 in) for the low position of the eccentric.*

   c)   *Measure the distance 'm' (Fig. 2.5), between the spring cap and the end of the pump spindle, this must not be less than 4 mm (0.16 in).*

8 Carburettors - general description

1   Two makes of carburettor are fitted, Solex and Weber. Both are of a downdraught twin choke type with manually operated choke control. Both types are conventional in operation and have a primary and main jet system and a mechanically operated acceleration pump. Both makes of carburettor incorporate exhaust emission control anti-pollution features except the Solex CIT 118 and 133 series.

9 Carburettor - removal and replacement (Solex and Weber)

1   The removal and replacement procedure is the same for both Solex and Weber carburettors.

2   Remove the air cleaner assembly, as described in Section 2.

3   Disconnect the choke and throttle cables from the carburettor.

4   Disconnect the flexible fuel feed pipe from the carburettor and blank the end with a 7 mm diameter bolt.

5   Remove the four securing nuts and lift off the carburettor and the insulation spacer.

6   Replacement of the carburettor is the reverse of the removal sequence. Clean off the old jointing compound from the carburettor mounting flange, the spacer and the heater box. Smear both faces of the spacer with   sealing compound and fit it on the intake manifold with the hole positioned on the right-hand side.

10 Carburettors (Solex) - general

1   The modification standard of Solex carburettors is recognised by a series of CIT numbers which are marked on the carburettors. Identification of the jets and their location is shown in Fig. 2.13.

2   The carburettor is set by the manufacturer. The position of the stop screws '2' and '4', shown in Fig. 2.6, for the butterflies of the primary and secondary chokes is obtained by using a micro-measuring device and these screws must not be altered under any circumstances. Only the idling air screw may be adjusted to obtain the correct idling speed.

3   If the engine is running badly check the condition of the following before carrying out any adjustments to the carburettor:

Air cleaner
Valve clearances
Ignition system

Spark plugs
Strobe timing of the distributor
Throttle and choke linkage

Adjustments should be carried out with the engine at normal running temperature, engine oil temperature 70 to 80ºC (158 to 176ºF).

4   If the car is not fitted with a tachometer, a workshop tachometer will have to be fitted for setting the idling speed, 900 to 950 rpm for models with manual transmission and 850 to 900 rpm for models with semi-automatic transmissions.

11 Idling - adjustment (Solex series CIT 118 and 133 carburettors)

1   Ensure that the throttle butterflies, for the primary and secondary chokes, close properly.

2   Slacken the pressure regulator bleed screw.

3   Preset screw '3' (Fig. 2.6) by screwing it in fully without forcing and then unscrew it six full turns. Preset screw '1' by screwing in fully and then unscrewing four complete turns.

4   Adjust the air screw '1' to bring the idling speed to that specified in Section 10.

5   Find the peak idling speed by slowly adjusting the volume control screw '3' in or out, as necessary, then screw it in so as to cause the idling speed to fall by between 10 and 20 rpm.

6   If the final speed obtained is different from that specified in Section 10, reset it, and repeat the operations as paragraph 5 above.

12 Choke control - adjustment (Solex series CIT 118 and 133 carburettors)

1   Refer to Fig. 2.7. With the choke lever in position indicated and peg 'a' in firm contact with lever '3', a 0.5 mm diameter rod must pass snugly, but freely, between the edge of the secondary throttle butterfly and the body of the carburettor. If necessary, adjust screw '2' to obtain this setting.

13 Idling - adjustment (Solex series CIT 137 and 131 carburettors)

1   Refer to Fig. 2.8. Do not alter the butterfly stop screws '2' and '4' of the primary and secondary chokes.

2   Connect up an exhaust gas analyser.

3   Slacken the hydraulic pressure regulator bleed screw.

4   With the engine running at normal temperature, adjust screw '1' to obtain an idling speed of 900 to 950rpm.

5   Using screw '3' adjust the mixture to obtain a CO reading of 2 to 3.5 percent and a CO_2 reading of 10 to 13 percent.

6   Operations 4 and 5 are to be carried out simultaneously until the specified idling speed is obtained with the CO and CO_2 readings within the specified limits.

14 Throttle closing damper - adjustment (Solex series CIT 137 carburettors)

1   The throttle closing damper is fitted to delay the rate of closure of the throttle when the accelerator pedal is released suddenly.

2   To check the closing delay run the engine at 2500rpm, release the accelerator pedal suddenly and check that the rpm falls to 1000 within 2 to 5 seconds.

3   Adjust the throttle closing damper, if necessary, as follows:

   a)   *Slacken the nut '1', Fig. 2.9.*

   b)   *Screw in the throttle closing damper to reduce the closing delay or screw it out to increase the closing delay.*

   c)   *Tighten the nut '1' and recheck the timing of the closing delay.*

Fig. 2.4. Checking the fuel pump pushrod travel

1 Insulation spacer   A Depth gauge

Fig. 2.5. Measuring the fuel pump spindle

Fig. 2.6. Solex carburettor adjusting screws

1 Idling air screw   3 Volume control screw
2 Primary butterfly stop screw   4 Secondary butterfly stop
                                      screw

Fig. 2.7. Choke adjustment (Solex)

1 Choke lever   3 Lever
2 Adjusting screw

15 Choke control - adjustment (Solex series CIT 137 carburettors)

1 With the choke control '5' (Fig. 2.8) at the first notch (starting from the no-choke position) check that a 0.35mm (0.014in) diameter rod goes through easily, but snugly, between the secondary throttle butterfly and the body of the carburettor. Adjust as necessary with screw '6' to obtain the correct setting.

16 Choke control - adjustment (Solex series CIT 131 carburettors)

1 On carburettors for cars produced up to June 1973 and fitted with the choke lever 'A' (Fig. 2.10), adjust as follows: With the choke lever positioned as shown in Fig. 2.11, peg 'C' in firm contact with lever '3', a 0.35 - 0.40mm (0.013 - 0.015in) diameter rod must pass freely, but snugly, between the edge of the secondary throttle butterfly and the body of the carburettor. If necessary, adjust screw '2' to obtain this setting.
2 On carburettors for cars produced since June 1973 and fitted with

choke lever 'B', adjust as for those fitted with lever 'A' except that a rod of 0.25 - 0.35mm (0.010 - 0.013in) is used.
3 It is important that before any adjustment of the choke control, the difference in profile of the slots in the choke levers should be noted: 'a' for lever 'A' and 'b' for lever 'B'. **Note:** It is recommended that the choke control assembly 'A' be replaced by the assembly 'B' to improve the choke control.

17 Float level - adjustment (Solex carburettors)

1 Remove the air cleaner, as described in Section 2. Disconnect the fuel feed pipe and remove the cover retaining screws. Lift off the cover and float assembly.
2 With the cover and float assembly positioned as shown in Fig. 2.12,

Fig. 2.8. Idling adjustment (Solex)

1 *Adjusting screw*	4 *Secondary butterfly stop screw*
2 *Primary butterfly stop screw*	5 *Choke control*
3 *Mixture screw*	6 *Choke adjusting screw*

Fig. 2.9. Throttle closing damper (Solex) adjustment

1 *Locking nut*	2 *Throttle closing damper*

the dimension measured between the float centre-line and the joint face of the cover (gasket fitted) must be:

    a) Carburettors CIT 118 series - 'h' = 20 ± 1mm (0.79 ± 0.04in)
    b) Carburettors all other series - 'h' = 18 ± 1mm (0.71 ± 0.04in)

If necessary, alter the position of the float by moving lug 'a' to obtain dimension 'h' for the type of carburettor being adjusted.
3 Fit the carburettor cover and ensure that the float does not touch the walls of the float chamber. Connect the fuel feed pipe. Fit the air cleaner assembly, refer to Section 2.

18 Cleaning - general (Solex carburettors)

Use only petrol and compressed air to clean jets and air bleeds. Do not clean them with probes as this may alter the calibration.
Remove the top cover as described in Section 17.
The position of the jets and air bleeds of a Solex 28 CIC 3 carburettor is illustrated in Fig. 2.13 and earlier series carburettors will not have all the jets as shown.

19 Carburettors (Weber) - general

The Weber 30DGS (W50.00) fitted to 1015cc engines and the Weber 30DGS1 (W51.00) fitted to 1222cc engines are very similar and the idling speed and the float adjustment is the same for both carburettors. The position of the jets and air bleeds of a 30DGS (W50.00) carburettor are illustrated in Fig. 2.14. Both carburettors have exhaust emission control anti-pollution systems and exhaust gas analyser equipment is required when adjusting the idling speed.

20 Idling speed - adjustment (Weber carburettors)

1 Before adjusting the idling speed, refer to Section 10 and carry out the checks listed in paragraph 3.
2 Do not alter the setting of the secondary butterfly stop screw as this is set, using a micro-measuring device, by the manufacturer.
3 Ensure that the throttle butterflies in the primary and secondary chokes close fully.
4 Run the engine to obtain a normal operating temperature of 70° to 80°C (158° to 176°F) and slacken the pressure regulator bleed screw.
5 Adjust screw '1' to obtain the correct idling speed:

    a) 850 to 900rpm - for cars with semi-automatic transmission
    b) 900 to 950rpm - for cars with manual transmission.

6 Using screw '5' adjust the mixture to obtain a CO reading 2 to 3.5 percent and a CO_2 reading of 10 to 13 percent. Obtain these readings with the engine idling speed as specified in paragraph 5 above. Both operations must be carried out simultaneously. The specified CO and CO_2 readings are for an ambient air temperature of between 15° and 30°C (61° and 86°F).

21 Primary butterfly - adjustment (Weber carburettors)

1 When the choke is operated, the linkage opens the primary butterfly by a preset amount. To adjust the setting it is necessary to remove the carburettor, as described in Section 9.
2 With the primary butterfly fully closed measure the gap between the edge of the butterfly and the body of the carburettor. For 30DGS (50.00) carburettors the gap should be 1.25 to 1.35mm (0.049 to 0.053in) and for 30DGS1 (51.00) 1.0 to 1.1mm (0.039 to 0.043in).
3 Adjust, if necessary, by bending the connecting rod, refer to Fig. 2.15 to obtain the correct setting.}

22 Float level - adjustment (Weber carburettors)

1 Remove the air cleaner assembly, as described in Section 2. Disconnect the fuel feed pipe.

Fig. 2.10. Choke lever assemblies

Fig. 2.13. Solex carburettor - cover removed

1 Bypass jet for primary choke
2 Air jet for secondary choke
3 Econostat for secondary choke
4 Constant richness idling jet

5 Accelerator pump injector
6 Idling jet
7 Air jet for primary choke

Main jet for primary choke at bottom of well for jet 7.
Main jet for secondary choke at bottom of well for jet 2.

Fig. 2.11. Choke adjustment (Solex)

1 Choke lever
2 Adjusting screw

3 Lever

Fig. 2.14. Weber carburettor - cover removed

1 Air correction jet for primary choke
2 Idling jet for primary choke
3 Mixture jet for primary choke
4 Accelerator pump injector
5 Mixture jet for secondary choke

6 Idling jet for secondary choke
7 Air correction jet for secondary choke
8 Main jet for secondary choke
9 Main jet for primary choke

Fig. 2.12. Float level adjustment (Solex)

Fig. 2.15. Weber carburettor adjustment

1 Primary butterfly stop screw
2 Circlip
3 Choke lever clamp screw
4 Connecting rod

5 Mixture screw
6 Clip
7 Secondary butterfly stop screw

2   Remove the carburettor cover. Refer to Fig. 2.15 and remove
the clip and its rubber washer and disconnect the connecting rod from
the throttle butterfly control lever. Disconnect the choke lever from
the carburettor body by removing the choke lever clamp screw and its
spring. Disconnect the control lever from the capsule by removing the
circlip. Remove the five cover securing screws and lift off the cover and
float assembly.
3   Hold the cover and float assembly vertically as shown in Fig. 2.16,
with the needle valve ball not depressed. Measure the distance 'a'
between the joint face of the cover (gasket in position) and the float.
This measurement must be 6.5 $\pm$ 0.25mm (0.255 $\pm$ 0.010in), if necessary, adjust lug 'b' to bring this dimension within the limits specified.
4   Ensure the gasket is in good condition, or renew it, and refit the
cover and float assembly in the reverse sequence of the removal
operations. Connect the fuel feed pipe and refit the air cleaner assembly.

23 Cleaning - general (Weber carburettors)

1   When cleaning the carburettor use only petrol and compressed air.
Never use a probe in the jets or air bleeds as this may well affect the
calibration.
2   Removal of the cover and float assembly, as described in Section 22,
gives access to the jets and air bleeds, the positions of which are shown
in Fig. 2.14.

24 Carburettor - dismantling (Solex and Weber)

1   Other than removing the carburettor cover and float assembly, as
described in Sections 17 and 22, it is unlikely that the owner will need
to further dismantle the carburettor, bearing in mind that the secondary
butterfly stop screws are set by the manufacturers and must not be
altered. If the butterfly spindles, which run directly in the body of the
carburettor, become worn a complete replacement carburettor will be
required.

25 Exhaust system - general

1   The exhaust system consists of separate pipes from each cylinder
head, joined in a 'V' section to the single pipe leading to the silencer.
2   The front piping as fitted to models using exhaust gases to heat the
inlet casing (early models use engine oil) is illustrated in Fig. 2.17..
3   When fitting the exhaust piping ensure that it is routed correctly
and that the clamps and securing bolts are tightened evenly. Components subject to stress and strains are liable to fracture.
4   When any one part of the system requires renewal, consideration
should be given to renewing the complete system as, apart from accidental damage, when one part fails the rest of the system is not likely
to last long.

Fig. 2.16 Float level adjustment
(Weber)

Fig. 2.17. Front pipes of exhaust system

26 Fault diagnosis - carburettors and fuel system

Unsatisfactory engine performance and excessive fuel consumption are not necessarily the fault of the fuel system or carburettor. In fact they more commonly occur as a result of ignition faults. Before working on the fuel system it is necessary to check the ignition system. Even though a fault may lie in the fuel system it will be difficult to trace unless the ignition is correct. The table below, therefore, assumes that the ignition system is in order.

Symptom	Reason/s	Remedy
Smell of petrol when engine is stopped	Leaking fuel lines or unions Leaking fuel tank	Repair or renew as necessary. Fill tank to capacity and examine seams and joints. Repair as necessary.
Smell of petrol when engine is idling	Leaking fuel line between pump and carburettor Overflow of fuel from float chamber due to wrong level setting or ineffective needle valve or punctured float	Check pipe and unions and tighten or repair. Check fuel level setting and condition of float and needle valve. Renew if necessary.
Excessive fuel consumption for reasons not covered by leaks or float chamber faults	Worn needle valve Sticking needle valve	Renew needle valve. Check correct movement of needle valve.
Difficult starting, uneven running, lack of power, cutting out	One or more jets blocked or restricted Float chamber fuel level too low or needle valve sticking Fuel pump not delivering sufficient fuel	Dismantle and clean out float chamber and jets. Dismantle and check fuel level and needle valve. Check pump delivery and renew if necessary.

Chapter 3 Ignition system

For modifications, and information applicable to later models, see Supplement at end of manual

Contents

Specifications

Spark plugs

To June 1972:

SEV - Marchal	34 S
Eyquem	755 S
Electrode gap	0.6/0.7 mm (0.024/0.028 in)

	Town traffic or operation in cold climates	Normal 'open road' conditions
1015 cc and 1129 cc engines, June 1972 on:		
Marchal	GT 34H	34 HS
AC	41-4-XLS	40-8XLS
Champion	N7Y	N6Y
Eyquem	755 LS	800 LS
Electrode gap	0.65/0.8 mm (0.026/0.032 in)	0.65/0.8 mm (0.026/0.032 in)
1222 cc engine, June 1972 on:		
Marchal	35 HS	34 HS
AC	42-XLS	40-8XLS
Champion	N9Y	N6Y
Eyquem	755 LS	800 LS
Electrode gap	0.65/0.8 mm (0.026/0.032 in)	0.65/0.8 mm (0.026/0.032 in)

Coil (alternatives)

Ducellier	2777 C
SEV-Marchal	E 44910312
Marelli	BZR 206 A

Distributor

	SEV-Marchal (cassette type)	Ducellier
January 71 to December 71	41301002	4310 A
December 71 to September 72	41301202	4431 A
From September 72	41301302	4451 A

Rotation (seen from drive end)	Clockwise
Firing order	1 - 4 - 3 - 2
Contact breaker gap	0.35 to 0.45 mm (0.014 to 0.018 in)
Cam dwell angle	55 to 59°

Ignition timing

Static setting	10° BTDC
Mark on flywheel:	
Cars to October 71	Rod hole corresponding to 10° initial advance before TDC
Cars from October 71	A chisel mark on flywheel and a sector graduated in crankshaft degrees fixed to the crankcase.
Condenser	0.25 - 0.30 UF

1 General description

In order that the engine can run it is necessary for an electrical spark to ignite the fuel/air mixture in the combustion chamber at exactly the right moment in relation to the engine speed and load.

The ignition system is based on feeding low tension voltage from the battery to the ignition coil where it is converted to high tension voltage. The high tension voltage is powerful enough to jump the spark plug gap in the cylinders many times a second under high compression pressures, providing that the system is in good condition and that all adjustments are correct.

The ignition system is divided into two parts, the low tension and the high tension circuits. The low tension (or primary) circuit consists of the battery, lead to the control box, lead to the ignition switch, lead from the ignition switch to the low tension or primary coil windings terminal and the lead from the low tension coil windings to the contact breaker points and condenser on the distributor. The high tension circuit consists of the high tension or secondary coil windings, the heavy duty ignition lead from the centre of the coil to the centre of the distributor cap, the rotor arm, the spark plug leads and spark plugs. The system functions in the following manner: High tension voltage is generated in the coil by the interruption of the low tension circuit. The interruption is effected by the opening of the contact breaker points in the low tension circuit.

High tension voltage is fed via the carbon brush, in the centre of the distributor cap, to the rotor arm of the distributor.

The rotor arm revolves at half engine speed inside the distributor cap and each time it comes in line with one of the four metal segments in the cap, which are in turn connected to the spark plug leads, the opening and closing of the contact breaker points causes the high tension voltage to build up, jump the gap from the rotor arm to the appropriate metal segment. From the sequence the electrical charge travels via the spark plug lead to the spark plug, where it finally jumps the spark plug gap before going to earth.

The ignition is advanced and retarded automatically, both mechanically and by a vacuum device, to ensure that the spark occurs at the right instant for the particular load at the prevailing engine speed. As engine speed increases centrifugal action of rotating weights pivoting against the tension of small springs advances the contact breaker cam in relation to the distributor shaft and so advances the timing. The vacuum control is connected via a small bore pipe to the carburettor and according to the varying intake depression it advances or retards the ignition timing.

Distributors of SEV-Marchal make have cassette type contact breaker sets which are discarded and replaced by a new cassette. Ducellier distributors have conventional type points. The distributor is fitted at the rear of the left-hand cylinder head and is secured on two studs which engage in elongated holes. To adjust the contact breaker points the distributor must first be removed from the engine as the points are not accessible when the engine is fitted in the car.

Fig. 3.1 diagrammatically illustrates the ignition circuit and the layout and numbering of the cylinders. The firing order, 1 - 4 - 3 - 2, is the same for both engines.

2   Distributor - removal and replacement

1   Mark the flanges of the distributor and its mounting so that the distributor can be refitted in its original position.
2   Remove the distributor cap and take note of the position of the rotor arm (photo).
3   Remove the retaining nuts and withdraw the distributor.
Note: Do not turn the crankshaft when the distributor is removed. If the crankshaft is moved whilst the distributor is removed, the ignition timing will have to be reset (photo).
4   No overhaul procedures are described for either make of distributor. Testing of the centrifugal and vacuum advance device requires special testing equipment and this should be entrusted to a service station which you know is equipped to test distributors.
5   To replace the distributor set the rotor arm to the same position it was at when the distributor was removed. Refit the distributor and the two retaining nuts, turn the distributor to line up the marks which were made on the flanges and tighten the retaining nuts (photo).
6   If a new distributor is being fitted the ignition will have to be retimed, as described in Section 8.

FRONT OF VEHICLE

Fig. 3.1. Ignition and cylinder layout diagram

3   Contact breaker points - adjustment

1   Remove the distributor as described in Section 2. Remove the rotor and the seal.
2   Turn the distributor shaft until one cam lobe lifts the contact heel to its highest point. Slacken the points locking screw and adjust the points gap to 0.35 to 0.045 mm (0.014 to 0.018 in) by moving the adjustable contact with a small screwdriver inserted through the adjacent slot (photo).
3   Tighten the locking screw and re-check the gap.
4   Replace the distributor as described in Section 2.

2.2 Distributor with cap, rotor and seal removed

2.3 Removing the distributor

2.5 Distributor fitted in position on the engine

3.2 Measuring the points gap with a feeler gauge

4 Contact breaker points - removal and replacement

1   Remove the distributor as described in Section 2. Remove the rotor and the seal.
2   SEV-Marchal distributors have a disposable, cassette type set of points. Remove the casette and fit a replacement cassette.
3   Ducellier distributors have a conventional set of points. Remove the two screws securing the top bearing housing and remove the housing. Remove the retaining clip and locking screw and lift out the contact points.
4   Check the condition of the points. If they are rough and pitted it will be necessary to renew them.
5   Fit the contact points and adjust the gap as described in Section 3. Refit the distributor, as described in Section 2.

5 Spark plugs and HT leads - general

1   The correct functioning of the spark plugs is vital for the correct running and efficient operation of the engine. The spark plugs fitted as standard are as listed in the Specifications at the beginning of this Chapter.
2   At intervals of 6,000 miles (10,000 Km) the plugs should be removed, examined and cleaned. If worn excessively they must be renewed. The condition of the spark plug can give some indication of the overall condition of the engine.
3   If the insulator nose of the spark plug is clean and white, with no deposits, it is an indication that the mixture is too weak, or that too hot a plug is fitted. (A hot plug transfers heat away from the electrode slowly - a cold plug transfers it away quickly).
4   If the tip and insulator nose is covered with sooty black deposits, then this is indicative that the mixture is too rich. Should the plug be black and oily, then it is likely that the engine cylinders and piston rings are worn, as well as the mixture being rich.
5   A properly tuned engine, under normal running conditions, will have a light deposit of a greyish brown colour on the electrodes.
6   If there are traces of long brown tapering stains on the outside of the white portion of the spark plug, then the plug will have to be renewed, as this shows that there is a faulty joint between the plug body and the insulator, and that pressure is being allowed to leak past.
7   If possible clean the spark plug in a sand blasting machine as this will remove carbon deposits more thoroughly than cleaning by hand. The machine will also test the condition of the spark plugs under pressure conditions. Any plug that fails to spark at the recommended pressure should be discarded.
8   The spark plug gap is of considerable importance as its efficiency will be seriously affected if the gap is too large or too small. Set the spark plug gap to specification.
9   Set the gap by measuring it with a feeler gauge, and then bend open, or close, the outer electrode until the correct gap is obtained. Never

bend the centre electrode as this will probably crack the insulation and cause plug failure.
10 To help get the spark plug thread correctly seated in the cylinder head when replacing the plugs, push a rubber tube over the insulator and screw the plug in as far as possible with the tube. Finish tightening the plug to 2 - 2.5 kg f m (14 - 18 lb f ft) with a torque wrench.
11 No routine maintenance is required for the plug leads other than being kept clean by wiping them regularly and checking for deterioration of the insulation and loose connections.

6 Coil and condenser - general

The coil is mounted on the left-hand wheel arch and the condenser is secured to the distributor by a clip. Checking the coil and condenser is dealt with in Section 9.

7 Ignition timing - general

1   There should be little need to retime the ignition except after engine overhaul or if the distributor has been renewed. When setting the timing it is essential that the contact breaker points are in good condition and that the gap is correctly set, as described in Section 3.
2   Two methods of determining the static timing point are used, on early 1015 cc engines, a 5 mm diameter rod is inserted in a hole in the crankcase to lock the flywheel and on all later 1015 cc engines and 1222 cc engines a graduated timing scale is attached to the crankcase and the flywheel is marked.

8 Ignition timing - static adjustment

1   On 1015 cc engines fitted with a distributor reference GA 2 - GD 1, proceed as follows:

   a) *Set No. 1 cylinder to TDC at the end of compression stroke (remove the rocker cover from the left-hand cylinder head and check that both valves are closed) and insert a 5 mm diameter rod through the hole in the left-hand side of the crankcase to engage with the hole in the flywheel. This determines the static timing position, 10° before TDC.*
   b) *Turn the distributor shaft until the rotor arm is pointing to the position of No. 1 segment of the distributor cap, refer to Fig. 3.1, and fit the distributor on its mounting studs. Fit the retaining nuts finger-tight.*
   c) *Connect a 12 volt timing lamp, 'A' in Fig. 3.2, between the earth and the terminal 'a' of the condenser on the distributor.*
   d) *Switch on the ignition and slowly turn the distributor body in the direction of the arrow shown in Fig. 3.4. Stop turning the distributor the moment the lamp lights up, indicating that the points are just opening. Tighten the retaining nuts and switch off the ignition. Disconnect the timing lamp and fit the distributor cover.*

2   For 1015 cc and 1222 cc engines fitted with distributors with reference numbers: GA2 - GD1, GA4 - GD1, GA5 - GD2 and GA3 - GD4 proceed as follows:

   a) *Set No. 1 cylinder to the end of the compression stroke (both valves closed), then turn the engine so that the mark, 'b' in Fig. 3.5 on the flywheel is aligned with the 10° graduation on the timing scale. Use of a mirror will help in aligning the mark accurately (photo).*
   b) *Turn the distributor shaft until the rotor arm is pointing to the position of No. 1 segment of the distributor cap and fit the distributor with the retaining nuts finger-tight.*
   c) *Connect a timing lamp between the terminal 'RUP' of the ignition coil and earth.*
   d) *Switch on the ignition and slowly turn the distributor body in the direction of the arrow in Fig. 3.4. Stop turning the distributor the moment the lamp lights up, indicating that the points are just opening.*
   e) *Tighten the retaining nuts and switch of the ignition. Disconnect the timing lamp and fit the distributor cap.*

Measuring plug gap. A feeler gauge of the correct size (see ignition system specifications) should have a slight 'drag' when slid between the electrodes. Adjust gap if necessary

Adjusting plug gap. The plug gap is adjusted by bending the earth electrode inwards, or outwards, as necessary until the correct clearance is obtained. Note the use of the correct tool

Normal. Grey-brown deposits, lightly coated core nose. Gap increasing by around 0.001 in (0.025 mm) per 1000 miles (1600 km). Plugs ideally suited to engine, and engine in good condition

Carbon fouling. Dry, black, sooty deposits. Will cause weak spark and eventually misfire. Fault: over-rich fuel mixture. Check: carburettor mixture settings, float level and jet sizes; choke operation and cleanliness of air filter. Plugs can be re-used after cleaning

Oil fouling. Wet, oily deposits. Will cause weak spark and eventually misfire. Fault: worn bores/piston rings or valve guides; sometimes occurs (temporarily) during running-in period. Plugs can be re-used after thorough cleaning

Overheating. Electrodes have glazed appearance, core nose very white – few deposits. Fault: plug overheating. Check: plug value, ignition timing, fuel octane rating (too low) and fuel mixture (too weak). Discard plugs and cure fault immediately

Electrode damage. Electrodes burned away; core nose has burned, glazed appearance. Fault: pre-ignition. Check: as for 'Overheating' but may be more severe. Discard plugs and remedy fault before piston or valve damage occurs

Split core nose (may appear initially as a crack). Damage is self-evident, but cracks will only show after cleaning. Fault: pre-ignition or wrong gap-setting technique. Check: ignition timing, cooling system, fuel octane rating (too low) and fuel mixture (too weak). Discard plugs, rectify fault immediately

Fig. 3.3. Timing the ignition

8.2 Setting the timing marks

Fig. 3.4. Setting the static ignition timing

1 *Distributor retaining bolts*

Fig. 3.5. Checking the timing

9 Fault diagnosis - ignition system (contact breaker type)

There are two main symptoms indicating ignition faults. Either the engine will not start or is difficult to start and misfires. If it is a regular misfire the fault is most likely to be in the secondary or high tension circuit. If the misfiring is intermittent, the fault could be in either the high or low tension circuits. If the engine stops suddenly, or will not start at all, it is likely that the fault is in the low tension circuit. Loss of power and overheating, apart from faulty carburation settings is normally due to faults in the distributor or incorrect ignition timing.

Engine fails to start

1   If the engine fails to start and the car was running normally when it was last used, first check that there is petrol in the fuel tank. If the engine turns over normally on the starter motor and the battery is evidently well charged, then the fault may be in either the high or low tension circuits. First check the HT circuit. **Note:** If the battery is known to be fully charged, the ignition warning light comes on and the starter motor fails to turn the engine, check the tightness of the leads on the battery terminals and also the secureness of the earth lead to its connection on the body. It is quite common for the leads to have worked loose, even if they look and feel secure. If one of the battery terminal posts get very hot when trying to operate the starter motor, this is a sure indication of a faulty connection to that terminal.
2   One of the commonest reasons for bad starting is wet or damp spark plug leads and distributor. If condensation is visible internally, dry the cap with a cloth and also wipe over the leads.
3   If the engine still fails to start, check that current is reaching the plugs. Disconnect each plug in turn at the spark plug end, and hold the end of the lead about 3/16th inch (5 mm) away from the cylinder head (not the rocker cover); turn the engine over on the starter. Sparking between the end of the cable and the cylinder head should be fairly strong with a regular blue spark. Hold the lead with rubber or plastic gloves to avoid electric shocks. If current is reaching the spark plugs, remove them, clean and reset the gap. The engine should now start.
4   If there is no spark at the plug leads take off the HT lead from the centre of the distributor cap and hold it to the cylinder head as before. Spin the engine on the starter. A rapid succession of blue sparks between the end of the lead and the cylinder head indicates that the coil is in order and that the distributor cap is cracked, the rotor arm faulty, or the carbon brush in the top of the distributor cap is not making good contact with the spring on the rotor arm. Possibly the contact breaker points are burnt, pitted or dirty, if so clean or renew them as described in Section 4.
5   If there are no sparks from the end of the lead from the coil, check the connection at the coil end of the lead and if it is in order check out the low tension circuit.

6   Switch on the ignition and turn the crankshaft so that the contact breaker points are open, then using a 12V bulb and two lengths of wire, or a zero-to-20 range voltmeter if available, test between the low tension wire to the coil and earth. No reading indicates a break in the supply from the ignition switch. Check the connections at the switch to see if any are loose and if so, refit them. A reading shows a faulty coil or condenser, or broken lead between the coil and the distributor.

7   Take the condenser wire off the points and with the points open, test between the moving point and earth. If there is now a reading then the condenser is faulty and will have to be renewed.

8   With no reading from the moving point to earth, take a reading between earth and the negative terminal of the coil. A reading here shows a broken wire, which will have to be renewed, between the coil and the distributor. No reading indicates that the coil is defective and must be replaced. Remember to fit the condenser wire to the points assembly. For these tests it is sufficient to separate the points with a piece of dry paper while testing with the points open.

Engine misfires

1   If the engine misfires regularly run it at a fast idling speed. Remove and replace each spark plug lead from its spark plug in turn. If the plug is firing properly this will accentuate the uneven running but will make no difference if the plug is defective. Remove the insulator from the lead to the faulty plug and hold the end about 3/16th inch (5 mm) away from the cylinder head (not the rocker cover) with the engine running. If the spark is strong and regular the fault must lie in the spark plug.

2   The plug may be loose, the insulation may be cracked, or the electrodes may have burnt away giving too wide a gap. Either renew the plug, or clean it, reset the gap and then test it.

3   If there is no spark at the end of the plug lead, or if it is weak and intermittent, check the ignition lead from the distributor to the plug. If the insulation is cracked or perished, renew the lead. Check the connection at the distributor cap.

4   If there is still no spark, examine the distributor cap carefully for tracking. This can be recognised by a very thin black line running between two or more segments, or between a segment and some other part of the distributor. These lines are paths which now conduct current across the cap, thus letting it run to earth; if this is the case it means the distributor cap will have to be renewed.

5   Apart from the ignition timing being incorrect, other causes of misfiring have already been dealt with in the previous sub-Section.

6   If the ignition timing is too far retarded, the engine will tend to overheat and there will be a noticeable drop in power. If this happens and the ignition timing is correct, then the carburettor should be checked as it is likely that this is where the fault lies.

Engine fires but will not run

1   If the engine fires when the starter motor is cranking, but dies when the ignition key is returned to the running position, it may be that the ballast resistor is at fault.

2   The ballast resistor is mounted on the ignition coil. It is normally wired in series with the coil primary (low tension) winding. When the starter motor is operated, the ballast resistor is temporarily bypassed and battery voltage is applied directly to the coil. This compensates for the voltage drop caused by the starter motor and gives a good spark for starting.

3   Should the ballast resistor be faulty, it must be renewed. Consult an auto-electrician or Citroen dealer. The resistor may be bypassed as a 'get-you-home' measure, but the coil itself may fail as a result of the increased primary current; contact breaker life will also be much reduced.

4   A ballast resistor is not used with the transistorised ignition system described in Chapter 13.

Chapter 4 Clutch and manual gearbox

For modifications, and information applicable to later models, see Supplement at end of manual

Contents

Specifications

Clutch
Type	Single dry plate, diaphragm spring
Driven plate (1015 cc engine)	6 springs all of the same colour
Driven plate (1222 cc engine)	2 grey, 2 blue, 2 white springs
Lining	Ferodo A755
Lining thickness - new	7.7 mm (0.30 in)

Gearbox
Number of gears	4 forward, 1 reverse
Ratios:	
1st	3.82 : 1
2nd	2.38 : 1
3rd	1.52 : 1
4th	1.12 : 1
Reverse	4.18 : 1
Speedometer drive	2.17 : 1

Differential unit
Location	Integral with gearbox
Ratio:	
1015 cc Engine	4.375 : 1
1222 cc Engine	4.125 : 1

Gearbox and differential tolerances
Endfloat of 1st/2nd synchro-hub (max)	0.05 mm (0.002 in)
Endfloat of 3rd/4th synchro-hub (max)	0.05 mm (0.002 in)
Clearance of half-washers between 2nd and 3rd gearwheels (max) ...	0.05 mm (0.002 in)
Crownwheel and pinion backlash (max)	0.13 to 0.27 mm (0.005 to 0.011 in)
Total preload on differential bearings	0.05 mm (0.002 in)

Oil grade	EP 80
Oil capacity	1.4 litre approx. (2.5 Imp. pints)

1 General description

1   Two types of transmissions are available on GS models, a manual transmission with a four speed gearbox, and a semi-automatic transmission. The drive, transmitted to the front wheels through the differential gearing in the gearbox and the drive shaft is very similar on both types. The semi-automatic transmission is described in Chapter 5.

2   The clutch is a cable operated single dry plate diaphragm type. When the clutch pedal is depressed the clutch spring is compressed which releases the pressure plate thereby freeing the driven plate (disc), which is splined to the gearbox primary shaft through the control shaft. When the clutch driven plate is freed there is no drive from the engine to the gearbox; but when engaged, drive is transmitted from the engine to the gearbox. Fig. 4.1 shows a cross-section through the clutch.

3   The four forward speed gears are in constant mesh through synchro units. Reverse gear is engaged through a separate layshaft and idler gear, and is meshed with a gear which is integral with the 1st and 2nd synchro-unit. Gear selection is obtained by the gear lever operating the selector forks, which select gears on the primary shaft which then mesh with the appropriate gear on the pinion shaft.

4   Various gear ratios have been used. The speedometer drive is taken from the gearbox. The power flow through the gearbox is shown in Fig. 4.4.

2 Clutch - maintenance

Routine maintenance is confined to checking the clutch pedal free-movement. (see Section 4). If all the adjustment is nearly taken up, this is an indication that the lining on the disc is almost at the limit of permissible wear.

Fig. 4.1. Cross-section through the clutch

Fig. 4.2. Longitudinal section - manual gearbox

Fig. 4.3. Transverse section - manual gearbox

3   Clutch cable - removal and replacement

1   Open the bonnet. Remove the spare wheel, slacken off the locknut and cable adjusting nut and release the pedal linkage cover from the bulkhead. Get an assistant to depress the clutch pedal while you chock the clutch release fork, release the pedal and remove the cable end from the release fork. Disconnect the other end from the pedal linkage on the bulkhead and remove the cable from its support on the gearbox casing (photos).

2   Replacement is the reverse of the removal sequence. Adjust the release bearing clearance as described in Section 4.

4   Clutch - adjustment

Note:
You may have to modify two open-ended spanners (16mm and 19mm) to carry out this operation as the nuts are not very accessible.

1   Remove the spare wheel.

2   Refer to photo 3.1a and slacken the locknut. Turn the adjusting nut to obtain a clearance of 3.2 to 4.8 mm (0.125 to 0.190 in) between the fixed tube and the adjusting nut. This setting will give the clutch pedal 15 to 20 mm (0.6 to 0.8 in) free movement.

3   Tighten the locknut and refit the spare wheel.

5   Clutch - removal

1   Removal of the clutch necessitates the removal of the engine as

described in Chapter 1, Section 6. Before removing the clutch cover bolts, mark the position of the cover in relation to the flywheel, so that it can be put back in the same position.

2   Restrain the flywheel from turning and slacken the cover assembly retaining bolts a little at a time, working in a progressive diagonal sequence so that the diaphragm spring pressure is released evenly to prevent any distortion.

3   When all the spring pressure on the bolts has been released, remove the bolts, washers, clutch cover assembly and clutch driven plate (photo).

6   Clutch - inspection and renovation

1   Examine the friction lining of the clutch driven plate for wear and contamination by oil. If the linings are dark in colour this indicates oil contamination caused by oil leaking past the crankshaft rear seal, or the gearbox seal. Check that there are no loose or broken damper springs or rivets on the driven plate and that the splines of the hub are in good condition.

2   Examine the friction faces of the flywheel and clutch pressure plate for scoring, caused by the heads of the rivets on the clutch driven plate, as a result of excessive wear of the linings. If there is deep scoring of the flywheel it will have to be machined, (this is specialist work), or renewed. Heavy scoring of the pressure plate or broken diaphragm spring necessitate the replacement of the clutch cover assembly.

3   Whenever the engine is removed for any reason, always examine the clutch operating mechanism and replace any worn parts as described in Section 16.

3.1a Disconnecting the clutch cable from the pedal linkage on the bulkhead. Cable nuts arrowed

3.1b Clutch cable support on the gearbox housing

5.3 Removing the clutch cover assembly and clutch driven plate

1st GEAR

2nd GEAR

3rd GEAR

4th GEAR

REVERSE GEAR

Note: The gears of the drive shaft are in constant mesh with the driven gears of the 1st, 2nd, 3rd and 4th gears.

Fig. 4.4. Power flow - manual gearbox

Fig. 4.5. Clutch adjustment (LHD vehicles)

1   Adjusting nut   3   Fixed tube
2   Locknut

7   Clutch - replacement

1   If the original clutch cover assembly is being refitted, line-up the
marks made at removal, position the driven plate and fit the cover
assembly to the flywheel. Fit the washers and retaining bolts, screw
them in evenly just enough to grip the driven plate but not enough to
prevent it being moved.
2   Before tightening the retaining bolts it is necessary to line-up the
centre of the driven plate with the centring bush of the crankshaft. This
is easily done if you have an old control shaft or a mandrel with the
same spigot and spline diameter as the control shaft. It can also be
lined up by eye, but this is not so reliable. If the driven plate is not
centred correctly, it will be impossible to fit the engine to the
gearbox and the control shaft may get damaged while attempting to do
so.
3   With the driven plate correctly positioned, proceed to tighten the
retaining bolts in a progressive and even manner at a torque of 1.8
kg f m (13 lb f ft). Remove the centralising tool.(photo).
4   Replace the engine in the car as described in Chapter 1.

7.3 Clutch cover assembly bolted in position on the flywheel

8   Gearbox - removal and replacement

The gearbox cannot be removed as a separate unit. It is removed
with the engine, as an engine and gearbox assembly, as described in
Chapter 1, Section 5. Separation of the gearbox from the engine is
described in Chapter 1, Section 7.

9   Gearbox - dismantling (general)

Before dismantling the gearbox decide if it is worthwhile from a
cost point of view. If it is in a generally poor condition then the cost of
parts could be more than an exchange unit. Another point to consider
is that special equipment is required to adjust the crownwheel and
pinion.

10 Gearbox - dismantling procedure (stage 1)

1   Drain off the oil and position the gearbox on the bench with the
left-hand half-casing lowermost. Remove the brake calipers, as
described in Chapter 8, Section 4.
2   On each side loosen the differential output shaft ring nuts with a
chain or strap wrench. Unscrew the ring nuts fully and withdraw the
shafts and bearings (if necessary, tap lightly with a mallet).
3   Remove the spring clip and the clutch thrust bearing. Remove the
fork shaft retaining screw and withdraw the shaft by passing it through
one of the vents of the clutch housing. Collect the spring, the anti-
rattle bushes and the fork.
4   Remove the rear cover and the clutch housing. Refer to Fig. 4.7,
and blank off the hole (a) with a finger, remove the split pin and
collect the blanking disc from the hole.
5   Remove the nuts and bolts securing the half-casings together and
lift off the right-hand casing, taking care to collect the lockball, the
ball and socket guide and the guide thrust spring.
6   Remove the plate which holds the return spring, the ball and
socket, the plunger, the spring and the lockball.
7   Remove the shaft and fork of the 3rd and 4th gear and the lockball.
Remove the control shaft and primary shaft assembly. Remove the
bevel pinion assembly.
8   Remove the differential assembly. Remove the roller bearing outer
races from the half-casings and mark them so as to identify them with
their corresponding bearings. To avoid having to reset the backlash on
reassembly, identify and mark the position of the adjusting shims.

Fig. 4.6. Clutch release mechanism

1   Screw   5   Spring clip
2   Fork   6   Thrust bearing
3   Bush   7   Spring
4   Shaft

Fig. 4.7. Removing blanking disc

Fig. 4.8. Dismantling the gearbox

1 Lockball	5 Plate
2 Spring	6 Ball and socket guide
3 Selector fork	7 Ball and socket
4 Plunger	8 Lockball

Fig. 4.9. Dismantling the gearbox

1 Differential unit	4 Lockball
2 Bevel pinion shaft assembly	5 Control shaft
3 Primary shaft	

11 Gearbox - dismantling procedure (stage 2)

1 Strip down the left-hand half-casing:

a) *Remove the cylindrical pin, which is free in its housing, the reverse idler gear shaft and the gear.*

b) *Remove the reverse gear lever by unscrewing the lever spindle from the underside of the half-casing and remove the lever.*

c) *Remove the reversing light switch (if fitted), or the blanking plug.*

d) *Place a finger over the hole (a) in Fig. 4.10, free the reverse gear control shaft towards the rear and collect the lockball and its spring from the housing.*

e) *Remove the circlip (if fitted) retaining the differential output shaft seal and drive out the seal with a suitable tube.*

2 Strip down the right-hand half-casing:

a) *Place a finger on the lockball hole and free the 1st and 2nd gear shaft and fork assembly towards the rear and collect the lockball and its spring. Remove the stop pin by positioning the shaft/fork assembly against the rear bearing to avoid any damage as the pin is removed using a 5 mm pin punch.*

b) *Remove the differential output shaft seal, refer to paragraph 1 (e) above.*

3 Strip down the control shaft/primary shaft assembly:

a) *Remove the circlip and separate the control shaft from the primary shaft.*

b) *Remove the needle bearing, the retaining nut, which is locked by peening, and the bearing.*

4 Strip down the bevel pinion shaft assembly:

Note: The bearing surfaces of the bevel pinion shaft have been subjected to a special surface treatment and it is essential that precautions are taken to prevent any scratches or other damage that could risk causing seizure of the operating parts.

a) *Remove the speedometer drive/nut, which is locked by peening, the bearing and the pinion shaft, adjusting shim, the idling pinion of the 4th gear and the synchro-ring. Identify the adjusting shim to avoid having to adjust the position of the pinion shaft in the casing unless the pinion shaft or casing is being renewed.*

b) *To avoid damage to the bearing surface of the shaft wrap a piece of 0.10 mm (0.004 in) thick foil, 'A' in Fig. 4.13,, round the shaft. Hold it against the circlip, separate the ends of the circlip with pliers and slip the foil under the circlip. Remove the circlip over the foil.*

c) *Remove the 3rd and 4th gear synchro-hub, the 3rd gear synchro-ring and idling pinion. The 3rd and 4th gear synchro-rings are identical but must be kept as a matched set with the corresponding pinions if they are not being renewed.*

d) *Release the washer and remove the two half-washers. Remove the 2nd gear pinion, the needle cage, (or the dowels and spring), and the 2nd gear synchro-ring.*

e) *Using a piece of foil as before, remove the circlip, as described in (b) above. Remove the 1st and 2nd gear synchro-hub, the 1st gear synchro-ring, the 1st gear idling pinion and the dowels and their springs.*

f) *If it is necessary to remove the front bearing inner race, a press and piece of tube of 50 mm diameter is required. Remove the circlip, the thrust washer and the bearing. Press off the inner race.*

5 To dismantle the differential assembly remove the locking pin and drive out the differential gear shaft. Remove the differential gears and the planet gears. Remove the crownwheel retaining bolts. If the bearings are to be replaced, remove them using a three claw extractor with a suitable centre pad.

6 Strip down the differential output shafts:

There are two types of output shaft, the earlier type 'A' in Fig. 4.17 and the later type, 'B' which does not have a nut (1).

a) *Grease the visible thread (b) and then remove the nut from 'type A' shaft.*

b) *Using a universal type extractor, having a central screw fitted with a ball to avoid damaging the end (a) of the shafts, remove the bearing.*

7 Release the speedometer socket from the rear cover and uncouple the speedometer drive gear. Remove the seals.

8 From the clutch housing remove the control shaft seal by levering it out with a screwdriver.

12 Gearbox components - preparation for reassembly (general)

1 Clean all the parts thoroughly and examine them for defects. Check the gears for chipping and cracks. If the bevel pinion shaft requires renewal, this will also mean a new crownwheel, and in that case you may think it more economical to exchange the gearbox. It is important that no grinding or any type of re-work be carried out on the specially treated surfaces of the pinion shaft. Oil all parts before fitting with EP 80 oil.

Fig. 4.10. Removing the reverse idler gear

1 Lever
2 Pin
3 Shaft
4 Idler gear
5 Reverse gear selector shaft

Fig. 4.13. Removing the circlip

A Foil
1 3rd & 4th synchro unit
2 Circlip
3 Pliers

Fig. 4.11. Control shaft and primary shaft assembly

1 Control shaft
2 Primary shaft
3 Nut
4 Bearing
5 Needle bearing
6 Circlip

Fig. 4.14. Bevel pinion shaft assembly - dismantling

1 Half-washers
2 Washer
3 Needle cage
4 2nd gear pinion
5 2nd gear synchro-ring

Fig. 4.12. Bevel pinion shaft assembly - dismantling

1 Speedometer drive/nut
2 Bearing
3 Shim
4 4th gear pinion
5 4th gear synchro ring

Fig. 4.15. Pinion shaft bearing removal

1 Dowels and spring (if fitted)
2 Circlip
3 Thrust washer
4 Bearing
5 Inner race

Fig. 4.16. The differential unit

1 Pin
2 Shaft
3 Differential gear
4 Planet gear
5 Crownwheel
6 Bearing

Fig. 4.17. The output shaft (early type on left)

1 Nut
2 Bush
3 Bearing
4 Ring nut

(a) Dimples (b) Nut threads

14 Bevel pinion - preparation for reassembly

1 Press on the inner race with the aid of a 45 mm inside diameter tube. Fit the roller bearing with the smaller bore of the bearing on the gear side of the pinion shaft. Fit the thrust washer with the engraved face away from the bearing. Fit the circlip using the same precautions and method as at removal. Refer to Section 11 (photos).

2 Fit the retarding dowels and their springs (if fitted), the 1st gear pinion, the 1st gear synchro-ring and the synchro unit of the 1st gear with the selector fork groove towards the 1st gear pinion (photos).

3 Adjust the axial clearance, 'J1' as in Fig. 4.18, of the synchro-hub of the 1st and 2nd gear by selecting a circlip of suitable thickness which will ensure that the clearance does not exceed 0.05 mm (0.002 in). A range of circlips, 1.30 to 1.58 mm thick, in steps of 0.04 mm are available. When fitting the circlip use the same precautions and method, as described at removal in Section 11 (photo).

4 Fit the 2nd gear synchro-ring, the retarding dowels and their springs and the 2nd gear pinion (photos).

5 Adjust the clearance of the thrust bearings of the 2nd and 3rd gear wheels by selecting adjusting half-washers of suitable thickness. Half-washers are available in steps of 0.03 mm (0.0012 in). With the half-washers in place, the clearance at 'J2' as in Fig. 4.19, between the half-washers and the side of the groove must not exceed 0.05 mm. The two half-washers fitted must be of the same thickness. Fit the retaining washer (photos).

6 Fit the 3rd gear pinion, the 3rd gear synchro-ring and its 3rd and 4th gear synchro-unit (photos).

7 Adjust the end clearance of the synchro-hub of the 3rd and 4th gears using the same procedure as for the synchro-hub of the 1st and 2nd gears. See paragraph 3. This clearance, 'J3' as in Fig. 4.19, must not exceed 0.05 mm (photo).

8 Fit the 4th gear synchro-ring and pinion, an adjusting shim of known thickness and the bearing, with the shoulder towards the rear of the bevel pinion shaft. Fit the speedometer drive/nut and tighten to 10 to 12 kg f m (72 to 86 lb f ft). Do not lock the nut, by peening, at this stage. **Note: To hold the bevel pinion shaft while tightening the nut clamp the 1st gear pinion, interlocked with the bevel pinion by the slider of the 1st and 2nd gears in a vice fitted with light-alloy vice grips (photo).**

13 Differential shafts - preparation for reassembly

1 Fit the ring nut in position and press on the bearing using a piece of tube with an inside diameter of 26 mm.

2 Fit the bush against which the seal bears; ensure that the bush does not have any scratches or damage (photo).

3 On the earlier type shafts fit the nut and tighten it to 14 to 16 kg f m (100 to 115 lb f ft).

15 Control shaft and primary shaft - reassembly

1 Fit the ball bearing to the primary shaft with the shoulder pointed towards the rear and fit the retaining nut. Tighten the nut to 7 to 8.5 kg f m (50 to 62 lb f ft) and lock by peening (photos).

2 Fit the needle bearing and couple up the control shaft to the primary shaft. Fit the retaining clips (photos).

13.2 Differential shaft with ring nut, bearing and bush fitted

14.1a Fitting the roller bearing on the bevel pinion shaft

14.1b Fitting the bevel pinion thrust washer

14.1c Using a piece of foil to protect the specially treated surfaces of the bevel pinion shaft while fitting the circlip

14.2a Replacing the retarding dowel and spring to the bevel pinion shaft

14.2b The retarding dowels in position while fitting the 1st gear pinion to the bevel pinion shaft

14.2c 1st gear synchro-ring and synchro-unit with selector fork groove towards 1st gear pinion

14.3 Fitting the circlip retaining the synchro-hub of 1st and 2nd gear on the bevel pinion shaft

14.4a Locating the spring and dowels of the 2nd gear pinion in the bevel pinion shaft

14.4b Fitting the 2nd gear pinion to the bevel pinion shaft

14.5a The adjusting half-washers on the bevel pinion shaft

14.5b The half-washers fitted in position and the retaining washer on the bevel pinion shaft

14.6a Fitting the 3rd gear pinion and 3rd gear synchro-ring to the bevel pinion shaft

14.6b The 3rd/4th gear synchro-unit

14.6c Fitting the 3rd/4th gear synchro-unit to the bevel pinion shaft

14.7 The circlip retaining the 3rd/4th gear synchro-unit

14.8a Fitting the 4th gear synchro-ring and pinion to the bevel pinion shaft

14.8b Fitting the adjusting shim to the bevel pinion shaft

14.8c Fitting the pinion shaft rear end bearing

14.8d Fitting the speedometer drive/nut to the bevel pinion shaft

14.8e Clamping the bevel pinion shaft in a vice with soft jaw grips and tightening the speedometer drive/nut

15.1a Fitting the primary shaft ball bearing

15.1b Fitting the bearing retaining nut to the primary shaft

15.1c Primary shaft retaining nut locked by peening

15.2a Fitting the needle bearing on the primary shaft

15.2b Coupling the control shaft to the primary shaft and securing it with spring clip

Fig. 4.18. Adjustment of 1st and 2nd gear synchro-unit axial clearance

1 1st gear pinion   3 Circlip
2 1st gear synchro hub   4 Synchro-unit

Fig. 4.19. Adjustment of 2nd and 3rd gear thrust bearings

1 Circlip   4 Washer
2 2nd gear pinion   5 3rd gear pinion
3 Half-washer   6 3rd & 4th gear synchro-unit

16 Clutch housing - preparation for reassembly

1 Fit a new control shaft seal in the clutch housing (photo).
2 Fit the two clutch release cross spindle bushes in the coils of the springs with the shoulders placed face-to-face. Lightly oil the spindle. Hold the fork and its spring in place, fit the spindle through one of the holes in the housing and then in the spring of the fork and its bearings.
3 Position the spindle and tighten the retaining screw. Fit the two free ends of the spring to rest on the bosses of the housing (Fig. 4.6).
4 Fit the thrust bearing and the spring clip locking the bearing to fork (photo).

17 Half-casings - preparation for reassembly

1 On each half-casing, grease the differential shaft bore and the edge of the seals. Fit the seals in the bore with the lip of the seal towards the inside of the half-casing. On gearboxes with a retaining circlip fitted, fit the seal and then fit the circlip so that one end of the circlip is 10 mm (0.40 in) from the drain hole in the bearing housing (photo).
2 In the right-hand half-casing, fit the selector fork shaft of the 1st and 3rd gears on the rear bearing with the notch towards the front. Fit the fork on the shaft and fit the locking pin. Position the fork and shaft assembly against the rear bearing when driving in the locking pin (photo).

3 Fit the spring and lockball into the housing. Use a 5 mm diameter rod to compress the spring while fitting the shaft into the front bearing. All five lockballs and their springs are identical.
4 In the left-hand half-casing fit the spring and lockball of the reverse gear selector shaft in the housing. Use a round bar to compress the spring and fit the selector shaft. Fit the reverse gear lever and tighten the spindle to 2.7 to 3.3 kg f m (21 to 25 lb f ft) (photos).
5 Fit the reverse idler pinion shaft in the rear boss. Fit the reverse pinion, with the groove towards the differential, and the spacer. Engage the reverse gear lever in the groove and complete fitting the reverse pinion shaft. Fit the locking pin fully in its housing. This pin which locks the primary shaft needle bearing must protrude slightly beyond the face of the bearing housing (photos).

18 Differential unit - reassembly

1 If the crownwheel, bearings or differential casing is being renewed, it will be necessary to determine the required thickness of the adjusting shims, as described in Section 21. Assembly should not take place until this has been done. If the above parts are not being renewed, proceed with the assembly.
2 Press the inner races on the casing and ensure that the roller bearings are identified and matched to their respective inner races. Fit the crownwheel, treat the threads of the retaining bolts with Loctite and tighten them to 4.8 to 5.5 kg f m (35 to 38 lb f ft).
3 Fit the two planet gears and hold them in place with the differential shafts. Fit the differential gears and shaft with the locking pin hole lined up correctly. Fit the locking pin.

Fig. 4.20. Gear selector shaft lockballs and springs

16.1 Fitting a new control shaft seal in the clutch housing

16.4 Clutch thrust bearing and retaining clips

17.1 Fitting the differential shaft seal in the half-casing bore

17.2 Fitting the 1st/3rd gear selector fork and shaft assembly

17.4a Fitting the reverse gear selector shaft detent spring in its housing

17.4b The lockball in its housing

17.4c Holding down the spring and lockball with a pin punch while fitting the selector shaft

17.4d The reverse gear lever fitted in position

17.5a Reverse gear shaft and pinion in position

17.5b Fitting the reverse gear shaft locking pin

19 Bevel pinion/crownwheel - adjustment (general)

1   The bevel pinion shim along with the differential shims are used to adjust the differential crownwheel and the bevel pinion to achieve the correct engagement of the gearteeth and to preload the differential bearings. This adjustment is most important. Giving the teeth the correct engagement will ensure silence and long service from the crownwheel and pinion.

2   The bevel pinion and crownwheel are paired and marked with identical inscriptions engraved on face, 'F1', of the pinion shaft and the side, 'F3', of the crownwheel as in Fig. 4.21. On some pairings the mark of the pinion is on the face, 'F2'. Never separate a crownwheel and pinion matched set.

3   In addition to the pairing marks, two dimensions are engraved on the side, 'F3', of the crownwheel. The larger dimension represents the distance 'L1' from the intersection 'a' of the bevel gear centre line to

the thrust face of the roller bearing on the bevel pinion shaft. The smaller dimension represents the distance 'L2' of the intersection 'a' of the bevel gear centre-line to the thrust face of the crownwheel on the casing. These dimensions are obtained by adjusting the position of the bevel pinion and of the crownwheel with shims whose thickness have to be determined. To do this a Citroen adjusting kit 3184-T (a dial gauge and a surface plate) will be required. If these can be borrowed proceed; if not, entrust the work to your dealer.

20 Bevel pinion - position adjustment

1   Fit the bevel pinion shaft assembly in the left-hand half-casing. Fit the rear cover and hold it in place with two bolts.

2   Fit the cap, 'A' of kit 3184-T, and hold in place with the screw 'a', screwed into the plastic cap on the end of the bevel pinion. Fit the

dial gauge on support 'B' and place the support on a surface plate. Zero the dial on the large needle of the gauge and note the position of the integrating needle, datum point.

3   Fit the support 'B' into the bore of the differential bearing, using handle 'C', pivot the support first in one direction and then in the other and stop at the exact point when the needle changes direction. Rotate the bevel pinion shaft and check any variation in the dial reading. If the variation exceeds 0.2 mm change the position of cap 'A'.

4   Pull rod 'd' to bring the needle to the datum point and then allow it to return slowly, counting the number of revolutions and fractions of a revolution made by the large needle until the stem again contacts the cap. This measurement is equivalent to dimension 'E' in Fig. 4.24. 'K1' + 'K2' is a gauge dimension of 78 mm and is marked on support 'B' at 'b' in Fig. 4.23.

5   If, for example, 'L1' in Fig. 4.21 is 82 mm and dimension 'E' is 4.44 mm, the position of the bevel pinion is 'K1' + 'K2' + 'E' or 78 + 4.44 - 82.44 mm. Therefore the pinion is too far from the differential centre line: 82.44 - 82 = 0.44 mm, and it is necessary to replace the existing adjusting shim with one that is 0.44 mm thicker. Shims are available in steps of 0.04 mm. If the distance read is smaller than the dimension on the bevel pinion then a thinner shim will be required.

6   Remove the adjusting equipment, the rear cover and the bevel pinion shaft assembly. Remove the nut from the pinion shaft and the bearing. Replace the existing shim with one of the correct thickness. Fit the bearing and the nut, tighten to 10 to 12 kg f m (72 to 86 lb f ft) and lock by peening into the groove on the shaft (photo).

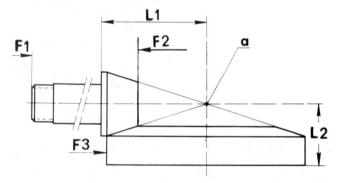

Fig. 4.21. Bevel wheel and crownwheel identification
For key see Section 19

Fig. 4.22. Crownwheel and pinion adjusting kit - 3184T

Fig. 4.23. Adjusting the bevel pinion shaft position
For key see Section 20

Fig. 4.24. Selecting bevel pinion shaft adjusting shim
For key see Section 20

20.6 Locking the speedometer drive/nut by peening

21 Crownwheel - position adjustment

1   Fit the outer races of the left- and right-hand differential bearings in their housings without the shims. Fit the differential roller bearings and fit the differential casing in the left-hand casing. Fit the mandrel 'C', in the pinion shaft position. Fit the right-hand half-casing and rear cover, as described in Section 16 (without sealing compound).

2   Fit the dial gauge on the straight edge 'D' and place it on a surface plate. Adjust the gauge position so that it will operate between 8 and 9 mm. Zero the dial opposite the large needle and note the position of the integrating needle (datum point). The dimension 'K1' + 'R', in Fig. 4.25, equals 35 mm. This dimension is engraved on the straight edge 'D'.

3 Fit the straight edge on the crownwheel bearing face of the differential casing, with the dial gauge probe touching the end of the mandrel. Move the differential casing back and forward and stop at the exact moment at which the needle changes direction. Note the gauge reading. Pull back the probe of the dial gauge to the datum point then, release it slowly and count the number of revolutions or fractions of a revolution made by the large needle until the probe touches the mandrel. This measurement is dimension 'E' in Fig. 4.25. .

4 If, for example, the large needle rotates through 7.46 turns, then dimension 'E' is 7.46 mm. The bearing face of the wheel is 35 + 7.46 = 42.46 mm distance from the bevel pinion centre line. Therefore, if 'L2' in Fig. 4.21 is 40 mm, to obtain this dimension would require a shim of 42.46 - 40 = 2.46 mm. As the preloading of the bearings is evaluated at 0.025 mm per bearing the thickness of the shim which must be fitted between the left-hand half-casing and the outer race is 2.46 + 0.025 = 2.485 mm. Shims are available in steps of 0.05 mm, so the nearest thickness would be 2.50 mm.

5 Place the gearbox with right-hand half-casing lowermost and measure dimension 'E' as described for the left-hand half-casing. Assume this to be 2.45 mm, therefore the crownwheel bearing face is 35 + 2.45 = 37.45 mm from the bevel pinion centre line. The shim required would be 40 - 37.45 = 2.55 mm. Without taking into consideration the bearing pre-loading the total thickness of shims (left and right) would be 2.46 + 2.55 = 5.01 mm. With preloading of 0.05 mm for the two bearings the total thickness would be 5.06 mm. As the shim for the left-hand side is 2.50 mm, the right-hand shim would be 5.06 - 2.50 = 2.56 mm, so the nearest thickness would be 2.55 mm.

6 Assemble the differential, as described in Section 12, paragraph 9.

22 Gearbox - reassembly procedure

1 Fit the differential in the left-hand half-casing. Check that the reverse gear idler is in the neutral position and fit the bevel pinion shaft assembly. Fit the control/primary shaft assembly, turn the needle bearing so that the end of the locking pin of the reverse gear shaft enters the locking notch in the bearing (photos).

2 At this stage, check the crownwheel to pinion backlash. If the crownwheel and pinion shaft adjustment has been carried out the backlash should be correct, however it is advisable to check it. Fit the right-hand half-casing and the rear cover. Tighten the rear cover bolts first and then the casing assembly bolts. Mount a dial gauge on the left-hand casing so that its probe rests on the side of a tooth of the crownwheel and measure the movement of the wheel while holding the bevel pinion. The backlash should be between 0.13 and 0.27 mm. Take three readings spaced at 120° intervals, the difference between any two

readings should not exceed 0.1 mm, otherwise the wheel is out of true, and must be renewed, or there is a foreign body between the crownwheel and the differential casing flange. Remove the dial gauge, the rear cover and the right-hand half-casing.

3 Oil the 3rd and 4th gear shaft and fork assembly, check that the 1st and 2nd gear and the 3rd and 4th gear synchro units are in neutral. Fit the 3rd and 4th gear fork and shaft and engage the fork with the groove in the synchro-unit. Fit the 3rd and 4th gear lockball and spring (photo).

4 Fit the interlock plunger of the 1st and 2nd and reverse gear shafts. Fit the spring holder plate noting that the springs are of different thickness wire. The one with its thicker wire should be fitted towards the reverse gear idler. Grease the ball joint and fit it in the left-hand half-casing, with the groove towards the right-hand half casing (photos).

5 On the right-hand half-casing, stick the lockball in its housing with grease. Stick the spring and guide of the ball joint in their housing with grease. Smear the joint faces of the two half-casings with suitable sealing compound. To prevent the sealing compound from entering the casing smear only the outer half width of the joint faces (photo).

6 Check that the planet gears are correctly positioned and fit the right-hand half-casing, ensuring that the 1st and 2nd gear fork engages correctly, that the spring holder plate fits into its housing and that the guide fits in the ball joint groove. Fit the assembly bolts but do not tighten fully until after the rear cover has been fitted (photo).

7 Fit a new seal and 'O' ring and replace the speedometer socket in the rear cover. Smear the joint face of the cover with sealing compound and fit the rear cover. Tighten the cover retaining bolts to a torque of 2.5 to 3 kg f m (18 to 21 lb f ft) then slightly loosen the bolts holding the rear cover to the right-hand half-casing. Finally tighten the assembly bolts of the half-casings to 1.4 to 1.5 kg f m (10 to 11 lb f ft) in the sequence shown in Fig. 4.26. Tighten the bolts holding the rear cover to the right-hand half-casing to 2.5 to 3 kg f m (18 to 21 lb f ft) (photos).

8 Fit the lockball, spring and disc of the 3rd and 4th gear selector fork shaft. Compress the disc and spring with a 5 mm diameter rod and fit a new split pin (photos).

9 Smear the outer half width of the clutch housing joint face with sealing compound and fit the housing, taking care that the oil seal is not damaged by the splines of the control shaft. Tighten the retaining nuts to 1.3 to 1.5 kg f m (9.5 to 11 lb f ft) (photo).

10 Fit the differential output shafts, tap them lightly with a mallet to position the bearing. Tighten the ring nuts to 6 to 10 kg f m (43 to 72 lb f ft) and lock them by peening. Fit the brake calipers as described in Chapter 8, Section 5 (photos).

11 Fit the drain, level and filler plugs. Fit the reversing light switch or blanking plug. When fitting the switch, smear the threads with gasket cement and tighten to 1.2 to 1.5 kg f m (9 to 10 lb f ft).

Fig. 4.25. Selecting differential bearing adjusting shims
For key see Section 21

Fig. 4.26. Tightening sequence of gearcase assembly bolts

22.1a The differential unit in position in the left-hand half-casing

22.1b Placing the bevel pinion shaft assembly in the left-hand half-casing

22.1c The control and primary shaft assembly fitted in position

22.3 Placing the 3rd/4th gear selector fork and shaft assembly in position

22.4a Fitting the interlock plunger of the 1st/2nd and reverse gear selector shafts

22.4b Fitting the spring holder plate

22.4c Positioning the ball joint with the groove upwards

22.5 Ball joint guide fitted in right-hand half-casing

22.6 Fitting the right-hand half-casing to the left-hand half-casing

22.7a Fitting the gearcase rear cover

22.7b Gearcase assembly bolts with cap nuts

22.8a Fitting the lockball of the 3rd/4th gear selector fork shaft in its housing ...

22.8b ... and then the spring ...

22.8c ... and the disc ...

22.8d ... retained by a split pin

22.9 Fitting the clutch housing to the gearbox

22.10a Fitting a differential shaft to the gearcase

22.10b Locking the differential ring nut by peening

23 Fault diagnosis - clutch

Symptom	Reason/s	Remedy
Judder when taking up drive	Loose engine/gearbox mountings or defective mountings.	Check for tightness. Replace faulty mountings.
	Badly worn friction surfaces or clutch disc contaminated with oil carbon deposit.	Remove engine and replace clutch as required. Rectify any oil leakage.
	Worn splines on the clutch disc or control shaft	Renew disc and or control shaft.
Clutch spin (or failure to disengage so that gears cannot be engaged)	Clutch pedal free movement too great.	Adjust clutch cable.
	Clutch disc sticking to pressure plate (usually after standing idle for some time)	As temporary remedy engage top gear, depress clutch and start engine. When running rev up engine and slip clutch until normal disengagement is possible.
	Damaged or misaligned clutch cover assembly	Replace clutch cover assembly.
Clutch slip (increase in engine speed without corresponding increase in car speed)	Too much clutch pedal free-movement	Adjust clutch cable.
	Clutch disc linings worn out or contaminated with oil	Replace clutch disc. Rectify any oil leak.

24 Fault diagnosis - gearbox

Symptom	Reason/s	Remedy
Ineffective synchromesh. Jumps out of one or more gears (on drive or overrun)	Worn synchro-units Weak lockball springs or worn selector forks or worn gears.	Dismantle and renew. Dismantle and renew.
Noisy, rough, whining and vibration	Worn bearings and gears Crownwheel and bevel pinion out of adjustment	Dismantle and renew. Dismantle and re-adjust.

Note: It is sometimes difficult to decide whether it is worthwhile removing and dismantling the gearbox for a fault which may be nothing more than a minor irritant, considering the amount of work and cost involved. Gearboxes which howl, or where the synchromesh can be 'beaten' by a quick gear change, may continue to perform for a long time in this state. A worn gearbox usually needs a complete rebuild to eliminate noise.

Chapter 5 Semi-automatic gearbox

For modifications, and information applicable to later models, see Supplement at end of manual

Contents

Specifications

Torque converter

Control switch contact gap	1.4 ± 0.05
Operating pressure	5.5 to 6.5 bar (80 to 90 psi) at 5000 ± 100 rpm
Oil capacity (including gearbox)	4 litres (7.1 Imp. pints) approx

Gearbox

Number of gears	3 forward, 1 reverse
Ratios:	
1st	2.79 : 1
2nd	1.70 : 1
3rd	1.12 : 1
Reverse	2.50 : 1
Differential unit	Refer to Chapter 4
Oil capacity (including converter)	4 litres (7.1 Imp. pints) approx
Oil change quantity	1.4 litres (2.5 Imp. pints) approx

Electro-valve switch contact gap

Up to September 1977	1.40 mm (0.055 in)
From September 1977	1.45 mm (0.057 in)

Fig. 5.1. Torque converter and gearbox

1 Pump
2 Torque converter
3 Clutch device
4 Distributor
5 Electro-valve control switch
6 Strainer

1 General description

1 Two types of transmission are available on GS models, a manual transmission with a four speed gearbox, and a semi-automatic transmission with a three speed gearbox. The drive, transmitted to the front wheels through the differential gearing in the gearbox and the driveshafts is very similar on both types. The manual transmission is described in Chapter 4.
2 A wet plate clutch and torque converter transmits the drive from the engine to the gearbox. Engagement and disengagement of the clutch is controlled by a hydraulic valve operated by a solenoid. This electrovalve is controlled in turn by switches operated by the movement of the gearbox selector shafts. The gearbox is a non-automatic type, gear selection is by a floor level gear lever. There is no clutch pedal, the clutch being operated by hydraulic pressure from a pump which is integral with the gearbox. The automatic clutch disengages the drive when a gear selection is being made and the gearing between the three fixed gear ratios is provided through the torque converter.

The oil is pumped from the gearbox through a strainer to the distributor unit where it is directed to operate the clutch, and excess oil is returned to the gearbox via an air cooled, oil cooler.

The clutch and torque converter assembly is a sealed unit and cannot be repaired or overhauled by an owner. If defective it must be renewed as a complete assembly.

2 Oil change - gearbox and torque converter

1 Position the car on level ground, preferably over a pit, or on a lift. Remove the spare wheel. Clean round the filler, level and drain plugs and remove them, draining the oil into a container. Remove the strainer, clean it and replace it, fitted with a new 'O' ring, and tighten it to 1 to 1.5 kg f m (7 to 11 lb f ft). Refit the drain plug and tighten to 3.5 to 4.5 kg f m (26 to 33 lb f ft).
2 Refill the gearbox through the filler plug opening to the oil level plug, approx 1.4 litres (2.5 Imp. pints) with oil of an approved specification. Refit the level plug and the filler plug.
3 Check that the level in the gearbox is correct as follows:

a) Chock the front wheels and apply the handbrake. Let the engine idle, and engage 3rd gear. Gently move the gear lever to energise the solenoid-operated valve controlling the clutch (it is energised when a faint click is heard). Repeat this operation ten times.
b) With the engine still idling and the gear engaged, remove the level plug and the filler plug and top up the oil level of the gearbox. Fit the level and filler plugs. Tighten the level plug to 3.5 to 4.5 kg f m (26 to 33 lb f ft) and the filler plug from 1 to 1.5 kg f m (7 to 11 lb f ft).

Note: The difference in the oil level between a 'cold' box and a 'hot' box is about 0.2 litres (0.75 Imp. pint). Because of this expansion, when checking the level on a 'hot' box some fluid may run out: do not top-up.
4 Fit the spare wheel.

Fig. 5.2. Power flow - 3-speed gearbox

Fig. 5.3. Location of drain and level plugs on
right-hand side of casing

1   Drain plug   2   Level plug

Fig. 5.4. Location of filler plug and strainer

1   Filler plug   2   Strainer

Fig. 5.5. Schematic diagram of torque converter - clutch engaged

Fig. 5.6. Schematic diagram of torque converter - clutch disengaged

3   Electro-valve switch - checking and adjustment

1   If the clutch is sluggish in operation or it disengages without the gearlever being moved, the cause could be incorrect adjustment of the contact gaps of the electro-valve switch.
2   Open the bonnet. Remove the spare wheel. Disconnect the earth strap from the negative terminal of the battery. Slacken the pressure regulator bleed screw to release the pressure from the hydraulic system. Remove the duct from the left-hand heater box.
3   Refer to Fig. 5.7 and remove the pin and clevis. Free the link rod from the control lever. Remove the screws fixing the gaiter to the console. Pull up the gearlever and remove the retaining and clevis pins. The fixing plate for the gaiter remains in the console, to remove it, the console must be removed. Remove the cover from the electro-valve control switch.
4   The procedure for checking and adjusting the contacts is the same for all four. In neutral, all points should be closed. Select a gear and ensure that it is fully engaged otherwise the check or adjustment would be incorrect. Using feeler gauges, A in Fig. 5.8, check the contact gap which should be as specified. To adjust slacken the securing screw of the fixed contact (3 mm Allen key) and slide the contact in its guide to obtain the correct gap, then moderately tighten the securing screw. Use the same method for the other gears. Refit the switch cover.
5   When replacing the gearlever, fit clips to retain the lower fixing plate and seal in position. Make the clips from two strips of metal 0.5 mm (0.02 in) thick by 10 mm (0.40 in) wide and 40 mm (1.6 in). Fold the strips as shown at 'b' in Fig. 5.9. Working through the console opening position the lower seal and fixing plate under the console, fold the end 'a' of the strip over the metal body of the console so that it holds the plate and seal in position. Replace the gearlever by reversing the removal sequence.
6   Check that when the gearlever is in first gear position, that it does not touch the base or the seats. If necessary move the base in its fixing slots.

4   Torque converter oil-feed system - pressure check

1   Drive the car to obtain a gearbox oil temperature of $70^{\circ} \pm 5^{\circ}$C.
2   Remove the spare wheel and spare wheel support. Remove the blanking plug from the electro-valve and fit a 6 or 7 mm union as required. Connect a pressure gauge, graduated from 0 to 10 bar (0 to 145 psi) to the union. Fit a workshop tachometer if one is not installed in the car.
3   Run the engine at 5000 ± 100 rpm and check that the pressure is between 5.5 and 6.5 bar (80 and 94 psi). Run the engine at $850 ^{+50}_{-0}$ rpm and check that the pressure is not less than 4 bar (58 psi).
4   If the pressure is incorrect, and before any other operation, check the gearbox oil level and the state of cleanliness of the suction strainer for the converter feed pump.

5   Gearbox - removal and replacement

1   Remove the engine/gearbox assembly, as described in Chapter 1, Section 5. Separate the gearbox and converter from the engine, as described in Chapter 1, Section 7.
2   Replacing the engine/gearbox assembly is described in Chapter 1, Section 19. Ensure that the converter and driveplate are aligned in the position marked when separating the gearbox from the engine.

6   Torque converter - removal

1   Drain the gearbox oil. With the converter retaining bracket in position (refer to Chapter 1, Section 6, paragraph 5) place the complete assembly in a vertical position with the converter resting on a bench. This prevents the oil from flowing out of the converter.
2   Remove the nuts securing the converter casing to the converter housing and lift off the gearbox. Remove the converter retaining bracket and lift off the converter housing leaving the converter on the bench. Remove the control shaft. Do not lose the spring 'a' in Fig. 5.10.

3   Drain the converter by turning it upside down over a suitable receptacle and allow to drain for several hours.
4   Change the starter ring gear if necessary, as described for the flywheel in Chapter 1, Section 11.

7   Torque converter - replacement

1   Place the converter face downwards on the bench. Fill the converter with about 1.5 litres (2.6 Imp. pints) of oil through the hole in the bore. Fill the converter in stages as it takes the oil some time to percolate through the various parts of the converter. The converter must not be completely filled until after the gearbox has been replaced in the car. The true capacity of the converter is about 2.3 litres (4 Imp. pints).
2   Replacement is the reverse of the removal sequence. Check that the two locating dowels are in position on the housing. When engaging the housing on the converter, turn the converter so that the drive pins engage in the notches of the pump gear. Check that the seals and circlip are fitted. Engage the control shaft in the rotor sleeve and in the converter splines and fit them in the end of the shaft.
3   It is essential that the converter retaining bracket is fitted to prevent damage to the driving pins.

8   Gearbox - dismantling (general)

1   The comments in Chapter 4, Section 9, apply equally to the gearbox of the semi-automatic transmission.
2   When removing and fitting the circlips of the bevel pinion shaft, use the method described in Chapter 4, Section 11, paragraph 4, to prevent damage to the special surface treatment of the shaft. Refer to Fig. 4.13.
3   The removal, dismantling and reassembly of the differential unit and output shafts is described in Chapter 4. Adjustment of the crown-wheel and bevel pinion, and checking of the backlash, is described in Chapter 4, Sections 20, 21 and 22. Removal and replacement of the brake calipers and discs is described in Chapter 8, Section 4 and 5.

9   Gearbox - dismantling procedure (stage 1)

1   Remove the torque converter, as described in Section 6. Remove the brake calipers and discs. Remove the differential output shafts. Remove the control switch body (4 mm Allen key), the rubber guards and the switch base (4 mm Allen key). Remove the bolts securing the rear cover. Carefully free the cover taking care not to bend the pins which operate the switch unit and remove the rear cover.
2   Refer to Fig. 4.7. Blank off the hole 'a' with a finger, remove ove the split pin and collect the blanking disc spring and lockball. Position the gearbox with the left-hand half-casing lowermost and remove the bolts securing the half-casings. Lift off the right-hand half-casing and collect the spring and balljoint guide of the gear selector rod. Remove the balljoint, the plate holding the return spring, the spring and lockball.
3   Remove the primary shaft assembly, the bevel pinion shaft assembly and the differential unit.

Fig. 5.7. Disconnecting the gearlever

1	Control lever	3	Clevis
2	Pin	4	Link rod

Fig. 5.8. Adjusting the switch contacts

1	Connector	3	Screw
2	Rubber seal	A	Feeler blades

Fig. 5.9. Seal and fixing plate retaining clips

1	Lower seal	3	Clips
2	Lower fixing plate	4	Console
	a and b Folds		

Fig. 5.10. Removing the torque converter

1	Distributor assembly	3	Converter housing
2	Control shaft	(a)	Spring housing

Fig. 5.11. Dismantling the semi-automatic gearbox

1	Balljoint	5	Bevel pinion assembly
2	Spring	6	Primary shaft
3	Lockball	7	Spring holder plate
4	Differential assembly	8	Spring

10 Gearbox - dismantling procedure (stage 2)

1 Dismantle the left-hand half-casing. Remove the pin which retains the reverse idler gearshaft. Drive out the pin holding the spacer on the shaft, (4 mm pin punch). Using a bronze drift, or similar tool, drive out the idler gearshaft. If necessary, remove the differential output shaft seal as described in Chapter 4, Section 11.

2 Dismantle the right-hand half-casing:

 a) *Move the 2nd/3rd gearshaft and fork assembly as far as possible to the rear, drive out the pin retaining the fork on the shaft (4 mm pin punch), free the shaft from the rear, remove the fork and the lockball.*

 b) *Move the 1st/reverse gearshaft and fork assembly as far as possible to the front and drive out the fork retaining pin (4 mm pin punch). Move the shaft to the rear with a finger over the hole, 'A' in Fig. 5.13, to avoid losing the lockball, collect the lockball and its spring. Lift out the fork.*

 c) *To remove the control lug which operates the reverse gearshaft, move the shaft as far as possible to the rear, so that the lug comes against the casing and drive out the retaining pin. Completely remove the pin by moving the lug to the front and swinging it into the recess below the ball joint socket. Remove the shaft and the control lug. If necessary, remove the pins which operate the control switch (2 mm pin punch).*

3 Dismantle the primary shaft: Remove the needle bearing, (the inner race is not interchangeable). Fit the shaft in a vice equipped with soft jaws and remove the bearing retaining nut and the bearing.

4 Dismantle the bevel pinion shaft assembly:

 a) *Fit the bevel pinion assembly in a vice with soft jaws, gripping the reverse gear pinion or the first gear pinion. Lock the bevel pinion by shifting the relevant synchro sleeve in the appropriate direction.*

 b) *Remove the speedometer drive/nut, the bearing, adjusting washer and the 3rd gear pinion and synchro-ring. If the gearbox is to be re-assembled without changing the casing, the bevel pinion or the bearing, identify and retain the adjusting washer to avoid having to adjust the bevel pinion position.*

 c) *Remove the circlip retaining the 2nd/3rd synchro-hub. Remove the hub, the 2nd gear synchro ring and the 2nd gear synchro sleeve. Identify and retain all synchro rings to their pinions.*

 d) *Remove the first gear synchro ring, the retaining washer and two half-washers. Remove the 1st gear pinion, its synchro ring and the needle cage.*

e) *Remove the circlip retaining the 1st/reverse gear synchro hub, the reverse gear synchro ring, the reverse pinion and the needle cage.*

f) *If it is necessary to remove the front bearing, remove the retaining circlip, the thrust washer, the bearing and the inner race, using a press and a 50 mm (2 in) diameter tube.*

Note: The bevel pinion shaft of semi-automatic transmissions does not have retarding dowels.

5 If necessary, remove the speedometer drive socket, and the drive gear and seals from the rear cover.

6 Dismantle the converter housing:

a) *Mark the oil pump in relation to the converter housing. Remove the pump retaining bolts, the pump casing and the pinions. Remove the seals.*

b) *Remove the oil strainer and 'O' ring seal.*

c) *If necessary, remove the pressure distributor retaining bolts (6 mm Allen key) and the distributor. Never separate the electro-valve from the distributor, these units cannot be overhauled by an owner; if either is defective, the assembly must be renewed. Do not remove the stator sleeve; if defective, the complete converter housing must be renewed.*

Fig. 5.12. The left-hand half-casing

1 Reverse idler shaft   4 Reverse idler gear
2 Pin   5 Pin
3 Spacer   6 Oil seal

Fig. 5.13. The right-hand half-casing

1 Control lug   4 2nd/3rd gear selector shaft
2 1st/reverse gear selector shaft 5 2nd/3rd gear fork
3 1st/reverse gear fork   6 Control switch operating pins

Fig. 5.14. The primary shaft

1 Needle bearing   3 Nut
2 Bearing   4 Inner race

Fig. 5.15. Dismantling the bevel pinion shaft assembly

1 3rd gear synchro-ring   4 Bearing
2 3rd gear pinion   5 Speedometer drive/nut
3 Adjusting washer

Fig. 5.16. Dismantling the bevel pinion shaft assembly

1 Needle bearing   4 Half-washers
2 1st gear synchro ring 5 Retaining washer
3 1st gear pinion

Fig. 5.17. Dismantling the bevel pinion shaft assembly

1 Circlip   4 Reverse gear pinion
2 Reverse/1st gear synchro-units 5 Needle bearing
3 Reverse gear synchro-ring

Fig. 5.18. Dismantling the bevel pinion shaft assembly

1	Inner race	3	Thrust washer
2	Roller bearing	4	Circlip

11 Gearbox components - preparation for reassembly

1   Carry out the procedures described in Chapter 4, Sections 1, 2 and 13.

2   Prepare the bevel pinion shaft assembly:

a) *Refer to Figs. 5.15, 5.16, 5.17 and 5.18. Fit the inner race, if it was removed, the roller bearing with the smaller diameter towards the bevel pinion, the thrust washer, with the face without markings towards the bearing, and the circlip.*

b) *Fit the needle cage, the reverse pinion, the reverse gear synchro ring and the reverse/1st gear synchro unit, with the selector fork groove towards the reverse gear pinion. Adjust the axial clearance of the reverse/1st gear synchro hub by selecting a circlip of a thickness which gives a maximum clearance of 0.05 mm (0.002 in) at 'J1' in Fig. 5.19. Fit the selected circlip.*

c) *Fit the needle cage, the 1st gear synchro ring and the 1st gear pinion. Fit the half washers and retaining washer. With the half washers fitted the clearance at 'J2' in Fig. 5.19, must not exceed 0.05 mm (0.002 in). Half washers are supplied in steps of 0.03 mm (0.0012 in) and the two fitted must be of the same thickness.*

d) *Fit the 2nd gear pinion, the 2nd gear synchro ring and the 2nd/3rd gear synchro unit. Adjust the axial clearance of the 2nd/3rd gear synchro unit as described in paragraph (b) above, so that the clearance at 'J3', in Fig. 5.19, does not exceed 0.05 mm (0.002 in). Fit the selected circlip.*

e) *Fit the 3rd gear synchro ring and the 3rd gear pinion. Fit an adjusting washer of known thickness, the bearing with the shoulder towards the rear and the speedometer drive/nut. Tighten the nut to 10 to 12 kg f m (72 to 86 lb f ft). Do not lock the nut by peening at this stage.*

3   Prepare the primary shaft: Refer to Fig. 5.14. Fit the ball bearing with the shoulder towards the rear. Fit and tighten the nut to 7 to 8.5 kg f m (50 to 62 lb f ft). Lock the nut by peening. Fit the needle bearing.

4   Prepare the control shaft: Oil the seals and fit them on the shaft from the splined end, 'a' in Fig. 5.20. Fit the circlip. The spring will only enter its housing when the shaft is fitted in the converter.

5   Fit the rubber seal and the 'O' ring on the speedometer drive socket. Grease the drive pinion and fit it in the socket. Fit the speedometer drive assembly into the rear cover with the groove of the socket aligned with the hole for the securing screw.

6   Fit the differential shaft seals in each half-casing as described in Chapter 4, Section 8.

7   Prepare the left-hand half-casing: Refer to Fig. 5.12. Preparation of the half-casing is the reverse of the dismantling sequence, described in Section 10. The pin (5) which locks the needle bearing of the primary shaft must stand slightly proud of the surface of this bearing.

8   Prepare the right-hand half-casing: Refer to Fig. 5.13. Preparation of the half-casing is the reverse of the dismantling sequence described in

Section 10. When fitting the pins which operate the control switch unit on the fork shaft, position the split of each pin perpendicular to the longitudinal axis of the fork shaft. The shafts are identified in Fig. 5.21. The projection of the control switch operating pins is given in millimetres. The shaft of the 2nd/3rd gear fork has a single notch at 'd' and two flats at 'a'. The shaft of the reverse/1st gear fork has two notches for the fork locking pins at 'b' and 'c'. The fork gap of the reverse/1st gear fork is greater than that of the 2nd/3rd gear fork.

9   Prepare the converter housing:

a) *Oil the pump pinion, stick the 'O' ring seal in its groove with grease and fit the pump to the casing, align the marks made at removal and fit the retaining bolts. Centre the pump assembly with a mandrel and tighten the bolts to 1.9 kg f m (13 lb f ft).*

b) *Smear the pressure distributor joint face with jointing compound. Fit the distributor on the converter casing with the electro-valve towards the right of the casing. Fit and tighten the retaining bolts to 1.2 to 1.7 kg f m (9 to 12 lb f ft).*

c) *Fit the 'O' ring seal on the strainer and screw the strainer into its housing on the converter casing and tighten it to 1 to 1.5 kg f m (7 to 11 lb f ft).*

Fig. 5.19. Axial clearance of gears and synchro-hubs

1	1st gear synchro-unit	6	2nd gear pinion
2	1st gear synchro-ring	7	2nd gear synchro-ring
3	1st gear pinion	8	2nd/3rd gear synchro-unit
4	Half-washers	9	Circlip
5	Retaining washer		

Fig. 5.20. The control shaft

1	Seal	3	Circlip
2	Seal	4	Spring

$$h1 = 14,4 \, ^{+1}_{\ 0}$$

$$h2 = 18,4 \, ^{+1}_{\ 0}$$

2nd/3rd gear fork shaft

Fig. 5.21. Selector fork shafts - identification

12 Gearbox - reassembly procedure

1 If any of the following have been renewed it will be necessary to
adjust the position of the crownwheel and pinion, as described in
Chapter 4, Sections 19, 20 and 21: the gearbox casing, the crownwheel
and pinion, the differential bearings and the differential casing.

2 Fit the differential in the left-hand half-casing. Fit the bevel pinion
shaft assembly. Fit the primary shaft assembly, turn the needle bearing
so that the end of the locking pin on the reverse gear shaft enters the
groove in the bearing.

3 Check the backlash of the crownwheel to pinion, as described in
Chapter 4, Section 22, paragraph 2.

4 On the left-hand half-casing fit the spring holder plate with the
spring having the thicker diameter wire fitted towards the reverse gear
idler pinion. Fit the ball joint with the groove towards the right-hand
casing side. Temporarily fit a differential shaft to centre the planet
wheels. Position both synchro units in neutral.

5 Grease the spring and balljoint guide and fit them in the right-hand
half-casing. Ensure that all locking between the reverse/1st gear shaft
and 2nd/3rd gear shaft is in place, and that the forks are in the neutral
position.

6 Smear the outer half of the joint faces of the half-casing with
jointing compound, avoid getting sealing compound inside the
casing. Fit the right-hand half-casing on the left-hand half-casing,
ensuring that the selector forks engage in the grooves of the synchro
units and, at the same time, guide the spring holder plate into its
housing in the right-hand casing. Make sure that the balljoint guide
enters the groove of the balljoint. Fit the assembly bolts finger tight,
final tightening is done after the rear cover is fitted.

7 Smear the joint face of the rear cover with jointing compound.
Fit the cover on the gearbox casing. Fit and tighten the retaining
bolts to 2.5 to 3 kg f m (18 to 21 lb f ft), then slightly slacken the
bolts retaining the cover to the right-hand half-casing. Refer to Fig.
4.26 and tighten the half-casing retaining bolts, following the numerical
sequence shown. On some casings the bolt (3) may be on the left-hand
half-casing. Finally tighten the half-casing bolts to 1 to 1.5 kg f m
(10 to 11 lb f ft). Retighten the slackened rear cover bolts.

8 Fit the 2nd/3rd gear selector shaft lockball, spring and disc,
secured with a split pin.

9 Fit the differential shafts and the brake calipers.

10 Smear the seal face of the control switch base plate with jointing
compound. Fit the plate on the rear cover (4 mm Allen key) with the
slot, (a) in Fig. 5.22, towards the front of the gearbox. Fit the rubber
seal on the switch and fit the switch on the base plate with the
connector towards the right-hand half-casing. Adjust the switch points
gap as described in Section 3. Fit the switch cover and the rubber
collar.

11 Replace the torque converter, as described in Section 7.

Fig. 5.22. Electro-valve control switch

1	Baseplate	3	Rubber collar
2	Rubber seal	4	Connector

13 Fault diagnosis - semi-automatic gearbox

Symptom	Reason/s	Remedy
Ineffective synchromesh	Worn synchro-units	Dismantle and renew
Jumps out of gear	Weak lockball springs or worn selector forks	Renew.
	Control switch out of adjustment	Re-adjust contact gaps.
Noisy, rough, whining and vibration	Worn bearings and gears	Dismantle and renew.
	Crownwheel and bevel pinion out of adjustment	Dismantle and re-adjust.
Gear changing difficult	Low oil pressure	See below.
	Electro-valve/distributor defective	Renew.
	Torque converter defective	Renew.
Oil pressure low	Oil strainer blocked	Remove and clean.
	Oil pump defective	Rectify as necessary.
Transmission overheating	Oil cooler ineffective	Check the air duct.
	Torque converter defective	Renew the torque converter assembly.

Chapter 6 Hydraulic system

For modifications, and information applicable to later models, see Supplement at end of manual

Contents

Specifications

Hydraulic pump

Type	Single cylinder piston type
Drive	Connecting rod from oil pump
Ratio pump speed/engine speed	1 : 2
Piston diameter	15 mm
Piston stroke	10 ± 0.05 mm
Output under load of 175 bar (2.490 psi)	0.9 cc per rev. at 250 rpm

Pressure regulator

Cut-out pressure	170 ± 5 bar (2418 ± 71 psi)
Cut-in pressure	145 ± 5 bar (2062 ± 71 psi)

Accumulator

Capacity	0.40 litre (24.4 cu in)
Inflation pressure:	
Until 3/1973	40 ± 5 bar (370 ± 71 psi)
From 3/1973	60 ± $\frac{5}{10}$ bar (711 to 925 psi)

Pressure switch range

Until 3/1973	60 to 80 bar (853 to 1138 psi)
From 3/1973	75 to 95 bar (1068 to 1351 psi)

Hydraulic fluid type ... ...

Mineral LHM (green colour)

Reservoir capacity (including reservoir):

Early models	3.5 litres (6.25 Imp pints)
Late models	4.2 litres (7.39 Imp pints)

1 General description

1 The hydropneumatic suspension and the braking system is pressurized by a common hydraulic system. The hydraulic system is illustrated diagrammatically in Fig. 6.2.
2 Hydraulic fluid is drawn from the hydraulic reservoir, mounted on the right-hand wing valance, and delivered under pressure to the hydraulic pressure regulator mounted on top of the clutch housing. From the pressure regulator, fluid passes to the four-way union. Fitted in the system is a pressure switch, wired to a warning lamp on the instrument panel which lights up when the hydraulic pressure is too low.
3 From the four-way union, fluid under pressure passes through the front and rear height correctors to their respective suspension cylinders. From the suspension cylinders the low pressure return fluid is returned through pipelines to the hydraulic reservoir.
4 The height correctors maintain the hydropneumatic suspension at the manually selected height by admitting fluid to, and releasing fluid from, the suspension cylinders according to the movement of the front and rear anti-roll bars to which they are connected. Three height positions can be selected by the manual height control. The normal

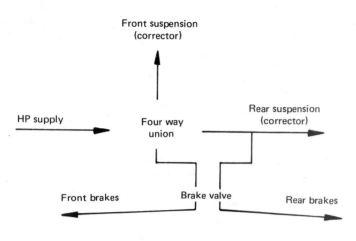

Fig. 6.1. Diagram of operation

driving position is with the lever in the first notch (towards the front), when travelling on good road surfaces. The intermediate position (ground clearance increased), can be used when driving on rough surfaces (very slowly). With the lever in the rear notch the ground clearance is increased to the maximum, 'high position'. This is intended for wheel changing and must not be selected when driving, except in exceptional cases to negotiate particularly difficult surfaces over short distances and at very low speed. As these height positions are obtained by hydraulic pressure they can only be maintained while the engine is running. When the engine is stopped the car sinks down against the bump stops.

5   Hydraulic pressure for the braking system is fed from the four-way union to a connection on the brake control valve for operation of the front brake calipers. The rear brake calipers are operated by hydraulic pressure which is passed to the brake control valve from the rear suspension. This arrangement results in the braking effort being biased in favour of the front brakes, and at the same time, regulates the braking effort on the rear wheels according to the load on the rear suspension - the heavier the load, the greater the pressure in the rear suspension, thus more braking effort.

6   Hydraulic pressure is released from the system by slackening the bleed screw on the pressure regulator. This allows the pressure fluid to bleed off to the reservoir.

Fig. 6.2. Hydraulic circuit diagram (lhd models shown)

1 Fluid reservoir	4 Four-way union	7 Front brake calipers	10 Rear suspension cylinders
2 High pressure pump	5 Front height corrector	8 Brake control valve	11 Rear brake calipers
3 Pressure regulator and accumulator	6 Front suspension cylinders	9 Rear height corrector	

2 Hydraulic system and components - precautions and depressurising

1 Cleanliness is of the utmost importance when working on the hydraulic system and its components. Clean all adjacent areas before disconnecting components, after removal, blank-off all orifices and ensure that components and pipes do not get contaminated.
2 Use only LHM mineral hydraulic fluid in the hydraulic system, the use of any other fluid will ruin the rubber rings and seals. LHM fluid is green in colour. Keep the fluid, carefully sealed, in its original container.
3 Use only genuine spare parts. Components are identified by painting or marking in green. All rubber parts are identified by their white or green colour and are of a special quality for use with LHM fluid.
4 Before starting work on the hydraulic system, the pressure must first be released and reference must be made to Chapter 13, Section 9 for details of system modifications and depressurizing method according to type.

3 Hydraulic system faults - preliminary checks

In the event of incorrect operation of the hydraulic system, carry out the following checks before dismantling the system:
1 Examine the controls and mechanical linkage to ensure that they are not sticking or are under stress.
2 With the engine idling, slacken the pressure regulator bleed screw one and a half turns, and check that the sound of leakage can be heard.
3 Tighten the bleed screw: cutting-out must occur, this is indicated by less noise from the hydraulic high pressure pump.
4 If cutting-out does not occur check that there is sufficient fluid in the reservoir and that the reservoir filter is clean and in good condition. Check also that there is no leak on the suction side of the pump.
5 Check that the pressure regulator relief screw is fully tightened.

4 Cleaning components and pipelines

1 Hydraulic units must be cleaned with petrol or white spirit and blown through with compressed air. Clean the rubber hoses also with petrol or white spirit and then dry out with compressed air.
2 Always renew all joints and seals at each dismantling.
3 After cleaning, lightly oil all internal parts of components, and block off all orifices.

5 Pipe joints - assembly

1 When connecting pipe joints, lightly oil the seal with LHM fluid, and position it as shown, 'a' in Fig. 6.3.
2 Centre the pipe in the housing by lining it up with the axis of the hole, avoiding all stress. Ensure that the end 'b' of the pipe enters in the small bore 'c'.
3 Start the union nut by hand. Tighten the nut in accordance with the following torque loading:

3.5 mm pipe \
4.5 mm pipe — *0.8 to 0.9 kg f m (5.8 to 6.6 lb f ft)* \
6.0 mm pipe — 0.9 to 1.1 kg f m (6.6 to 8 lb f ft)

4 Do not overtighten, the design of joint ensures that the sealing action increases with fluid pressure. Overtightening can cause deformation of the pipe and result in leakage.

6 Routine maintenance

1 Every 6000 miles (10,000 km) the hydraulic filter must be cleared. Unclip the filter and remove it from the top of the hydraulic reservoir.
2 Clean the filter in petrol or white spirit and dry it with compressed

air. Refit the filter, check the fluid level and top-up, if necessary. Loosen the bleed screw on the pressure regulator and allow any trapped air to escape. Re-tighten the screw (photo).
3 Every 18,000 miles (30,000 km) change the fluid in the hydraulic system. To drain the system place the manual height control lever in the 'normal' position, open the pressure regulator bleed screw then move the manual control lever to the 'high' position. Slacken the clip securing the fluid level sight tube, disconnect the tube and connect it to a length of hose with the other end in a container to collect the fluid. Remove the filter and drain the high pressure pump suction line. Clean the filter as described above.
4 Reconnect the sight tube, fit the filter and prime the high pressure pump with fluid through the pump suction pipe. Fill the reservoir with LHM fluid, run the engine then tighten the pressure regulator bleed screw. Select the 'high' position and top up the reservoir. **Note:** *On later models the fluid level is registered by an indicator mounted on top of the reservoir. The same principle applies, a yellow disc, indicating the fluid level must be maintained between minimum and maximum level marks.*

7 Hydraulic system components - checking (general)

1 The checks must be carried out in the sequence described, if a unit proves to be defective it must be repaired or changed before proceeding with the next check. Units which have been removed from the car can only be tested on a hydraulic test bench and should be taken to a Citroen agent with the appropriate testing equipment.
2 To carry out the checks with the units in position, the equipment illustrated in Fig. 6.5 will be required. The female blanking plug (C) can be made from a two-way union AM-453-37.
3 Before proceeding with the checks, ensure that the filter in the hydraulic reservoir is clean and that the hydraulic fluid is at operating temperature. Drive the car on the road first, if necessary. Check that the fluid level in the reservoir is correct.
4 Release the pressure from the hydraulic system as described in Section 2. Remove the heater distribution box and ducts. Disconnect the supply pipes from the two-way union and connect them to the three-way union, 'B' in Fig. 6.6, fitted with the pressure gauge 'A'. The assembly consisting of the three-way union and the pressure gauge remains in position throughout the checks.

8 Main accumulator - checking

1 From the four-way union disconnect the supply pipes to the front brakes, front suspension and rear suspension. Blank-off the openings with the blanking plugs 'D'.
2 Disconnect the ignition lead to the contact breaker, to prevent the engine from starting. Tighten the pressure regulator bleed screw.

6.2 Pressure regulator bleed screw (arrowed)

Fig. 6.3. Pipe joint assembly

Fig. 6.5. Hydraulic system testing equipment

Fig. 6.4. Draining the hydraulic system

1 Pump suction pipe   4 Filter
2 Fluid level sight tube   5 Fluid level marks
3 Clip   6 Pressure regulator

Fig. 6.6. Three-way union and test gauge

Fig. 6.7. Four-way union connections

1 Front suspension   4 Front brakes
2 Rear suspension   5 Pressure switch
3 Four-way union

3   Operate the starter motor and check that the needle of the pressure gauge rises gradually and then stabilizes. This value is the inflation pressure of the accumulator and should be between 35 and 45 bar (500 and 640 psi) on models dated until March 1973 and between 50 and 65 bar (715 and 925 psi) on models dated from March 1973. Connect the contact breaker lead.

9   Pressure regulator - checking

1   Check the cut-out pressure as follows:
   a) *Start the engine. With the pressure regulator bleed screw closed check that the cut-out pressure is between 165 and 175 bar (2350 and 2490 psi), indicated when the gauge needle stops rising.*
   b) *When the cut-out pressure is reached let the engine run until the pressure stabilizes. Stop the engine and note the pressure drop over a period of three minutes. If the drop is more than 10 bar (140 psi) check the plugs 'D' for leaks and repeat the operation. If the pressure drop is still outside the limit the pressure regulator is defective and must be replaced.*
2   Check the cut-in pressure as follows:
   a) *Start the engine. When cut-out occurs open the pressure regulator bleed screw slightly. The pressure will fall gradually then rise again when the high pressure pump begins to charge.*

b) The minimum reading on the gauge is the cut-in pressure and must be between 140 and 150 bar (1990 and 2130 psi).

3   If the cut-out or cut-in pressure is outside the permitted limits the pressure regulator is defective and must be renewed.

10 Hydraulic brake control unit - checking

1   Slacken the pressure regulator bleed screw. Remove the blanking plug from the front brakes connection of the four-way union and connect the supply pipe for the front brakes.
2   Tighten the pressure regulator bleed screw and start the engine. After cut-out, allow the pressure to stabilize then stop the engine.
3   Note the pressure drop over a period of three minutes. If the pressure drops by more than 10 bar (140 psi) repeat the operation. If the drop is outside the limit, the brake control unit is defective and must be replaced.

11 Pressure switch - checking

1   With the test equipment connected as in Section 10, run the engine to obtain the cut-out pressure. Stop the engine.
2   Operate the brake pedal until the hydraulic pressure warning light is permanently on and note the reading on the pressure gauge. This should be between 60 and 80 bar (870 and 1160 psi) for vehicles up to 1973, and 75 to 95 bar (1087 and 1377 psi) for later models.

12 Front suspension - checking

1   Slacken the pressure regulator bleed screw. Remove the blanking plug from the front suspension connection of the four-way union and connect the front suspension supply pipe.
2   Tighten the bleed screw and run the engine. Place the manual height control lever in the 'normal' road position, wait until the front of the car rises and cut-out takes place. Allow the pressure to stabilize and stop the engine. Note the pressure drop over a period of three minutes, if it exceeds 10 bar (140 psi) repeat the operation.
3   If the pressure drop exceeds the permitted limit, this means the front height corrector on one, or both, of the front suspension cylinders are defective. Check these two units by successive elimination, as described in Sections 13 and 14.

13 Front height corrector - checking

1   Remove the three screws and the guard protecting the height corrector. Slacken the pressure regulator bleed screw and place the manual height control lever in the 'high' position.
2   Disconnect the supply pipe to the front suspension cylinders and blank the opening with a blanking plug. Tighten the bleed screw. Place the manual height control lever in the 'normal' position and start the engine.
3   Allow the pressure to stabilize and stop the engine. Note the pressure drop over a period of three minutes, if it exceeds 10 bar (140 psi) repeat the operation.
4   If the pressure drop is outside the permitted limit, the front height corrector is defective and must be replaced. Remove the blanking plug and connect the front suspension supply pipe to the corrector. Refit the corrector guard plate.

14 Front suspension cylinders - checking

1   Slacken the pressure regulator bleed screw. Place the manual height control lever in the 'high' position. Disconnect and remove the supply pipe to the front right hand cylinder.
2   Fit a blanking plug to the opening in the three-way union and repeat the check as described in Section 13. If the front right-hand suspension cylinder is defective it must be replaced. Remove the blanking plug and refit the supply pipe.

3   If, after having checked the front height corrector and the front right-hand suspension cylinder, the drop in pressure still exists then the left-hand suspension cylinder is defective and must be replaced.

15 Rear suspension - checking

1   Slacken the pressure regulator bleed screw and place the manual height control lever in the 'high' position. Remove the blanking plug from the rear suspension connection of the four-way union and connect the supply pipe.
2   Disconnect the supply pipe for the rear brakes at the brake control valve and fit a blanking plug to the pipe opening. Tighten the pressure regulator bleed screw and place the manual control in the 'normal' road position.
3   Carry out the procedure for checking the front suspension, as described in Sections 12, 13 and 14. Renew defective units. Remove the checking equipment and connect the supply pipe for the rear brakes to the brake control valve and reconnect the supply pipes to the two-way union.

16 Brake control valve - simplified check for leakage

1   Slacken the pressure regulator bleed screw and place the manual height control in the 'high' position. Disconnect the rubber, brake return line from the reservoir and attach a transparent plastic tube to the end and support it vertically.
2   Tighten the bleed screw, select 'normal' road position on the manual height control and start the engine. When the car has settled, depress the brake pedal until fluid appears in the plastic tube. Release the brake pedal and check that the fluid level in the plastic tube remains virtually constant. If it does not, replace the brake control unit, as described in Chapter 8, Section 14.

17 Hydraulic pump - general

1   The hydraulic pump is mounted at the front of the engine behind the fan cowl. It is a piston type pump and is driven by a connecting rod from an eccentric on the engine oil pump.
2   Removal of the pump on earlier models required the removal of the fan cowl, on later models access is provided by an aperture in the fan cowl.
3   Removal of the pump is described in Chapter 1, Section 10 and replacement in Chapter 1, Section 18. After fitting the pump always prime it by removing the suction pipe from the reservoir and filling it with LHM fluid.

Fig. 6.8. Front height corrector

1   Supply pipe to front   2   Blanking plug
  suspension

18 Pressure regulator and accumulater - general

1   The pressure regulator and accumulator supplies and maintains a supply of hydraulic fluid pressure of between 140 and 175 bar (1190 and 2490 psi), the minimum cut-in pressure and the maximum cut-out pressure respectively.
2   Checking the pressure regulator and accumulator for leakage, inflation pressure and cut-out and cut-in pressures are described in Sections 8 and 9. No overhaul procedures are described; if the unit is defective it should be renewed.
3   Removal and replacement is as follows:

a) *Release the hydraulic pressure from the system, as described in Section 2. Disconnect the earth strap from the negative terminal of the battery. Note the pipe connections and disconnect them from the pressure regulator and accumulator. Remove the securing bolts and lift off the pressure regulator.*
b) *Replacement is the reversal of removal, always fit new seals to the pipe connections.*

19 Pressure switch - electrical check

1   The pressure switch is fitted at the four-way union and is wired into a warning light on the instrument panel. When the pressure in the hydraulic system is below the specified pressure range (see Section 11) the warning light is illuminated.
2   When the engine is stopped (no pressure in the hydraulic system) and the ignition switched-on, the instrument panel warning light should be on, if not, check the bulb and wiring. It is important that the warning light is working correctly as it indicates when the pressure in the brake system is below the safety level.
3   The pressure switch is removed by disconnecting the wiring and unscrewing the switch from the four-way union. When replacing the switch tighten it to a torque of 1.1 to 1.2 kg f m (8 to 9 lb f ft).

20 Front height corrector - removal and replacement

1   Jack-up and support the front of the car. Release the hydraulic pressure from the system, as described in Section 2. Remove the right-hand roadwheel. Remove the height corrector guard plate and the anti-roll bar bearing guard plate from the right-hand side. Disconnect the pipes from the corrector.
2   Remove the anti-roll bar right-hand bearing bolts and the corrector support retaining bolt. Remove the corrector with its support.
3   Replacement is the reverse of the removal sequence. Carry out the anti-roll bar adjustment as described in Chapter 7, Section 9. Start the engine, tighten the pressure regulator bleed screw and check for leaks. Lower the car and check the suspension heights as described in Section 25.

21 Rear height corrector - removal and replacement

1   Release the pressure from the hydraulic system, as described in Section 2. Disconnect the pipes from the height corrector.
2   Set the manual control to 'normal' position and disconnect the ball joint. Mark the position of the corrector, remove the retaining bolts and the corrector.
3   Replacement is the reverse of the removal sequence. Start the engine, tighten the pressure regulator bleed screw and check for leaks. Check the suspension heights, as described in Section 25.

22 Front suspension cylinder - removal and replacement

1   Position the car as described in Chapter 7, Section 4, for the removal of a suspension arm, and disengage the ball and socket from the suspension arm. Disconnect the pipes from the cylinder.

2   With a strap wrench remove the spheres. Remove the cylinder retaining bolts, turn it 90° raise the suspension arm and remove the cylinder.
3   There is no repair instruction for the cylinders; defective cylinders must be renewed.
4   Replacement is the reverse of the removal sequence. When assembly is complete, start the engine, tighten the pressure regulator bleed screw and check for leaks. Check the suspension heights as described in Section 25.

23 Rear suspension cylinder - removal and replacement

1   Position the car as described in Chapter 11, Section 3 for the removal of a suspension arm, and disconnect the ball and socket from the suspension arm. Disconnect the pipes from the cylinder.
2   Remove the retaining collar. Jack-up the suspension arm fully and remove the suspension cylinder and sphere.
3   Replacement is the reverse of the removal sequence. When assembly is complete, start the engine, tighten the pressure regulator bleed screw and check for leaks. Check the suspension heights, as described in Section 25.

24 Suspension heights - presetting

1   Presetting the heights enables an approximate adjustment to be made. It should be carried out whenever major components of the suspension are replaced.
2   Support the car, front and rear, as described for the removal of the suspension arms in Chapters 7 and 10. Remove the guard plate from the front corrector and the inspection panel in the floor of the boot. Slacken the bolt securing the clamp of the front automatic control rod. Slacken the screws securing the rear corrector, slide them to the centre of their slots and tighten the screws.
3   Set the manual control lever to the 'normal' road position. Relieve the stress on the corrector slide valves as necessary by displacing the sector and slackening the plastic fork end (old type control) or bush nut of the control rod.
4   With a jack and a cross beam placed under the suspension arms, raise the arms until the beam is up against the axle unit. In this position the lever 'A' of the front wishbones is halfway between the travel stops (Fig. 6.10), ie 'J1' = 'J2' $\pm$ 2 mm (0.08 in) and the rear suspension arms on both sides are at an equal distance from the travel stops, ie 'J1' = 'J2' $\pm$ 2 mm (0.08 in) in Fig. 6.11.
5   Ensure that the slide valves of the front and rear correctors are at the neutral position. Tighten the clamps of the front and rear automatic control rods, taking care not to jam the ball joint of the front corrector tie rod in its fork, and at the rear not to touch the edge of the hole with the rod of the automatic control rod. Tighten the clamps to 0.8-0.9 kg f m (6 to 6.5 lb f ft).
6   Fit the roadwheels, lower the car and run the engine. Tighten the pressure regulator bleed screw. Adjust the suspension heights as described in Section 26.

25 Suspension heights - checking

1   Place the manual control lever in the 'normal' road position and allow the engine to idle. Check the suspension heights with the car on level ground and the tyres at the correct pressure.
2   Lift the front of the car, by hand, as high as possible. When released, the car will drop, then rise again, and settle. Measure the distance between the lower point of the centre of the anti-roll bar, 'a' in Fig. 6.12, and the ground.
3   Push the front of the car down by hand as far as possible and then release it. The car will rise, drop again and then settle. Measure the front height again. Calculate the average of the two measurements, it should be between 179 and 199mm (7 and 7.8in).
4   Measure the rear suspension height in the same manner. The height is measured between the centre of the rear flanged edge of the sub-frame, 'b' in Fig. 6.13, and the ground. It should be between 262 and 282mm (10.3 and 11.1in). If the heights are not within the specified range, adjust the suspension heights as described in Section 26.

Fig. 6.9. Front height corrector removal

1	Corrector	4	Anti-roll bar bearing
2	Support	5	Manual control
3	Lever	6	Nut

Fig. 6.10. Presetting the front suspension height
For key see Section 24

Fig. 6.11. Presetting the rear suspension height
For key see Section 24

Fig. 6.12. Measuring the front suspension height

1   Clamp   (a) Lowest point of anti-roll bar

Fig. 6.13. Measuring the rear suspension height
(b) Sub frame

26 Suspension height - adjustment

1   The suspension height adjustment can be made without presetting, if the heights of the car only require slight alteration.

2   Remove the front corrector guard plate and the inspection panel on the floor of the boot. Set the manual control lever to the 'normal' road position. Start the engine and allow it to idle.

3   Disconnect the manual control from the front and rear correctors. At the front, slightly slacken the clamp bolt, '1' in Fig. 6.12, and adjust the clamp to obtain a front height of 189mm (7.4in). Tighten the clamp bolt to 1.3 to 1.5 kg f m (9 to 10 lb f ft). At the rear, slacken the screws securing the corrector and adjust the position of the corrector to obtain a rear suspension height of 272mm (10.7in). Retighten the corrector securing screws.

4   Adjust the manual height control linkage, as described in Section 27, so that the linkage can be connected without altering the corrector to a higher or lower height setting. After connecting the manual height control linkage check the suspension heights, as described in Section 25.

27 Manual height control - adjustment

1   On models produced until March 1972 refer to Fig. 6.14 and proceed as follows:

a) *Remove the inspection panel on the floor of the boot to give access to the rear corrector. Set the manual control lever to the 'normal' road position. Underneath the front axle check that the pin of the front fork is in the centre of the slot. If not, slacken the sector plate securing screws and move the sector to achieve this position. If this adjustment cannot be obtained position the sector plate in the centre and tighten the securing screws. Slacken the control rod clamp and adjust its length until the pin of the fork is in the middle of the slot. Tighten the clamp.*

b) *Check that the pin of the rear fork is in the centre of the slot. If not, slacken the plastic fork screw and adjust to obtain this position. Tighten the fork screw.*

c) *Operate the manual control and return to the 'normal' road position. Check the adjustment. Refit the inspection panel in the boot.*

2   On models produced since March 1972 refer to Fig. 6.17 and proceed as follows:

a) *Remove the guard plate from the front corrector and the inspection panel in the floor of the boot. Set the manual control lever to the 'normal' road position.*

b) *On the front corrector control check that the lever '2' in Fig. 6.15 is not pressing on the adjusting screw. Allow a clearance of approximately 5mm (0.2in). On the rear corrector control the clearance 'J1' and 'J2' must be as nearly equal as possible on each side of the fork.*

c) *Move the manual height control lever to the intermediate position and check that the height increases by 30 to 40mm (1.2 to 1.6in). If necessary, adjust at the fork and/or the adjusting screw to obtain this condition.*

d) *Move the manual control lever to the 'normal' road position and check the suspension heights as described in Section 25. Refit the front corrector guard plate and the inspection panel in the floor of the boot.*

Fig. 6.14. Manual height control (before March 1972)

| 1 Clamp | 3 Sector plate | 5 Fork screw | (a) Control lever 'normal' |
| 2 Front fork | 4 Securing screws | 6 Slot | position |

Fig. 6.15. Manual control adjustment

1   *Adjusting screw*   2   *Lever*

Fig. 6.16. Manual control linkage

1   *Fork   For J1 & J2 see Section 27*

Fig. 6.17. Manual height control (from March 1972)

a *Normal*   c *High*
b *Intermediate*
            For J1 and J2 see Section 27

---

28 Fault diagnosis - hydraulic system

Before diagnosing faults from the following chart, check that the hydraulic reservoir is filled to the correct level, that the pressure regulator bleed screw is tightened and that there are no visual leaks in the system, with the engine running.

Symptom	Reason/s	Remedy
No hydraulic pressure	Reservoir filter blocked	Clean the filter.
	Suction pipe from pump leaking	Tighten connection or renew pipe.
	High pressure pump defective	Renew pump.
	Pressure regulator defective	Renew pressure regulator.
Hydraulic pressure too low	Partially blocked reservoir filter	Clean the filter.
	High pressure pump defective	Renew the pump.
	Pressure regulator cut-out setting too low	Renew pressure regulator.
Hydraulic pressure too high	Pressure regulator not cutting-out	Renew pressure regulator.
Suspension not maintaining the car at selected height	Suspension cylinder defective	Renew defective cylinder.
	Manual control linkage worn or sticking	Dismantle and replace as necessary.
	Presetting of height incorrect	Carry out presetting procedure.
	Height corrector defective	Renew the corrector.
	Height adjustment incorrect	Re-adjust the suspension height.
	Clamp loose on anti-roll bar	Re-adjust the height and ensure clamp is tightened.
Car fails to rise when the engine is started	Reservoir filter blocked	Clean the filter.
	Pump suction pipe leakage	Tighten connections or renew pipe.
	Pump defective	Renew the pump.
	Pressure regulator defective	Renew the pressure regulator.
	Defective suspension cylinder	Renew.
	Defective height corrector	Renew.
	Clamp loose on anti-roll bar	Re-adjust suspension height.
Vibration and rattles	Steering defective	Check the steering system.
	Suspension ball and sockets worn	Renew as necessary.
	Rear axle unit flexible mountings defective	Renew the rear flexible mountings.
	Loose components or piping	Check and rectify as necessary.

Chapter 7 Front axle and suspension

For modifications, and information applicable to later models, see Supplement at end of manual

Contents

Specifications

Suspension

Type	Independent, double wishbone
Springing	Hydropneumatic cylinders
Damping	Integral with hydropneumatic cylinders
Anti-roll bar	21 mm diameter
Suspension height (normal)	189 ± 10 mm (7.44 ± 0.4 in)
Suspension cylinder spheres:	
Inflation pressure:	
Until February 1973	$50 \pm \frac{5}{10}$ bar ($710 \pm \frac{70}{140}$ psi)
From February 1973	$55 \pm \frac{5}{10}$ bar ($780 \pm \frac{70}{140}$ psi)

Driveshafts	Ball-type constant velocity joint at wheel end. Tri-axial joint at gearbox end.

1 General description

1 The front axle which is a subframe bolted to the bodyframe, carries the engine and transmission, the anti-roll bar, upper and lower suspension arms and swivel assemblies, the steering system and the suspension cylinders.

2 The height of the suspension can be selected manually to provide three different settings. Stop and bump buffers are fitted for the upper suspension arms. The wheel hubs run on ball bearings which are secured by ring nuts. The driveshafts are bolted to the differential output shafts, with the brake discs between them, and splined to the hubs.

3 The anti-roll bar is connected by ball jointed connecting rods to the upper suspension arms. Connected to the anti-roll bar is the height corrector which maintains the hydropneumatic suspension at the manually selected height.

2 Maintenance - general

Although there is no routine maintenance prescribed for the front axle and suspension system, visual and manual inspection of moving parts should be made periodically for wear or damage. Check the rubber bellows and the suspension arm bushes for splitting or deterioration. Damaged rubber bellows allow the ingress of dirt and grit which can result in expensive repairs. On all models from November 1972 the rubber bellows type dust shields protecting the suspension ball joints

contain 7cc (0.42 cu. in) of LHM fluid, it is therefore most important that they are maintained in good condition.

3 Suspension balls - lubrication

1 Jack-up and support the front of the car with the roadwheels hanging free. Release the pressure from the hydraulic system, as described in Chapter 6, Section 2. Remove the front wheels and thoroughly clean the working area.

2 Remove the pin securing the socket into the arm, and the thimble clip. Disengage the protective thimble and push the dust shield back along the pushrod.

3 Remove the clip and disengage the socket securing pin, Fig. 7.2, from the pushrod. Remove the ball and socket.

4 Thoroughly clean the pushrod and the ball and socket, smear the socket with multi-purpose grease and insert the ball into its socket.

5 Reassembly is the reverse of the disassembly sequence.

4 Upper suspension arm - removal and replacement

1 Jack-up and support the front of the car. Release the pressure from the hydraulic system, as described in Chapter 6, Section 2, and remove the roadwheel. If a right-hand suspension arm is being removed remove the height corrector guard plate.

Fig. 7.1. Front suspension

1 Suspension cylinder
2 Ball and socket
3 Upper suspension arm
4 Upper ball joint
5 Hub
6 Lower ball joint
7 Lower suspension arm
8 Link rod
9 Travel stops
10 Height corrector
11 Anti-roll bar

2 To disconnect the anti-roll bar, slacken the castellated nut by a few threads and tap it sharply to free the ball joint, remove the nut and disconnect the link rod. Remove the pin securing the socket into the arm.

3 Slacken the nut, securing the upper ball joint, by a few threads and using a suitable extractor, release the ball joint. Remove the nut.

4 Remove the pivot pin nut, drive out the pivot pin and remove the suspension arm, shim and protective caps.

5 Replacement is the reverse of the removal sequence. The right and left-hand arms are different. The boss 'a' in Fig. 7.4 must face forward when the arm is fitted on the car. Check the ball joint seals, if defective replace the ball joints. Check the movement of the suspension arm, there should be no endplay, if necessary, adjust with different thickness of shim. Always fit new NYLSTOP nuts after each dismantling. Tighten the pivot pin nut to 5.9 to 6.5 kg f m (43 to 47 lb f ft). Tighten the castellated nut to 2.5 to 3 kg f m (18 to 22 lb f ft) and the upper ball joint nut to 2.7 to 3 kg f m (20 to 22 lb f ft).

5 Lower suspension arm - removal and replacement

1 Carry out the procedure described in Section 4, paragraph 1.

2 Slacken the lower ball joint nut by a few threads and using a suitable extractor, release the lower ball joint from the suspension arm. Remove the nut and disconnect the joint.

3 Slide back the steering trackrod rubber bellows, as described in Chapter 9, to give access to the lower suspension arm pivot pin. Remove the pivot pin nut and the pivot pin, if necessary prise the wheel arch slightly. Remove the lower arm.

4 Examine the rubber seal of the ball joint, if it is in poor condition replace the ball joint assembly. Examine the fluidbloc bushes and replace, if necessary, as described in Section 6.

5 Replacement of the suspension arm is the reversal of the removal sequence. Always fit new NYLSTOP nuts after each dismantling. Tighten the pivot pin nut to 8 to 9 kg f m (58 to 84 lb f ft) and the ball joint nut to 2.7 to 3 kg f m (20 to 22 lb f ft).

6 Lower suspension arm bushes - removal and replacement

1 Remove the lower suspension arm, as described in Section 5.

2 Use of an 8mm expanding pin (Rawlpin or similar type) as shown in Fig. 7.5 simplifies the removal of the bushes. Fit the expanding pin with a threaded rod and a nut. Insert the pin in the bush and tighten the nut to open the two legs of the pin until they grip the bush. Pull on the rod while rotating the bush until the bush is withdrawn. Discard the bush. Remove the other bush.

3 Clean the bore of the arm and grease the metal cups and the thrust face of the fluidbloc bushes with a multi-purpose grease. Fit the bushes in the bore and tap them home with a mallet.

7 Anti-roll bar - removal

1 The anti-roll bar must be mounted with an axial preload of 35 to 40 kg (77 to 88 lb) on the clamp bearings. To set this preloading the Citroen tool 2067-T is required, if this tool is not available to the owner this work will have to be left to your local agent.

2 Jack-up, and support, the front of the car. Release the pressure from the hydraulic system as described in Chapter 6, Section 2. Remove the roadwheels. Remove the height corrector guard plate.

3 Remove the castellated nuts and disconnect the connecting rods from the upper suspension arms. Remove the plates protecting the anti-roll bar bearings. Disconnect the automatic height control rod from the anti-roll bar, by removing the clamp bolt, and leave the automatic control system in position on the suspension unit.

4 Remove the bolts holding the anti-roll bar bearings and remove the assembly of bar and bearings. Take care not to lose the plastic shells of the automatic control rod, located in the right-hand bearing. If necessary, using a suitable extractor remove the connecting rods from the anti-roll bar. Dismantle and clean the anti-roll bar. Renew bearings and dust shields, as necessary.

8 Anti-roll bar - assembly and replacement

1   Refer to Fig. 7.7 and fit the inner dust shields. Fit the clamps positioned so that 'a' = 93mm (3.66in) and the heads of the clamp bolts face forward and the clamps are perpendicular to the bar. Fit the bearing. Note that the bearings are different, the right-hand bearing has a housing for the plastic bearing of the automatic height control rod. Fit the outer dust shields. Fit the connecting rods, note the rods are different, and tighten the ball joint nuts to 2.5 to 3.0 kgf m (18 to 22 lbf ft).

2   Place a cross bar supported by a jack under the lower suspension arm ball joints and raise the bar until it bears against the axle-frame. Offer up the anti-roll bar and couple the connecting rods to the upper suspension arms. Tighten the ball joint nuts to 2.5 to 3 kg f m (18 to 22 lb f ft).

3   Grease the nylon shells and fit them in the bearings. On the right-hand side fit the plastic shells on the automatic height control rod.

4   Raise the anti-roll bar until it is possible to fit the retaining bolts and nuts. Engage the nuts by a few threads, check that the automatic control rod bearing is in its housing and continue to raise the bar by its centre until one of the bearings comes into contact with the axle frame. If the other bearing does not make contact with the frame, insert shims between this bearing and the frame until it can be secured without any stress on the anti-roll bar. Tighten the retaining nuts to 1 to 2.1 kg f m (13 to 15 lb f ft).

5   Preload the bearings as described in Section 9. Preset the height control, as described in Chapter 6, Section 24.

6   Remove the jack and crossbar. Fit the corrector and bearing guard plates, and the roadwheels. Lower the car, run the engine and tighten the pressure regulator bleed screw. Check the heights, as described in Chapter 6, Section 25.

Fig. 7.2. Suspension ball lubrication

1   Clip   2   Securing pin

Fig. 7.5. Removing suspension arm bush

1   Threaded rod   3   Expanding pin
2   Nut

Fig. 7.3. Upper suspension arm removal

1   Pivot pin nut   5   Ball joint seal
2   Castellated nut   6   Nut
3   Ball joint   7   Link rod seal
4   Corrector guard bolts   8   Pin

Fig. 7.4. Upper suspension arm

1   Protective caps   2   Shim

Fig. 7.6. Removing the anti-roll bar

1   Corrector guard plate   3   Nut
2   Connecting rod

9 Anti-roll bar - adjustment

Note: Citroen tool 2067-T is required to preload the clamp bearings.
1   Place the car on a lift or over a pit. Remove the bearing protective plates and disengage the lower part of the inner dust shields.
2   Slacken one bolt of the left-hand clamp. Compress the springs of tool 2067-T by screwing in the nut '4' in Fig. 7.9. Position the tool so that the forked ends are located on the two stop clamps, completely unscrew the nut '4' so that the tool exerts the correct preload on the two bearings of 35 to 40 kg (77 to 88 lb). Tighten the clamp bolt to 1 to 1.1 kg f m (7 to 8 lb f ft) and remove the tool 2067-T.
3   Fit the dust shields and the bearing protective plates. If the plates touch the anti-roll bar fit a plain washer between the plate and the axle frame at the front securing points.

10 Driveshaft - removal and refitting

1   Remove the wheel disc. Remove the split pin and slacken the hub retaining nut. Jack-up and support the front of the car. Release the pressure from the hydraulic system, as described in Chapter 6, Section 2. Remove the roadwheel. Remove the retaining nut.
2   Remove the nuts securing the driveshaft to the output shaft. Disconnect the lower suspension arm and the steering linkage from the hub carrier, as described in Section 6 and Chapter 9, respectively.
3   Detach and remove the upper suspension arm bump stop then swing the hub outwards, without disengaging the swivels of the inner universal joint, and withdraw the driveshaft splines from the hub and remove the shaft.
4   Refitting is a reversal of the removal procedure. Lubricate the seal ring in the hub with grease before inserting the driveshaft. Tighten the respective retaining nuts and bolts to their specified torque wrench settings.

11 Hub - removal and replacement

1   Disconnect the driveshaft from the hub, as described in Section 10. Disconnect the steering tie-rod from the steering arm, as described in Chapter 9. Disconnect the upper and lower suspension arm, as described in Sections 4 and 5.
2   Push back on the end of the driveshafts, so that the inner universal joint does not separate, disengage the splines from the hub and remove the hub.
3   Replacement is the reversal of the removal sequence.

12 Hub - dismantling and reassembly

1   Remove the inner seal. Using a 4mm drill clear the peening, locking the ring nut. Remove the ring nut (Citroen supply special tools for this, 3321-T and 3320-T). Using an extractor (Citroen tool 1893-T) remove the hub. Remove the outer seal and the hub bearing.
2   Examine the bearing and seals and renew as necessary. Smear the bearing with grease and using a suitable mandrel and a press, fit the bearing with the projecting part, (b in Fig. 7.10), of the ball race facing outwards. Fit the inner race. Fit the ring nut and tighten it to 40 to 50 kg f m (290 to 360 lb f ft). Lock the ring by peening it in two places.
3   Fit the outer seal, leaving a clearance between it and the ball race, 'g' in Fig. 7.10. Grease the inner lip of the seal and the bearing. Using a suitable mandrel and a press, bearing on the inner race, fit the hub. Fit the inner seal and press it fully home into the housing.

13 Front axle unit - removal

1   Removal of the front axle unit is a major operation and the owner should ensure that adequate facilities and assistance is available before undertaking the task. When stripping down the unit after removal and when preparing a unit for refitting, reference should be made to the relevant Chapters in the manual for removal and replacement procedures of the various components.
2   Remove the engine/gearbox assembly, as described in Chapter 1. Remove the bolt securing the Cardan shaft to the pinion of the steering box. On each side remove the plates between the chassis and axle unit, and the plates protecting the suspension spheres. Using a strap wrench

remove the spheres from the suspension cylinders and blank off the cylinders.
3   Remove the bolts holding the four-way union and the union for the overflow return pipes. Disconnect the supply union from the height corrector and the overflow return pipes from the suspension cylinders and remove them from the clips. Remove the bolts holding the anti-roll

Fig. 7.7. Anti-roll bar bearing assembly

1   Inner dust shield
2   Clamp
3   Bearing
4   Outer dust shield
(a) 3.66 in (93 mm)
(b) Machined surface

Fig. 7.8. Anti-roll bar adjustment

1   Bearing
2   Nuts
3   Guard plate
4   Front securing point

Fig. 7.9. Preloading the anti-roll bar

1   Dustshields
2   Stop clamp screw
3   Stop clamp
4   Nut

bar right-hand bearing and the linkage rod from the manual height control. Remove the driveshafts (Section 10).

4   Place a jack and a crossbeam under the axle unit to support it while removing the retaining bolts. Lift up the carpet under the pedals and at each side remove the rear retaining bolts, refer to Fig. 7.11. Remove the two front retaining bolts. Free the hydraulic pipes from their brackets.

5   Make a careful check to ensure that all pipes and components have been disconnected. Hold the height corrector so that it will not get damaged, lower the jack and remove the unit. Collect the shims fitted between the chassis and the lower unit mounting '1' in Fig. 7.11.

14 Front axle unit - replacement

1   Replacement is the reverse of the removal sequence. When replacing and connecting components refer to the relevant Chapter for procedure and adjustments.

2   Refer to Fig. 7.11 and fit the mounting bolts. Fit bolts '2' and '4' and tighten bolt '2' to 2 kg f m (14 lb f ft). Fit bolt '3' and tighten the bolts '4', '2' and '3' (in that order) to 4.5 to 5 kg f m (33 to 36 lb f ft). Fit shims at bolt '1' between the chassis and axle unit to give a maximum clearance of 0.5mm (0.020in) and tighten the bolts to 9 to 10 kg f m (65 to 72 lb f ft).

Fig. 7.10. Front hub assembly

1 Outer seal	4 Inner race
2 Ring nut	5 Outer race
3 Inner seal	6 Hub

For b and g see Section 12

Fig. 7.11. Axle unit retaining bolts

1 Rear bolt	3 Rear bolt
2 Rear bolt	4 Front bolt

15 Fault diagnosis - front axle and suspension

Before diagnosing faults from the following chart, check that any irregularities are not caused by:

1   *Defective steering*
2   *Incorrect tyre pressures*
3   *Incorrect 'mix' of tyres*
4   *Incorrect wheel alignment*

Symptom	Reason/s	Remedy
Vibration and rattles	Worn suspension arm ball joints	Renew as necessary.
	Worn suspension arm pivot pin and/or bearing	Renew.
	Suspension cylinder loose	Tighten cylinder retaining bolts.
	Suspension cylinder ball and socket worn	Renew cylinder.
	Pipe securing clips and brackets loose	Tighten as necessary.
	Axle unit securing bolts and nuts loose	Tighten as necessary.
	Hub bearings worn	Renew bearings.
Suspension bottoming	Fault in hydraulic system	Check through the hydraulic system.
	Defective suspension cylinder/s	Renew as necessary.
	Suspension heights set incorrectly	Re-adjust the suspension heights.

Chapter 8 Braking system

For modifications, and information applicable to later models, see Supplement at end of manual

Contents

Specifications

Type
Front and rear brakes	Hydraulically operated disc brakes	
Parking brake	Mechanically operated, acting on front discs	

Footbrakes

	Front	Rear
Disc diameter	270 mm (10.6 in)	178 mm (7 in)
Disc thickness (G10 engines until September 1972)	7 mm (0.28 in)	6 mm (0.24 in)
Disc thickness (all types from September 1972)	9 mm (0.35 in)	6 mm (0.23 in)
Minimum thickness after wear:		
Up to September 1972	4 mm (0.16 in)	4 mm (0.16 in)
From September 1972	6 mm (0.24 in)	4 mm (0.16 in)
Maximum run-out of disc	0.2 mm (0.008 in)	0.2 mm (0.008 in)
Thickness of pad (without wear leads)	8.55 mm (0.34 in)	7.55 mm (0.30 in)
Thickness of pads (with wear leads)	12 mm (0.47 in)	12 mm (0.47 in)

Handbrake
Thickness of pad	3.65 mm (0.14 in)

1 General description

1   The dual circuit braking system, with disc brakes fitted to all four wheels is hydraulically operated from the main hydraulic system. The front brakes are supplied from the hydraulic pressure regulator and the rear brakes are supplied from the rear suspension system. This arrangement favours the front brakes and imposes a braking effort limitation on the rear axle in relation to the load. The braking action is applied through the brake pedal operating a hydraulic control valve which allows pressure to the braking system.

2   The front discs are mounted inboard of the front wheel driveshafts and are secured between the differential output shafts and driveshafts. The two-piston type calipers are mounted on the gearbox. The friction pads fitted in each caliper are renewable. As the brake pads wear, they are automatically adjusted and when the wear limit of the pad is reached a wire in the pad lining contacts the disc, and a warning light on the instrument panel lights up. On earlier models which are not fitted with a pad wear warning device, the pads must be checked visually at regular intervals.

3   The rear brake discs are bolted to the inner face of the wheel hubs. The calipers are mounted on the rear suspension arms. Brake adjustment is automatic but unlike the front brakes there is no warning light, therefore the pad thickness must be checked visually at regular intervals.

4   The handbrake is applied through a "spade handle" control and flexible cables operating the calipers (separate from the main front hydraulic brakes) which forces the friction pads against the brake disc.

2 Routine maintenance

1   Visually check the thickness of the brake friction pad linings every 10,000 km (6,000 miles). When replacing pads always fit new pads to both calipers on each axle.

2   Every 10,000 km (6,000 miles) adjust the parking brake as described in Section 15.

3   Every 40,000 km (24,000 miles) check that the thickness of the brake discs is not less than 4 mm (0.16 in) and variation in thickness does not exceed 0.02 mm (0.008 in).

4   To check the wear in the front pads, use a mirror and torch so that you will view the pads from above.

5   The rear pads usually wear at a much slower rate than the front especially if the vehicle is run in a lightly loaded state. To check these pads, jack up the vehicle and remove each rear roadwheel in turn. Remove the cover plate (which hides the pads) by unscrewing the 8 mm bolt and again use a mirror to check the thickness of the friction material.

3 Brake pads (front brakes) - renewal

1   Remove the spare wheel and the heater distributor box with its ducting. Disconnect the wear detector leads (if fitted) and extract the clip securing the pad retaining spindle (photo).

2   On cars fitted with old type calipers (Fig. 8.1) push on the ends 'a' of the pads with the hand, to push back the pistons, in the direction of the arrows. Pull on the end 'b' of the pad retaining spring with

a wire hook and then pull the pad forward to release it. Alternatively prise the spring by inserting a screwdriver behind it. Remove the other pad in the same way. Do not depress the brake pedal until the new pads are fitted. Fit the pads into the caliper by pushing it as far as possible to the rear so that the spigots engage in their corresponding slots. Lock the pads by raising the ends so that the spring arms engage in the pad arm notches. Connect the wear detector leads (if fitted).
3   On cars fitted with new type calipers, Fig. 8.2, push the pad at 'c' with a screwdriver and remove the pin. Hold the pad by the wear detector lead and push out the spindle. Remove the spindle and the spring. Remove the pads from above (photos).
Note: Do not depress the brake pedal until the new pads are fitted.
4   Press the caliper pistons back into their bores with a suitable blunt tool. Fit the inner pad first. Hold the pad with a hook inserted in the hole 'd' of the pad. Fit the spring. Insert the spindle into the brake caliper and into the upper hole of the pad after interposing the spring below the spindle. Repeat the same operation for the other pad. Push home the spindle and fit the pin. Connect the wear detector leads.
5   Operate the brake pedal a few times to settle the brake pads and ensure that the pedal travel remains normal.
6   Fit the heater distributor box, ducting and spare wheel.

4   Caliper (front brakes) - removal

1   Place the manual height control in 'high' position and slacken the pressure regulator bleed screw. Disconnect the earth strap from the negative terminal of the battery. Remove the spare wheel. If the right-hand caliper is being removed it is necessary to remove the heater distributor box and ducting.
2   Disconnect the caliper hydraulic connection pipe and, if a left-hand caliper, disconnect the feed pipe and release it from its support bracket. Slacken the caliper attaching bolts, remove the rear bolt, swing the caliper upwards and refit the bolt. Fit a nut to the bolt and tighten to retain the two halves of the caliper together (photos).
3   Remove the locknuts and nuts of the handbrake cable, withdraw the cable and collect the spring.
4   Remove the front attaching bolt and lift out the caliper. If it is the

old type caliper collect the shim, located between the caliper and the gearbox, used for positioning the caliper in relation to the brake disc.

5   Calipers (front brakes) - replacement

1   Check that the contact faces of the caliper and gearbox are clean and smooth. Scrape off any burrs.
2   With the two halves of the caliper held together by the rear attaching bolt and nut, offer up the complete caliper, fitted with the handbrake pads, and in the case of the old type caliper, the original shim removed. Fit the front attaching bolt, finger-tight. Remove the nut from the rear attaching bolt, swing the caliper into position and fit the rear bolt. Check that the shim is in position (old type caliper) and tighten the bolts to 4.5 to 5 kg f m (33 to 36 lb f ft) on old type calipers and to 6 kg f m (43 lb f ft) on new type.
3   Fit the main brake pads, as described in Section 3.
4   Adjust the clearance of the handbrake pads, as described in Section 15. Connect up and adjust the handbrake cable, as described in Section 15.
5   Connect up the feed pipe and connection pipe. Fit new seals and tighten the unions to 0.8 to 0.9 kg f m (5.8 to 6.5 lb f ft).
6   Bleed the front brakes, as described in Section 18.
7   Fit the heater distributor box and ducting. Fit the spare wheel and connect the earth strap to the negative terminal of the battery.

6   Disc (front brakes) - removal and replacement

1   Remove the caliper, as described in Section 4, but do not disconnect the parking brake cable. Disconnect the driveshaft inner universal joint from the differential output shaft, as described in Chapter 7, Section 10.
2   Using a suitable stud extractor, remove the six studs from the differential output shaft flange and remove the disc from above (photo).
3   Check that the thickness of the discs is not less than 4 mm (0.16 in) and that variation in thickness round the disc does not exceed 0.02 mm (0.008 in). Check that maximum run-out of the disc does not exceed 0.2 mm (0.008 in) when fitted.
4   Replacement is the reverse of the removal sequence.

3.1 Detach front brake wear indicator lead and extract clip

3.3a Withdraw the disc pads retaining pin and clip (arrowed) . . .

3.3b . . . and lift out the brake pads

4.2a Hydraulic connection (black arrow). White arrow indicates bleed nipple

4.2b Removing the front caliper retaining bolts

6.2 Removing the studs in the differential shafts

Fig. 8.1. Old type caliper

1   Pad retaining spring

Fig. 8.2. New type caliper

1 Pin	*3 Wear lead*
2 Spindle	*4 Spring*

7   Calipers (front brakes) - renovation

1   Remove the calipers, as described in Section 4, and remove the brake pads, as described in Section 3. Separate the two halves of the caliper.
2   Apply a controlled supply of compressed air to the hydraulic pipe connections and carefully blow the pistons from their bores.
3   Examine the pistons and bores for scoring, corrosion or damage. Renew any defective parts and reassemble with new seals.
4   Replace the pads and refit the caliper, as described in Sections 3 and 4.

8   Brake pads (rear brakes) - renewal

1   Jack-up the rear of the car and remove the wheels.
Note: All four pads should be renewed at the same time.
2   Unscrew the nut and withdraw the central locating bolt (or remove the split pin on later models). Remove the pad shield and pads. Do not depress the brake pedal until the pads have been refitted.
3   Using a suitable blunt tool press the pistons into their bores. Fit the new pads and the pad shield. Fit the locating bolt (or slot pin).
4   When all four pads have been refitted, depress the brake pedal several times to settle the pads and to ensure that the brake pedal travel is normal.

9   Calipers (rear brakes) - removal

1   Jack-up and support the rear of the car. Slacken the pressure regulator bleed screw to release the pressure from the hydraulic

system. Remove the roadwheel.
2   Disconnect the hydraulic feed pipe. Slacken both retaining nuts and remove the nut and bolt on the bleed screwside. Swing the caliper upwards, refit the bolt and tighten the nut to retain both halves of the caliper together. Remove the other nut and bolt and remove the caliper.

10   Calipers (rear brakes) - replacement

1   Replacement is the reverse of the removal sequence. Tighten the nuts of the retaining bolts to 3.6 to 4 kg f m (26 to 29 lb f ft). Fit a new seal in the feed pipe connection and tighten to 0.8 to 0.9 kg f m (6 to 6.5 lb f ft).
2   Start the engine. Tighten the pressure regulator bleed screw. Place the manual height control to 'high' position and, if necessary, move the rear suspension arms to cause the pressure to rise. Bleed the brakes as described in Section 19. Check for leaks.
3   Fit the roadwheel and lower the car to the ground.

11   Disc (rear brakes) - removal and replacement

1   Removal and replacement of the rear disc is described in Chapter 11, Sections 7 and 8.
2   Check the condition of the disc, as described in Section 6.

12   Calipers (rear brakes) - renovation

Renovation of the rear calipers is the same as described for the front calipers in Section 7.

13   Brake pedal and stoplamp switch adjustment

1   Refer to Fig. 8.4. The clearance 'J' between the brake and the control valve must be maintained between 0.1 and 0.5 mm (0.004 and 0.020 in). Adjustment is by slackening the locknut and turning the stop screw, (or by bending the metal plate if a stop screw is not fitted), then tightening the locknut.
2   To check the operation of the brake pedal set the manual height control to the normal road position, slacken the pressure regulator bleed screw then select the 'high' position. Operate the pedal three or four times, to move the control slide valve to the end of its stroke, and ensure that the pedal returns freely and is maintained against its stop by the return spring.
3   The stoplamp switch contacts are kept open, when the brake pedal is against its stop, by the contact plate. When the pedal is operated the stoplamp must light up as soon as the pedal contacts the control valve. Adjust as necessary by bending the switch support plate to achieve this condition.

Fig. 8.3. Rear brake caliper removal

1 Locating bolt (split pin on later models)	*3 Retaining nuts and bolts*
2 Caliper	*4 Feed pipe*

14 Control valve - removal and replacement

1   Jack-up and support the front of the car. Remove the right-hand roadwheel. Remove the spare wheel.
2   Slacken the hydraulic pressure regulator bleed valve and move the manual height control to the 'high' position to release the pressure from the hydraulic system.
3   Remove the control valve guard plate. Note the pipe connections and disconnect the pipes from the control valve. Remove the retaining bolts and the control valve.
4   Replacement is the reverse of the removal sequence. Tighten the retaining bolts to 1.7 to 1.8 kg f m (12 to 13 lb f ft). Check the adjustment of the brake pedal, as described in Section 13. Bleed the brakes as described in Sections 18 and 19.

15 Handbrake - adjustment

1   Jack-up and support the front of the car on stands. Remove the spare wheel. Release the handbrake. Remove the heater distributor box and flexible ducts.
2   Refer to Fig. 8.6. On each brake unit slacken the locknuts and back-off the nuts for adjusting the handbrake cables.
3   Slacken the screw securing the eccentric adjusters and set the eccentrics to the position which gives the maximum clearance. Ensure that the arms are against their stops at 'a'.
4   Turn the eccentrics in the direction of the arrows until a clearance of 0.1 mm (0.004 in) is obtained between the pad backplates and the heel 'b' of each arm. The use of a mirror helps when checking this clearance. Ensure this clearance is adjusted at the point of maximum disc run-out (photo).
5   When the clearance has been set, tighten the screw securing the eccentric to 4 kg f m (29 lb f ft). Re-check the clearance between the pad backplate and the heel of the arm.
6   Check that each end of the cables is located in the cable sheath ends. Screw on the adjusting nut until it contacts the arm (pull on the cable to facilitate this operation). Screw on the nuts alternately so that the length of thread protruding through the adjusting nuts is the same on both sides to within 5 mm (0.20 in). Tighten the locknuts to 1.5 kg f m (11 lb f ft).
7   Operate the handbrake handle several times, ensuring that the adjustment does not alter and that the handle locks in position when the brake is applied.
8   Replace the heater distributor box and ducting and the spare wheel. Lower the car to the ground.

16 Handbrake pads - removal and replacement

1   For even braking, the four handbrake pads must always be renewed at the same time.
2   If old type calipers are fitted remove them, as described in Section 4, and remove the pads.
3   Slacken the screws locking the eccentric adjusters and turn the eccentrics to the position giving the maximum clearance at the pads (direction of arrows in Fig. 8.7). Fit the pads and check that the anti-noise springs are correctly positioned.
4   Fit the calipers as described in Section 5. Adjust the pad clearance and brake cable, as described in Section 15.
5   If later type calipers are fitted, proceed as follows. Remove the heater distribution box and associated ducts for accessibility, then detach the handbrake cable.
6   Remove the divisional coil spring from its location between the adjuster arms, then unscrew and remove the adjuster arm bolts, together with their washers. The cam and lever assemblies can now be withdrawn and the pads removed (photos).
7   To refit the pads lift the spring and locate the pad into its support, then reassemble the cam and lever assemblies in reverse order to removal. Locate the coil spring, then adjust the pad clearance and brake cable as described in Section 15.

17 Bleeding the hydraulic braking system - general

1   When any part of the system has been dismantled or after changing the fluid in the hydraulic system the brakes will have to be bled to remove any air from the braking system. While bleeding the brakes ensure that the fluid in the hydraulic reservoir does not fall below the minimum level.
2   Bleeding the brakes is a two man job, as the brake pedal has to be held depressed during the bleeding operation.

18 Bleeding the front brakes

Note: This operation must be carried out without pressure to prevent emulsifying the fluid with air, which could later result in the formation of air bubbles in the system.
1   With the engine stopped, slacken the hydraulic pressure regulator bleed screw. Select the 'normal' position on the manual height control.
2   Clean round the bleed screw and remove the protective cap from the right-hand brake unit. Connect a transparent bleed tube to the bleed screw with the other end into the hydraulic reservoir (photo).
3   Depress the brake pedal and slacken the brake unit bleed screw. Keep the pedal depressed and start the engine.
4   Tighten the hydraulic pressure regulator bleed screw and allow fluid to flow through the bleed tube, into the reservoir, until the bleed tube is free from air bubbles, then tighten the brake unit bleed screw.
5   Release the brake pedal and remove the bleed tube. Push down hard on the brake pedal and check that the brake unit bleed screw is not leaking. Stop the engine and replace the rubber protective cap over the brake unit bleed screw.

19 Bleeding the rear brakes

1   Place the manual height control lever in the 'high' position so that a cross-beam of timber supported on a jack can be located beneath the vehicle directly below the rear seats. Now set the height control lever to the 'normal' position and slacken the screw on the pressure regulator. Return the height control lever to the 'high' position and wait for the vehicle to sink down.
2   Jack-up the car, place it on stands and remove the rear wheels. With the aid of a jack, lift one rear suspension arm (the rear height corrector will then be in the 'inlet' position).
3   Clean round the brake unit bleed screws, remove the rubber protective caps and connect a transparent bleed tube to each bleed screw with the other end placed in a clean container. Open the brake bleed screws and push the pedal hard down (photo).
4   Keeping the brake pedal depressed, tighten the hydraulic pressure regulator bleed screw and start the engine. Allow fluid to flow through the bleed tubes until they are free from air bubbles, then tighten the brake bleed screws. Release the brake pedal.
Note: The pressure should now build up in the hydraulic system, with the suspension arms assuming the high position. If this fails to occur, increase the engine speed to approximately 3000 rpm, unscrew the pressure regulator bleed screw and leave it open for 30 seconds. Close the bleed screw, allow the engine to idle and recheck the position of the suspension arms.
5   Remove the jack from the suspension arm. Remove the bleed tubes, depress the brake pedal and check the brake bleed screws for leaks. Fit the rubber caps.
6   Stop the engine. Fit the roadwheels, remove the supports and lower the car to the ground.

20 Control valve - renovation

1   Remove the control valve as described in Section 14. Remove the operating pad, the retaining ring and withdraw the boot. Remove the circlip, the piston, the spring and the collar. From the other end of the valve remove the circlip and the plug seal. Collect the spring and the other piston.
2   Examine the parts and renew as necessary. Always fit a new 'O' ring at every dismantling. If a piston is defective, both pistons and the body must be renewed, as they are supplied as a matched set.
3   Lightly oil the parts with LHM fluid and reassemble in the reverse of the removal sequence. Replace the control valve, as described in Section 14, and bleed the brakes, as described in Sections 18 and 19.

15.4 Adjusting front caliper handbrake eccentrics with the help of a mirror

16.6a Removing the cam and lever assembly (later models)

16.6b Withdraw the handbrake pad

18.2 The single front brake bleed screw (left hand caliper)

19.3 Rear offside caliper brake bleed screw

Fig. 8.4. Brake pedal adjustment

1 Stopscrew 5 Contact plate
2 Locknut 6 Control valve
3 Stoplamp switch 7 Return spring
4 Support plate

Fig. 8.6. Handbrake adjustment

1 Arm 4 Locknut
2 Spring 5 Eccentric adjuster
3 Adjusting nut 6 Lockscrew

For 'a' and 'b' see text

Fig. 8.5. Brake control valve

Fig. 8.7. Handbrake pad replacement (old type front disc caliper)

1 Eccentric adjusters   3 Pads
2 Lockscrews

Fig. 8.8. Handbrake pad replacement (new type front disc caliper)

1 Eccentric adjusters   3 Spring
2 Lockscrew

21 Fault diagnosis - braking system

Before diagnosing faults from the following chart, check that any braking irregularities are not caused by:
1 *Uneven or incorrect tyre pressures*
2 *Incorrect 'mix' of radial and crossply tyres*
3 *Wear in the steering mechanism*
4 *Defects in the suspension*
5 *Misalignment of the bodyframe*

Symptom	Reason/s	Remedy
Stopping ability poor	Brake pads and/or discs badly worn or scored	Dismantle, check and renew as required.
	Brake control valve faulty	Remove, dismantle and renew parts as necessary.
	Brake caliper seals defective	Dismantle and renew.
	Leak in the hydraulic system	Identify and rectify.
	Air in the hydraulic system	Bleed the system.
	Low main hydraulic system pressure	Check the main hydraulic system, Chapter 6.
Uneven braking, brakes grabbing or pulling to one side	Brake pads contaminated with oil	Renew brake pads, identify and rectify source of oil
	Brake disc distorted	Check and renew if necessary.
	Piston seized in a brake caliper	Dismantle and renew.
Parking brake inefficient	Worn brake pads	Renew brake-pads.
	Brake adjustment incorrect	Re-adjust.

Chapter 9 Steering, wheels and tyres

For modifications, and information applicable to later models, see Supplement at end of manual

Contents

Specifications

Steering

Type	Rack and pinion
Lock angle	44° 36' (not adjustable)
Ratio	1 : 19
Turning radius:	
Between walls (approx.)	5.10 m (17 ft 0.2 in)
Between kerbs (approx)	4.70 m (15 ft 9.6 in)
Steering wheel turns (lock-to-lock)	3.8
Wheel alignment	0 to 2 mm (0 to 0.07 in) toe-in
Camber angle	1° positive to 1° negative
Castor angle	$1° 15' {}^{+\ 1°\ 25'}_{-\ 1°\ 15'}$

Wheels

Type	Vent disc, 3 stud fixing 4½J x 15
Size	4½J x 15 in

Tyres

Size	145 - 15 ZX (tubeless)

Pressures (all models)

Front	1.8 kg/sq cm (26 psi)
Rear	1.9 kg/sq cm (28 psi)

1 General description

1 The rack and pinion type steering unit is mounted on the front axle unit. A steering arm is connected to each end of the rack by a tie-rod which is adjustable for setting the wheel alignment. Camber and castor angles are not adjustable: if they are suspect consult your Citroen agent.

2 When removing the steering, it is necessary to remove the steering column as the wheel is integral with the steering column shaft and cannot be removed separately. When the roadwheels are in the straight-ahead position the spoke of the steering wheel is positioned 30° below the horizontal towards the outside of the car.

3 The drive from the steering column to the steering unit is transmitted through a Cardan shaft, the universal joints of which are not identical, so care must be taken to ensure that it is fitted correctly.

4 Rubber bellows type dust covers are fitted over the axial joints between each end of the steering rack and the tie-rods.

2 Maintenance

1 No routine maintenance, as such, is required for the steering mechanism, but a visual examination should be made periodically to check the condition of the rubber bellows. They should be checked for cracking and general deterioration of the rubber. Defective bellows will allow the ingress of dirt and water and could lead to failure of the steering unit.

2 If there is any sign of excessive free-movement in the steering, check the tie-rod ball joints for wear. If the ball joints are worn, the complete tie-rod must be renewed as the balljoints are integral with the tie-rods. Check the wheel alignment periodically, as described in Section 6. Incorrect wheel alignment can ruin tyres very quickly.

3 Steering unit - removal

1 Raise and support the front of the car. Remove the front wheels.

2 Move the rubber bellows back and unlock the tabwashers. Unscrew the tie-rod ball joints, while holding the rack to prevent it turning. Remove the plastic sheath from the rack.

3 Before removing the Cardan shaft, mark the position of the ends so that it can be refitted correctly, as both ends are not identical. Slacken the nut holding the lower universal joint and remove the bolt holding the upper universal joint. Note relative position of steering wheel then free the steering column from the support tube and remove the Cardan shaft.

4   Remove the two bolts securing the steering unit to the front axle and remove the control rod from the front height corrector (mark the position of the collar on the rod). The height settings are not altered by removing the control rod of the height corrector.
5   Remove the steering unit from the car.

4   Steering unit - replacement

1   Fit the steering unit into its recess on the front axle unit. Fit the securing bolts, with washers under the heads, and torque tighten to 3.6 to 4 kg f m (26 to 29 lb f ft).
2   Place the Cardan shaft in position with the universal joints located as marked at removal. Engage the lower universal joint with the pinion.
3   Adjust the position of the rack so that an equal amount protrudes from each side of the casing and fit the steering column into the support tube. Insert the nylon washer.
4   Position the spoke of the steering wheel 30° below the horizontal towards the outside of the car (early models), 30° below the horizontal towards the centre of car (later models) or with the spoke pointing vertically downwards (latest models). Connect the steering column to the upper universal joint of the Cardan shaft. Fit the securing bolt and nut. Always fit a new Nylstop nut whenever the bolt is removed. Tighten the nut to 1.3 to 1.4 kg f m (9.5 to 10 lb f ft).
5   Fit the lower universal joint of the shaft to the pinion so as to give a clearance of 1 to 1.5 mm (0.040 to 0.060 in) between the nylon washer and the support tube (Fig. 9.3). Fit the clamping bolt and new nut. tighten to 1.3 to 1.4 kg f m (9.5 to 10 lb f ft).
6   Fit the plastic sheaths on the housing. Fit the stop washer and tabwasher, and screw the tie-rod ball joints fully home on the rack. Hold the rack from turning and torque tighten the ball joints to 3.6 to 4 kg f m (26 to 29 lb f ft). Bend the tab of the tabwasher back onto the flat of the ball joint.
7   Connect the control rod to the front height connector, if necessary, operate the height control to adjust to the marks made when the collar was removed.
8   Fit the front wheels and lower the car to the ground.
9   Check the toe-in of the front wheels, as described in Section 6.
10 Fit the rubber bellows over the plastic sheaths and adjust them so that, with the wheels in the straight-ahead position, their length is 155 ± 3 mm (6.10 ± 0.12 in), 'a' in Fig. 9.4.

5   Tie-rods - removal and replacement

1   Movement is transmitted from the rack of the steering unit to each wheel by a tie-rod which is secured, at its outer end, by a ball joint to the steering arm on the front hub. If the tie-rods are bent, or the ball joints are worn, the wheels will be out of alignment or have excessive free-movement independent of the steering unit, this will result in inaccurate steering and abnormal tyre wear.
2   Disconnect the tie-rods from the steering rack, as described in Section 3.
3   Remove the nut holding the tie-rod ball joint in the steering arm, and using a suitable extractor, remove the ball joint. If an extractor is not available, try holding a hammer to one side of the steering arm eye and striking the opposite side a sharp blow with a hammer, this will usually free the joint.
4   Replacement is the reversal of the removal sequence. Always fit a new tabwasher. When screwing the tie-rod swivel joint onto the steering rack prevent the rack from turning while tightening the joint to 3.6 to 4 kg f m (26 to 29 lb f ft). Tighten the nuts securing the ball joints to the steering arms to 1.8 to 2 kg f m (13 to 14.5 lb f ft).
5   Check the wheel alignment, and adjust as necessary, refer to Section 6.
6   Replace the rubber bellows, as described in Section 4.

6   Wheel alignment - checking and adjustment

1   The alignment of the front wheels does not normally alter unless the steering linkage or front suspension has been subject to abnormal stress or the tie-rods have been disturbed or renewed.
2   Before checking the wheel alignment the front and rear heights of the car must be correctly adjusted (refer to the relevant Chapters) and the tyre pressures must be correct.

3   Position the car on level ground with the wheels in the straight-ahead position and the manual height control set to the 'normal' road position.
4   With the engine running measure the toe-in of the front wheels using a wheel alignment gauge, of which there are various types available, and check that the toe-in is between 0 and 2 mm (0 and 0.080 in).
5   If adjustment of the toe-in is necessary, proceed as follows:

   a) *Slide the rubber bellows back to uncover the tie-rod ball joints and slacken the locknuts.*
   b) *Turn the ball joint ends a fraction of a turn at a time to obtain the correct adjustment. Make sure both ends are turned an equal amount. One complete turn of each ball joint end alters the adjustment by approximately 4 mm (0.16 in).*

6   Tighten the locknuts to a torque of 3.6 to 4 kg f m (26 to 29 lb f ft) and re-check the alignment. Check that the length of the threaded portion visible on the left and right-hand tie-rods ('b' in Fig. 9.5), is the same to within 2 mm (0.08 in).
7   Refit the rubber bellows, as described in Section 4.

7   Steering wheel and column - removal and replacement

1   Disconnect the Cardan shaft from the steering column assembly, as described in Section 3.
2   Disconnect the earth strap from the negative terminal of the battery. Disconnect the speedometer drive. Loosen the parcel shelf and disconnect the wiring.
3   Remove the dashboard screws and withdraw the dashboard sufficiently to allow for the removal of the steering column upper securing bracket. Remove the screws holding the lower bracket and withdraw the steering wheel and column assembly.
4   Replacement of the assembly is the reversal of the removal procedure. Ensure that the steering shaft position is adjusted, as described in Section 4.

8   Wheels and tyres - general

1   To provide equal and minimum wear from all the tyres, they should be rotated on the car at intervals of 6,000 miles (10,000 km) to the following pattern, but only if the wheels have been balanced off the vehicle.

   Front to rear and rear to front on the same side of the vehicle, not side to side.

   Wheels should be rebalanced when this is done. If two tyres only are being renewed, the new pair should always be fitted to the front wheels, as these are the most important from the safety aspect of steering and braking.
2   Never mix tyres of radial and crossply construction on the same car, as the basic design differences can cause unusual and, in certain conditions, very dangerous handling and braking characteristics. If an emergency should force the use of two different types, make sure the radials are on the rear wheels and drive particularly carefully. If three of the five wheels are fitted with radial tyres, make sure that no more than two radials are in use on the car (and these at the rear). Rationalise the tyres at the earliest possible opportunity.
3   Wheels are not normally subject to servicing problems, but when tyres are renewed or changed the wheels should be balanced to reduce vibration and wear. If a wheel is suspected of damage, caused by hitting the kerb or a pothole which could distort it out of true, change it and have it checked for balance and true running at the earliest opportunity.
4   When fitting the wheels, do not overtighten the nuts. The maximum possible manual torque applied by the manufacturers wheel brace is adequate. It also prevents difficulties when the same wheel brace has to be used for removal of the wheels!

Fig. 9.1. Cross-section of the steering rack housing

Fig. 9.2. Tie-rod to steering rack ball joint

1 Rubber bellows   4 Plastic sheath
2 Stop washer   5 Ball joint
3 Tabwasher

Fig. 9.4. Rubber bellows measurement

1 Rubber bellows

Fig. 9.3. Cardan shaft and support tube

1 Cardan shaft   3 Nylon washer
2 Support tube   4 Upper universal clamping bolt

Fig. 9.5. Tie-rod adjustment

1 Ball joint   2 Locknut

9   Fault diagnosis - steering, wheels and tyres

Symptom	Reason/s	Remedy
Excessive free movement in steering wheel	Wear in steering linkage, gear and Cardan shaft joints	Check condition of all joints and steering gear. Renew as required.
Wander	As above	As above.
	Wheels out of alignment	Check alignment.
	Uneven tyre pressure	Check pressures.
	Worn suspension arm pivot bushes	Renew pivot bushes.
Steering stiff and heavy	Ball joints seized	Renew.
	Incorrect wheel alignment	Check wheel alignment.
Wheel wobble and vibration	Roadwheels out of balance	Balance wheels.
	Wheels out of alignment	Check alignment.
	Worn wheel bearings	Renew bearings.
	Worn ball joints	Renew tie-rods

Chapter 10 Electrical system

For modifications, and information applicable to later models, see Supplement at end of manual

Contents

Specifications

Battery

Type	Steco 71901 or Fulmen ÁS209W
Voltage	12
Capacity	40 amp/hour
Earth	Negative

Alternator

Ducellier	7540A and B three phase
	7562A single phase
Paris-Rhone	A11M7 single phase
	A11R1 three phase

Regulator

Type	Ducellier 8366A or Paris-Rhone AYC 213

Starter motor

Type	Paris-Rhone D8E 103
	Ducellier 6208B until March 1972
	Ducellier 6217 from March 1972
	Ducellier 6217B from November 1972

Windscreen wipers ... ...   Electric motor - 2 speed

Fuses ... ...   8 (6 of 16 amp and 2 of 10 amp)

Lights

Headlamps ... ...   SEV Marchal 80/90 watt

Bulbs:

Lamp	Watt
Head	45/40
Direction indicator	21
Stop	21
Reversing	21
Front side	5
Tail	5
Number plate	5
Interior	7
Boot	5
Speedometer	4

Tachometer and clock	...	...	...	...	...	...	...	...	2
Battery indicator and fuel gauge	...	...	...	...	...	...	...	2

Warning lights:

Engine oil pressure	...	...	...	...	...	...	...	...	2
Brake pressure	...	...	...	...	...	...	...	...	2
Sidelamps	...	...	...	...	...	...	...	...	2
Headlamps	...	...	...	...	...	...	...	...	2
Direction indicators	...	...	...	...	...	...	...	2
Engine oil temperature	...	...	...	...	...	...	...	2
and brake pad wear	...	...	...	...	...	...	...	2
Heated rear window	...	...	...	...	...	...	...	2
Converter oil temperature	...	...	...	...	...	...	...	2

1 General description

The electrical system of all models covered by this manual is of the 12 volt type and the major components comprise, a 12 volt battery, of which the negative terminal is earthed, an alternator which is mounted on top of the engine at the front and is belt driven from the fan mounted on the front of the crankshaft, and a starter motor which is fitted on the rear left-hand side of the engine.

The battery supplies the power required to operate the starter motor, which places a heavy demand on it. The battery also provides the current for the ignition, lighting and other electrically operated equipment when the current being consumed exceeds the output of the alternator. It is kept fully charged by the alternator, the output of which is controlled by the regulator mounted on the side of the battery.

Do not connect a charging unit to the battery and never carry out any electrical welding repairs on the car unless both the negative and positive leads are disconnected from the battery, as serious damage can be caused to the electrical systems.

2 Battery - removal and replacement

1 The battery is housed in the engine compartment at the rear, left-hand side.
2 Disconnect the negative terminal first and then the positive terminal (screw or clamp).
3 Remove the regulator mounted in front of the battery by pulling it vertically to slide it out of its holder.
4 Unscrew the retaining nut and remove the clamp. Slide the battery towards the left to free it, and lift it out.
5 Before fitting the battery, make sure that both terminal posts and clamps are clean and free from corrosion, then smear them with petroleum jelly (not grease) to prevent corrosion.
6 Replacement is the direct reversal of removal. Before connecting the negative lead ensure that there is no flow of current. This is established by briefly touching the negative terminal with the lead end: any sparking indicates a short circuit which must be corrected first, or an electrical accessory left switched on.

3 Battery - maintenance and inspection

1 Normal weekly battery maintenance consists of checking the electrolyte level of each cell to ensure that the separators are covered by 6.35 mm (0.25in) of electrolyte. If the level has fallen, top up the battery using distilled water only. Do not overfill. If any electrolyte is spilled, the spillage must be wiped away immediately as electrolyte attacks and corrodes very quickly, any metal with which it comes in contact.
2 As well as keeping the terminals clean and covered with petroleum jelly, the top of the battery, and especially the top of the cells, should be kept clean and dry. This helps prevent corrosion and ensures that the battery does not become partially discharged by leakage through dampness and dirt.
3 Once every three months, remove the battery and inspect the battery tray and battery leads for corrosion (white fluffy deposits on the metal which are brittle to touch). If any corrosion is found, clean off the deposits with ammonia. Paint over the clean metal with an anti-rust/anti-acid paint.

4 At the same time inspect the battery for cracks. If a crack is found, the battery will have to be renewed. Cracks are frequently caused in the top of the battery cases by topping-up with distilled water in the middle of winter after instead of BEFORE a run. This gives the water no chance to mix with the electrolyte and so the former freezes and splits the battery case.
5 If topping-up the battery becomes excessive and the case has been inspected for cracks that could cause leakage, but none are found, the battery is being over-charged and the voltage regulator will have to be checked.
6 With the battery on the bench at the three monthly check, measure the specific gravity with a hydrometer to determine the state of charge and condition of the electrolyte. There should be very little variation between the different cells and if a variation in excess of 0.025 is present it will be due to either:

a) *Loss of electrolyte from the battery at some time caused by spillage, resulting in a drop in the specific gravity of the electrolyte when the deficiency was replaced with distilled water instead of fresh electrolyte.*
b) *An internal short-circuit caused by buckling of the plates or a similar malady pointing to the likelihood of total battery failure in the near future.*

7 The specific gravity of the electrolyte for fully charged conditions at the electrolyte temperature indicated, is listed in Table A. The specific gravity of a fully discharged battery at different temperatures of the electrolyte is given in Table B.

TABLE A

Specific gravity - battery fully charged
1.268 at 38°C (100°F) electrolyte temperature
1.272 at 32°C (90°F) electrolyte temperature
1.276 at 27°C (80°F) electrolyte temperature
1.280 at 21°C (70°F) electrolyte temperature
1.284 at 16°C (60°F) electrolyte temperature
1.288 at 10°C (50°F) electrolyte temperature
1.292 at 4°C (40°F) electrolyte temperature
1.296 at -1.5°C (30°F) electrolyte temperature

TABLE B

Specific gravity - battery fully discharged
1.098 at 38°C (100°F) electrolyte temperature
1.102 at 32°C (90°F) electrolyte temperature
1.106 at 27°C (80°F) electrolyte temperature
1.110 at 21°C (70°F) electrolyte temperature
1.114 at 16°C (60°F) electrolyte temperature
1.118 at 10°C (50°F) electrolyte temperature
1.122 at 4°C (40°F) electrolyte temperature
1.126 at -1.5°C (30°F) electrolyte temperature

4 Battery - electrolyte replenishment

1 If the battery is in a fully charged state and one of the cells maintains a specific gravity reading which is 0.025 or more lower than the

others, and a check of each cell has been made with a voltage meter to check for short circuits (a four to seven seconds test should give a steady reading of between 1.2 and 1.8 volts), then it is likely that electrolyte has been lost from the cell with the low reading.

2 If a significant quantity of electrolyte has been lost through spillage it will not suffice to merely refill with distilled water. Top-up the cell with electrolyte which is a mixture of sulphuric acid and water in the ratio of 2 parts acid to 5 parts water and the ready mixed solution should be obtained from battery specialists or large garages. The 'normal' solution can be added if the battery is in a fully charged state. If the battery is in a low state of charge, use the normal solution, charge the battery then empty out the electrolyte. Swill the battery out with clean water then refill with a new charge of electrolyte.

5 Battery - charging

1 In winter when a heavy demand is placed on the battery, such as when starting from cold, and much electrical equipment is continually in use, it is a good idea to occasionally have the battery fully charged from an external source at a rate of 3.5 to 4 amps.

2 Continue to charge the battery at this rate until no further rise in specific gravity is noted over a four hour period.

3 Alternatively, a trickle charger, charging at the rate of 1.5 amps can be safely used overnight.

4 Special rapid 'boost' charges which are claimed to restore the power of the battery in 1 to 2 hours are most dangerous unless they are thermostatically controlled as they can cause serious damage to the battery plates through overheating.

5 While charging the battery ensure that the temperature of the electrolyte never exceeds 37.8°C (100°F).

Caution: *If the battery is being charged from an external power source whilst the battery is fitted in the car, both battery leads must be disconnected to prevent damage to the electrical circuits.*

6 Alternator - general description

1 The use of alternators for generating the current required to operate car electrical systems is now more commonplace. Their main advantage over the dynamo type generator is that they provide a higher output for lower revolutions and are lighter in weight/output ratio.

2 The alternator generates alternating current and this current is rectified by diodes into direct current which is the current needed for battery storage.

3 The regulator, which controls the voltage output, is a transistorized unit and is permanently sealed. It requires no attention and will last indefinitely providing all wiring connections are correctly made, refer to Fig. 10.1.

Fig. 10.1. Alternator regulator connections

(a) Positive terminal   *(b) Yellow lead*

7 Alternator - safety precautions

1 If there are indications that the charging system is malfunctioning in any way, care must be taken to diagnose faults properly, otherwise damage of a serious and expensive nature may occur to parts which are in fact quite serviceable.

2 The following basic requirements must be observed at all times:

  a) *All alternator systems use a negative earth. Even the simple mistake of connecting a battery the wrong way round could burn out the alternator diodes in a few seconds.*
  b) *Before disconnecting any wires in the system the engine and ignition circuits should be switched off. This will minimise accidental short circuits.*
  c) *The alternator must never be run with the output wire disconnected.*
  d) *Always disconnect the battery from the car's electrical system if an external charging source is being used.*
  e) *Do not use test wire connections that could move accidentally and short circuit against nearby terminals. Short circuits will not blow fuses - they will blow diodes or transistors.*
  f) *Always disconnect the battery cables and alternator output leads before carrying out any electric welding work on the car.*
  g) *Never lever on the alternator body when adjusting its drive belt. The casing is easily fractured.*

8 Alternator - removal and replacement

1 Disconnect the earth lead from the negative terminal of the battery. Remove the front grille as described in Chapter 1.

2 Make a note of the connections and disconnect the three leads from the alternator.

3 Remove the adjusting arm bolt, slacken the pivot bolt and remove the drivebelt from the pulley. Remove the pivot bolt and the alternator.

4 Replacement of the alternator is the reverse of the removal sequence. Adjust the drivebelt tension by pivoting the alternator upwards on the pivot bolt, then tightening the adjusting arm bolt and the pivot bolt. When correctly tensioned a 10mm (0.4in) deflection of the belt should be possible.

9 Alternator - fault diagnosis

Special equipment is required for the testing of the alternator and the regulator. If a fault develops it is recommended that checks are made by a service station equipped for this work.

10 Starter motor - testing in the car

1 If the starter motor fails to operate then check the condition of the battery by switching on the headlamps. If they glow brightly for several seconds and then gradually dim, the battery is in an uncharged condition.

2 If the headlamps continue to glow brightly and it is obvious that the battery is in good condition, then check the tightness of the battery connections, particularly the earth lead from the battery terminal to its connection on the bodyframe. Check all connections from battery to solenoid switch and cable to starter for cleanliness and tightness.

3 If the starter motor still fails to turn check the solenoid by putting a voltmeter or bulb across the main cable connections on the starter side of the solenoid and earth. When the switch is operated there should be a reading or lighted bulb, if not the solenoid switch is faulty. If it is established that the solenoid is not faulty and 12 volts are getting to the starter then the fault must be in the starter motor.

11 Starter motor - removal and replacement

1 Disconnect the battery earth strap from the negative terminal of the battery. Take note of the connections and disconnect the wiring

from the starter motor.

2   Remove the six screws securing the left-hand upper cooling duct, disengage the two sealing rings and remove the upper cooling duct.

3   Remove the left-hand induction pipe assembly and blank off the open orifices in the cylinder heads and intake manifold, and carburettor assembly.

4   Remove the starter motor retaining bolts and draw the starter motor forward and remove it.

5   Replacement is the reverse of the removal sequence. Tighten the retaining bolts to 1.8 kg f m (13 lb f ft).

12 Starter motor (Ducellier) - dismantling and reassembly

1   Disconnect the field coil supply lead. Remove the three nuts securing the bearing endplate and remove the rear cover. Remove the plastic cover.

2   Drive out the fork hinge pin. Hold the drive gear and remove the bolt and washer from the commutator end of the shaft. Remove the bearing endplate and release the positive brush and its guide.

3   Remove the yoke from the two assembly rods. Remove the solenoid securing nuts and the solenoid. Remove the pinion fork and the armature.

4   Dismantle the solenoid by holding the solenoid core by the two flats, (a) in Fig. 10.2, and removing the two studs, the bolts, the spring with its washer, the adjustment sleeve and its nut.

5   From the armature assembly remove the celeron washer, the steel washer, the thrust bearing snap ring, the thrust bearing and the driving gear.

6   If necessary, unsolder the positive brush from the yoke and the negative brush from the bearing endplate.

7   Clean all the parts, take care that the cleaning fluid does not get on to the field coils or armature windings. Examine all the parts carefully, if the armature commutator is scored slightly it can be cleaned-up with fine glass paper (never use emery cloth as the carborundum particles will become embedded in the copper surfaces). If necessary undercut the mica insulation using an old hacksaw blade ground to suit. If the commutator is badly worn it will require skimming on a lathe and should be left to an electrical engineer. The minimum diameter of the commutator after machining must not be less than 30mm (1.181in). Check the length of the brushes, the minimum wear length is 7mm (0.275in), and ensure that they slide freely in the brush holders.

8   Using an ohmmeter connected between the solenoid supply terminal (flat blade) and the terminal marked DEM, check that the insulation resistance of the pull-in coil is approximately 0.24 ohms. With the ohmmeter connected between the solenoid supply terminal and the solenoid body check that the resistance of the hold-in coil is 1.08 ohms. Renew a solenoid which does not satisfy these conditions.

9   If the armature or field coil windings are suspect this is a job best left to an electrical engineer with the necessary test equipment.

10 Assembly is the reversal of the removal sequence. When assembling the armature, lightly oil the steel washer, the celeron washer and the splines with a very thin oil. Preset the adjusting sleeve halfway along its travel in the nut, (18) in Fig. 10.2.

11 Adjust the travel of the drive pinion as described in Section 13 and fit the plastic cover.

Fig. 10.2. Ducellier starter motor - dismantling

1 Fork pin	8 Bolt	15 Studs
2 Plastic cover	9 Bearing endplate	16 Spring
3 Endplate nuts	10 Solenoid	17 Washer
4 Rear cover	11 Yoke	18 Nut
5 Supply lead	12 Armature	19 Adjustment sleeve
6 Nuts	13 Assembly rods	20 Bolt
7 Steel washer	14 Pinion fork	

Fig. 10.3. Armature assembly

1 Thrust bearing   4 Steel washer
2 Driving gear   5 Celeron washer
3 Armature

Fig. 10.4. Starter motor solenoid

1 Pull-in coil   A Pinion fork
2 Hold-in coil

13 Starter motor (Ducellier) - adjustment of drive pinion

1 Remove the plastic cover. Energise the solenoid by connecting the positive terminal of a 12 volt battery to the flat blade connector on the solenoid and the battery negative to the terminal marked DEM. This will engage the drive pinion.
2 With the pinion in the engaged position measure dimension (a) in Fig. 10.5. This should not exceed 37.5mm (1.47in).
3 Disconnect the supply from the battery and measure the dimension (b) (drive pinion in its free position). Dimension (b) must be between 47.3 and 48.5mm (1.86 and 1.91in).
4 Adjustment is by altering the position of the adjusting sleeve on the solenoid. If the dimensions specified cannot be obtained by adjustment of the sleeve the starter must be dismantled.
5 Fit the plastic cover.

14 Starter motor (Paris-Rhone) - dismantling and reassembly

1 Disconnect the field coil cable from the solenoid. Remove the three retaining nuts, the clamp plate, the fibre seal and the solenoid.
2 Remove the plastic cap. Drive out the hinge pin of the operating lever and its support.
3 Remove the two assembly bolts. Partly separate the endplate, commutator end from the yoke and lift the positive brush from its guide. Remove the driving end starter bearing, the operating lever, the endplate, armature and starter drive assembly and the starter drive.
4 Remove the endplate from the armature by removing the retaining bolt, the thrust washer and the friction washer. Release the endplate, the bakelite coated washer, the steel washer, the flexible washer and the second steel washer.
5 If necessary, unsolder the negative brush from the endplate and the positive brush from the yoke.
6 Cleaning, examination and servicing is the same as described for Ducellier starter motors as described in Section 12 except that the commutator diameter must not be less than 35mm (1.378in) and the resistance of the solenoid pull-in coil and hold-in coil should be 3 ohms and 1 ohm respectively.
7 Assembly is the reversal of the removal sequence. When fitting the assembly bolts fit the bolt with the insulating tape between the two brush holders. Tighten the bolts to 0.8 to 1.1 kg f m (6 to 8 lb f ft).
8 Adjust the travel of the drive pinion as described in Section 15.

15 Starter motor (Paris-Rhone) - adjustment of drive pinion

The check and adjusting procedure is the same as for the Ducellier starter motor except that dimension (a) is 38.3mm (1.51in) maximum and dimension (b) is between 47.4 and 48mm (1.86 and 1.89in), obtained by adjusting the sleeve, Fig. 10.6, after having removed the solenoid securing flange.

Fig. 10.5. Ducellier starter motor - drive pinion adjustment

1 DEM terminal   2 Plastic cover

Fig. 10.6. Paris-Rhone starter motor - drive pinion adjustment

1 Adjusting sleeve

16 Fuses - general

1   There are two fuse boxes, each containing four fuses, mounted on the inner valance of the left-hand front wing, adjacent to the battery box. The front box contains fuses 1 to 4 and fuses 6 to 9 are in the rear box.
2   The circuits they protect (some accessories are optional and may not be fitted) are as follows:

Front box
(a) Yellow marking (10A) - Front and rear LH sidelamps - Number plate light - Clock light - Tachometer light - Battery indicator light - Fuel gauge light - Side and tail lamps warning light - Speedometer light.
(b) Green marking (16A) - Direction indicators - Fresh air blower - Rear window heating - Regulator - Cigarette lighter - Clock - Radio - Reversing lamps.
(c) Red marking (16A) - Battery charging indicator - Fuel gauge - Windscreen wipers - Windscreen washers - Oil pressure warning light - Hydraulic pressure warning light - Torque converter oil temperature warning light - Engine oil temperature and brake pad wear warning light - Stop lamps - Boot lighting - Interior light - Torque converter clutch relay - Heater blower.
(d) Blue marking (10A) - Front and rear RH sidelamps.

Rear box 2
(a) Green marking (16A) - Headlamp dipped beam, LH.
(b) Red marking (16A) - Headlamp dipped beam, RH.
(c) Yellow marking (16A) - Headlamp main beam, LH.
(d) White marking (16A) - Headlamp main beam, RH.

3   The following are not protected by fuses:

Horn - Starter solenoid - Torque converter clutch solenoid - Coil - Tachometer - Feed for headlamp flasher - Main beam warning light.

4   If the car is fitted with supplementary heating, a 16A fuse (mauve) will be found inside the rear box.
5   Always replace fuses with the correct type. When a fuse blows, check the circuits on that fuse, trace and rectify the fault before replacing the fuse. The circuits are all included in the wiring diagrams Fig. 10.14 and 10.15.

17 Headlamp - adjustment

The headlamps can only be adjusted correctly using beam alignment equipment and this work should be left to a service station so equipped. The headlamp beam adjusters are shown in Fig. 10.7.

Fig. 10.7. Headlamp adjusters

1   Horizontal adjuster   3   Vertical adjuster
2   Horizontal adjuster

18 Heating system - general

1   Warm air is drawn through the heating ducts and the heater box by the electrically driven fan motor.
2   If the fan does not operate check that the fuse is not blown and that the wiring and connections are in good condition. If the motor is defective it should be removed for exchange or repair by an auto-electrician.

19 Fan motor - removal and replacement

1   Disconnect the battery earth strap and remove the spare wheel.
2   Remove the rubber collar between the heater box and the fan. Note the connections and disconnect the wiring from the motor. Remove the securing screws and the motor assembly.
3   Replacement is the reversal of the removal sequence.

20 Windscreen wiper motor and mechanism - fault diagnosis

1   If the wipers fail to operate first check that current is reaching the motor. This can be done by switching on and using a voltmeter or 12 volt bulb and two wires between the positive terminal on the motor and earth.
2   If no current is reaching the motor check if there is any at the switch. If there is then a break has occurred in the wiring between switch and motor.
3   If there is no current at the switch go back to the ignition switch and so isolate the area of fault.
4   If current is reaching the motor but the wipers do not operate, switch on and give the wiper arm a push - they or the motor could be jammed. Switch off immediately if the wipers do not operate, as damage to the motor may occur. If the wipers do operate the reason for them jamming is most likely to be due to wear in the linkage of the wiper mechanism or the motor.
5   If the wipers run too slowly it will be due to something restricting the free operation of the linkage or a fault in the motor.
6   At this stage remove the motor, this is a fairly easy task, and have it checked out by an auto-electrician before going on to the removal of the wiper linkage mechanism as this is a much more involved task.

21 Windscreen wiper motor - removal and replacement

1   Disconnect the battery earth strap. Remove the bonnet as described in Chapter 1.
2   Remove the seal and ventilation panel, Fig. 10.8. Remove the crank arm retaining nut and the crank arm, Fig. 10.9.
3   Remove the support plate retaining bolts and the bolts which secure the motor to the support plate.
4   Note the connections, disconnect the wiring and remove the motor.
5   Replacement is the reverse of the removal sequences. Tighten the support plate retaining bolts to 0.35 to 0.4 kg f m (2.5 to 3 lb f ft) and the motor securing bolts to 0.5 kg f m (3.6 lb f ft). The crank arm must be fitted with the motor in the 'automatic stop' position. To ensure this, connect up the battery, switch on the ignition for about 5 seconds and then switch off again. Now fit the crank arm on the motor spindle and in alignment with the connecting rod as shown in Fig. 10.9. Tighten the crank arm retaining nut to 0.45 to 0.5 kg f m (3.2 to 3.6 lb f ft). Check the operation of the windscreen wipers.

22 Windscreen wiper mechanism - removal and replacement

1   Remove the battery earth strap and the bonnet. Remove the seal and ventilation panel.
2   Remove the nut securing the crank arm to the motor spindle and lift off the arm. Remove the wiper arms.
3   Disconnect the choke cable from the carburettor, the heater flap operating cable, the parking brake handle from the operating lever, the gear lever from the selector fork operating lever and the speedometer cable from the speedometer.

4   Refer to Fig. 10.10 and remove the instrument panel as follows:

 a) *Remove the cover by pushing it forward and removing it from the back. Disconnect the leads from the switch (or switches according to model).*

 b) *Remove the two fixing bolts and remove the panel from the dashboard by pulling downwards on the right-hand and then on the left-hand side, press lightly at (a) on the dashboard to assist the removal.*

 c) *Disconnect the connector or connectors (according to model) of the different leads on the panel and remove the panel.*

5   Remove the dashboard as follows:

 a) *Remove the parking brake handle and the knobs controlling the heater and demister (pull them out).*

 b) *Disconnect the electrical plugs.*

 c) *Remove the steering wheel as described in Chapter 9.*

 d) *Remove the seven screws holding the dashboard, Fig. 10.11, and remove the dashboard.*

6   Remove the shelf by removing the six retaining screws, refer to Fig. 10.12.

7   Remove the bolts securing the duct and the bolts securing the console, pull the console a little way to the rear.

8   Remove the bolt holding the pipe and free it. Remove the bolts holding the windscreen wiper bearings on the dashboard. Remove the nut, cap washer and seal from each spindle. Remove the mechanism from the dashboard.

9   Examine the mechanism and wiper bearing for wear or damage and replace as necessary.

10 Replacement is the reverse of the removal sequence. Ensure the crank arm is replaced as described in Section 22. When replacing the windscreen wiper arms position them as shown in Fig. 10.13 so that; 'A' = 60 $\pm$ 10mm (2.40 $\pm$ 0.4in) and 'B' = 35 $\pm$ 10mm (1.40 $\pm$ 0.4in). Tighten the retaining nuts to 0.9 kg f m (6.5 lb f ft) (photos).

23 Instruments and instrument panel bulbs - general

1   Access to the instruments and warning or light bulbs necessitates the removal of the instrument panel as described in Section 22.

2   If a warning lamp or light bulb fails check the relevant fuse before removing the instrument panel.

3   If the speedometer fails to register check the cable drive from the gearbox before removing the instrument. Fluctuation of the speedometer reading can usually be alleviated by lubricating the main cable with a light smear of general purpose grease at the 90° connector at the speedometer end.

4   If the fuel tank contents gauge fails to register, check the fuse first. If the fuse is all right remove the transmitter cover as described in Chapter 2. Short circuit the transmitter leads and switch on the ignition briefly. A reading on the gauge indicates that the gauge is serviceable. Check the wiring and connections to the transmitter at the tank, if necessary remove the transmitter for checking as described in Chapter 2.

Fig. 10.9. Windscreen wiper motor removal

1	Crank arm	4	Support plate
2	Retaining nut	5	Support plate retaining bolts
3	Connecting rod	6	Windscreen wiper motor securing bolts

Fig. 10.10. Removing the instrument panel

1	Switch	3	Fixing bolts
2	Cover	4	Flasher relay

Fig. 10.8. Ventilation panel removal

1	Panel	2 Seal

22.10a Fitting the windscreen wiper arm and retaining nut

Fig. 10.11. Dashboard securing screws

22.10b Fitting the windscreen wiper blade

Fig. 10.12. Shelf removal

1 Pipe   4 Bolts
2 Bolt   5 Shelf
3 Duct   6 Console
(a - f) Retaining screws

Fig. 10.13. Windscreen wiper arm adjustment

1 Arm retaining nuts   For (a) and (b) see text

24 Bulb - renewal

1   Before replacing a headlamp bulb always check the relevant fuse. If both front and rear right-hand sidelights fail at the same time, check the fuse as most likely cause of failure.

2   To replace a European-Dip type bulb, swing the springs retaining the bulb flange clear. Pull back the black plastic connector to withdraw it from the reflector. Remove the bulb, pulling it by its flange, from the connector carrying the feed leads. Fit the new bulb into the connector, then fit the unit into the reflector by rotating it until the flange locator fits into the slot. Swing the retaining springs back into place (photo).

3   To replace a quartz-halogen bulb, withdraw the bulb holder unit by turning it, it will come out automatically. (On some designs a restrainer has to be depressed.) Disconnect the bulb from the feed lead. When fitting the new bulb hold it by the metal part taking care not to touch the glass with your fingers, as this will shorten the life of the bulb and reduce its light output. If it is inadvertently touched

by the fingers it should be wiped clean immediately with a clean cloth dipped in methylated spirit.

4   Side and tail-lamp, direction indicator, stop and reversing lamp bulb. Remove the two screws securing the front side-lamp transparent cover. The tail-lamp cover is secured with three screws (photos).

5   Number plate lamp, remove the two screws securing the protector.

6   Interior lamp, hinge down the cover about the front, then disengage it or pivot the cover by means of the slot at the rear, then disengage it from the front, according to type fitted.

25 Heated rear window - general

If the rear window is not being heated check the fuse. If the fuse and the wiring to the window is in order, a failure of the wiring in the window is indicated. In this case it is advisable to take the car to a Citroen agent who can test it and if necessary repair a break in the wiring.

24.2 Replacing a headlamp bulb

24.4a Removing the transparent cover from a rear light cluster

24.4b Replacing a rear light bulb

24.4c Interior light with cover fitted

24.4d Replacing an interior light bulb

26 Fault diagnosis - electrical system

Symptom	Reason/s	Remedy
Starter fails to turn engine	Battery discharged.	Charge battery.
	Battery terminal leads loose or earth lead not securely attached to body.	Tighten.
	Loose or broken connections in starter motor circuit.	Repair.
	Starter motor switch or solenoid faulty.	Renew as necessary.
	Starter brushes badly worn, sticking or brush wire connections loose.	Renew or repair as necessary.
	Commutator dirty or worn.	Clean or skim.
	Starter motor armature faulty.	Renew.
	Field coils earthed.	Renew.
Starter motor turns engine very slowly	Battery in discharged condition.	Charge battery.
	Starter brushes worn, sticking or brush wires loose.	Renew or repair as necessary.
	Loose wires in starter motor circuit.	Tighten connections.
Starter spins but does not turn engine.	Starter pinion sticking	Dismantle and clean.
	Pinion or flywheel gear teeth broken or badly worn.	Renew components.
Starter motor noisy or excessively rough engagement	Pinion or flywheel gear teeth broken or badly worn.	Renew components.
	Starter motor retaining bolts loose.	Renew components.
Battery will not hold charge for more than a few days	Battery defective internally.	Renew battery.
	Electrolyte level too low or electrolyte too weak due to leakage.	Top up and check with hydrometer.
	Battery terminal connections loose or corroded.	Clean and tighten.
	Alternator drivebelt slipping.	Re-tension.
	Alternator not charging.	Check connections at output.
	Regulator defective.	Renew sealed unit.
Charging rate indicator records discharge	Alternator drivebelt loose or broken.	Tension or renew.
	Regulator faulty.	Renew sealed unit.
	No output from alternator.	Check alternator at auto-electrician.
Lights do not come on	Engine not running, battery discharged.	Charge or renew battery.
	Loose, disconnected or broken connections.	Re-make connections.
	Light switch faulty.	Repair switch.
	Bulb filament burnt out or blown fuse.	Renew fuse or bulb.
Lights work erratically	Battery terminal or earth connections loose.	Tighten connections.
	Lights not earthed properly.	Clean and re-make connections.
	Lights switch faulty.	Renew switch.
Horn operates all the time	Horn cable to horn switch earthed.	Repair insulation.
	Horn switch faulty.	Renew switch.
Horn fails to operate	Cable connections loose, broken or disconnected.	Reconnect.
	Blown fuse.	Renew fuse.
	Horn faulty.	Repair or renew horn.
Horn operates intermittently	Loose connections.	Secure connections.
Windscreen wipers fail to work	Blown fuse.	Renew fuse.
	Wiring connections loose, disconnected or broken.	Secure connections.
	Wiper motor faulty.	Repair or renew.
	Wiper mechanism jammed or seized.	Free, repair and refit.
Wiper arms move sluggishly	Wiper motor faulty.	Repair and renew motor.
	Wiper mechanism sticking or worn.	Free, repair or renew.

Fig. 10.14 Typical wiring diagram - LH drive models

Key

Club and Comfort
Club only
All types since 4.71
Options

Colour Code

White	Bc
Blue	Bl
Grey	Gr
Yellow	J
Brown	Mr
Mauve	Mv
Black	N
Red	R
Green	Ve
Violet	Vi

Fig. 10.14. Wiring diagram - LH drive models

1 Direction indicator and sidelamp right-hand
2 Headlamp, right-hand
3 Alternator
4 Headlamp, left-hand
5 Direction indicator and side lamp, left-hand
6 Horn
7 Engine oil pressure switch
8 Starter with solenoid
9 Ignition coil
10 Distributor
11 Fuse box
12 Windscreen washer
13 Brake system pressure switch
14 Electro-valve (torque converter option)
15 Oil temperature switch
16 Voltage regulator
17 Windscreen wiper motor
18 Warm air blower
19 Switch on gearbox (torque converter option)
20 Reversing lamp switch (Club)

21 Stoplamp switch
22 Battery
23 Fresh air blower (option)
24 Door pillar switch, right-hand
25 Terminal for accessories
26 Door pillar switch, left-hand
27 Lighting rheostat for tachometer, clock and battery meter (Club)
28 Speedometer light rheostat
29 Cigar lighter (Club)
30 Lighting switch
31 Relay (torque converter option)
32 Ignition and starter switch
33 Printed circuit connector for tachometer and clock unit (Club)
34 Speedometer light
35 Printed circuit connector for instrument and warning lamp unit
36 Printed circuit connector for warning lamps
37 Fresh air blower switch (option)
38 Warm air blower switch
39 Heated rear window switch (option)
40 Flasher unit

41 Direction indicator switch
42 Windscreen wiper and washer switch
43 Fuel gauge tank unit
44 Interior lamp
45 Boot lamp switch
46 Rear heated window
47 Boot lamp
48 Reversing lamp, right-hand (Club)
49 Tail lamp, right-hand
50 Stoplamp, right-hand
51 Rear direction indicator, right-hand
52 Number plate lamp
53 Rear direction indicator, left-hand
54 Stop lamp, left-hand
55 Tail lamp, left-hand
56 Reversing lamp, left-hand (Club)
62 Front brake unit, right-hand
63 Engine oil temperature thermal switch
64 Front brake unit, left-hand

Fig. 10.15. Wiring diagram - RH drive models

1 Front RH lamp cluster
2 Front RH headlamp
3 Front LH headlamp
4 Front LH lamp cluster
5 Alternator
6 Horn
7 RH brake unit
8 Oil temperature warning switch
9 LH brake unit
10 Fluid temperature warning switch (torque converter)
11 Starter motor
12 Oil pressure warning switch
13 Ignition coil
14 Front fusebox
15 Windscreen washer motor
16 Windscreen wiper motor
17 Hydraulic pressure warning switch
18 Solenoid valve (semi-automatic transmission)
19 Warm air blower
20 Control switch (semi-automatic transmission)
21 Distributor

22 Reversing light switch
23 Battery
24 Regulator
25 Rear fusebox
26 RH door switch
27 Fresh air blower motor
28 Accessory terminal
29 Brake warning light switch
30 LH door switch
31 Torque converter relay
32 Fresh air blower motor switch
33 Rear window heater switch
34 Warm air blower motor switch
35 Fluid temperature warning light (torque converter)
36 Rear window heater warning light
37 Fuel gauge
38 Warning light (brake pads and engine oil temperature
39 Direction indicator warning light
40 Speedometer light
41 Hydraulic pressure warning light
42 Side and tail lamps warning light

43 Clock and light
44 Panel lighting rheostat
45 Headlamp main beam warning light
46 Engine oil pressure warning light
47 Tachometer and light
48 Charging rate indicator and light
49 Ignition switch
50 Windscreen wiper and washer switch
51 Direction indicator, horns and headlamp flasher switch
52 Direction indicator flasher unit
53 Lighting switch
54 Cigar lighter
55 Fuel gauge transmitter
56 Rear window heater
57 Interior light
58 Luggage compartment light
59 Luggage compartment light switch
60 Rear RH lamp cluster
61 Number plate light
62 Rear LH lamp cluster
63 Second horn

Fig. 10.15 Typical wiring diagram - right-hand drive models

Colour Code

Bc : White	Mr : Brown
Bl : Blue	Mv : Mauve
Gr : Grey	N : Black
J : Yellow	R : Red
Ve : Green	

F : symbol | Insulation colour

Chapter 11 Rear axle and suspension

For modifications, and information applicable to later models, see Supplement at end of manual

Contents

Specifications

Suspension

Type	Independent, trailing arms
Springing	Hydropneumatic cylinders
Damping	Integral with suspension cylinders
Anti-roll bar	18mm diameter
Suspension height (normal)	272 ± 10mm (10.71 ± 0.4in)
Suspension cylinder spheres:	
Inflation pressure	$35 \pm \frac{5}{10}$ bar ($500 \pm \frac{70}{140}$ psi)

Rear wheel alignment (not adjustable)

Cars until September 1973	4mm (0.16in) toe-in to 4mm toe-out
Cars from September 1973	0 to 2mm (0 to 0.08in) toe-in
Camber angle (not adjustable)	$0^o \pm 40'$

1 General description

1 The rear axle unit is attached to the bodyframe by four flexible mountings. The suspension and damping effect is through the hydro-pneumatic cylinder units acting on each end of the trailing suspension arms which pivot on needle bearings. As on the front suspension three different heights can be selected manually.

2 The stub axles are integral with the ends of the suspension arms and carry the wheel hubs which run on ball bearings. The brake discs are part of the hub assembly and the brake calipers are mounted on the suspension arms.

2 Rear suspension balls - lubrication

The procedure for lubricating the suspension balls is the same as described in Chapter 7, for the front suspension balls, except that on cars from November 1972 the dust shields contain 25cc (1.52cu in) of LHM fluid.

3 Suspension arm - removal

1 Jack-up and support the rear of the car. Release the pressure from the hydraulic system. Remove the rear wheels. Refer to Fig. 11.2. Remove the pin and push back the piston rod of the suspension cylinder. Should there still be pressure in the suspension circuit, operate the manual control several times until the piston rod is free.

2 Slacken the collar and disconnect the union. Bend back the tab of the lockplate and remove the retaining bolt, the lockplate and, if fitted, the shims from behind the lockplate.

3 Using an extractor (Citroen tool 2068-T) in place of the bolt, screw in the extractor bolt to release the suspension arm from the anti-roll bar. Remove the extractor and the arm.

4 Suspension arm - replacement

1 The suspension arms are attached to each end of the anti-roll bar and the distance between them determines their lateral play. This play is adjusted by fitting shims behind the retaining bolt lockplate on only one of the two arms. The adjustment must always be reset whichever arm is removed (the one with or without shims).

2 If the bearing face 'c' (Fig. 11.3) of the support tube shows signs of binding, clean it up with a fine grade stone. Carefully clean the support tube, the bearing surface 'b' of the anti-roll bar and the suspension arm. Using a multi-purpose grease lubricate the face 'c' and the bearing surfaces of the support tube, and the bearings of the arm hub.

3 When fitting an arm without shims proceed as follows:

a) *Engage the hub of the arm on the support tube and connect it to the anti-roll bar with the mark 'a' on the face of the anti-roll bar in line with the gap of a missing spline in the arm hub. Check that the arms are fitted in the same plane without twisting the bar.*

b) *Remove the retaining bolt from the other arm.*

c) *Using a threaded rod and nut, (Citroen tool 2069-T) as shown in Fig. 11.4, fit the arm by screwing the rod A into the anti-roll bar then tightening the nut B until the arm is in place, with the face of the support tube bearing on the friction washer in the arm hub. Remove the tool.*

d) *Fit the lockplate, smear the threads of the bolt with jointing compound, fit and tighten the bolt to 1.8 to 2 kg f m (13 to 14 lb f ft). Lock the bolt by bending over a tab of the lockplate.*

e) *Set the lateral play of the arms by adjustment of the shimming at the other suspension arm as described in Section 5.*

4   Fitting an arm with shims is the same procedure as described in paragraph 3 above. Adjust the lateral play, as described in Section 5.

5   Suspension arms - lateral play adjustment

1   Position the tool (2069-T) as shown in Fig. 11.4, screw the central bolt 'A' into the anti-roll bar. Tighten the nut 'B' while moving the arm, when the arm falls slowly under its own weight, stop tightening the nut. This indicates that the support tube is bearing on the friction washer in the hub of the arm causing slight friction. Remove the tool.

2   Using a straightedge and a depth gauge measure the distance between the face of the anti-roll bar and the face of the arm hub. This dimension plus 0.05mm (0.002in) indicates the thickness of shimming required on the end of the anti-roll bar.

3   Using tool 2068-T bring the anti-roll bar out by 2 to 3mm (0.08 to 0.12in). Remove the tool 2068-T.

4   Place the required thickness of shims on the end of the anti-roll bar and fit the tool 2069-T. Tighten the nut 'B' moderately until the shims are in contact with the end face of the anti-roll bar. Never use the retaining bolt for this operation as the splines are a very close fit and the bolt would be subjected to abnormal stress. Remove the tool 2069-T taking care that the shims remain in place. Smear the threads of the retaining bolt and the faces of the lockplate with jointing compound. Fit the lockplate and retaining bolt and tighten to 1.8 to 2 kg f m (13 to 14 lb f ft). Bend over a tab of the lockplate to lock the bolt.

5   Position the rod of the suspension cylinder and fit the lock pin. Connect the pipe to the union (use a new seal) and tighten it to 0.8 to 0.9 kg f m (6 to 6.5 lb f ft). Tighten the collar.

6   Start the engine. Tighten the pressure regulator bleed screw. Bleed the rear brakes, as described in Chapter 8. Fit the rear wheels and lower the car to the ground.

Fig. 11.1. Rear suspension

Fig. 11.2. Removing a suspension arm

1	Bolt	3	Collar
2	Union	4	Pin

Fig. 11.3. Support tube and anti-roll bar

1   *Support tube*   2   *Anti-roll bar*

Fig. 11.4. Replacing a suspension arm

Fig. 11.5. Suspension arm extractor (A) - tool 2068-T

6   Suspension arm hub - replacing bearings, seal and friction washer

1   Remove the suspension arm as described in Section 3. Refer to
Fig. 11.6. If necessary, remove the arm hub deflector. Remove the
seal. Using an extractor remove the bearing. (The Citroen extractor is
tool 1671-T fitted with an' end piece 2070-T). Remove the friction
washer.
2   Carefully clean the inside of the suspension arm hub and the
support tube. Grease the bearing areas of the support tube. Smear
both faces of the friction washer with grease and fit it in the hub.
Always fit a new friction washer at each dismantling.
3   The needle bearings are fitted with seals 'a' in Fig. 11.6. These
must be fitted the right way round, the edge with the seal must be
positioned in the direction of the arrow 'F1' for the bearing '5' and
in the direction of the arrow 'F2' for the bearing '4'. To ensure
correct positioning of the bearings use Citroen mandrel 2071-T 'A' with
sockets 'B' and 'C'. Place the mandrel 2071-T 'A' inside the suspension
arm hub, fit the bearing '5' on the mandrel, and using the socket 'B',
push on the bearing until the socket comes in contact with the end
of the mandrel. The length of the socket determines the correct
position of the bearing. Bearing '4' is fitted in the same way using
socket 'C'.
4   Remove the assembly tool and smear the needle bearings with
multi-purpose grease. Fit the seal with the face having the inscription
on it, towards the outside of the hub (direction of arrow 'F2') and
in contact with the bearing. If necessary, fit the deflector, this must
be set in from the edge of the hub by 2 to 3mm (0.08 to 0.12in).
5   Replace the suspension arm, as described in Section 4.

Fig. 11.6. Suspension arm hub

1	Support tube	4	Inner bearing
2	Seal	5	Outer bearing
3	Deflector	6	Friction washer

7 Hub, bearing and brake disc - removal

1   Remove the brake caliper, as described in Chapter 8, Section 9.
2   Using a drill, relieve the peening on the ring nut.
3   Unless the official tool is available (3321 and 3304-T) the hub will now have to be held against rotation while the ring nut (and later the hub nut), are unscrewed. To do this, first bolt a length of flat steel to two of the wheel studs and use it as a lever. Mark the relative position of the slots in the ring nut to the adjacent faces of the hub. If the official tool is not being used, release the ring nut with a C-spanner or by using a hammer and drift. The nut is very tight.
4   Relieve the peening on the hub nut and again holding the hub against rotation, unscrew and remove it. This nut is also very tight.
5   Use a three legged extractor to withdraw the hub.
6   Unscrew the disc securing bolts, remove the disc, the bearing plate and then draw off the hub bearing.

8 Hub, bearing and brake disc - replacement

1   Fit the disc with the bearing plate between the disc and the hub, fit the securing bolts and tighten to 4.5 to 5 kg f m (33 to 36 lb f ft).
2   Position the new bearing with the sealed side facing the brake disc and press it into the hub.
3   Offer up the hub assembly to the stub axle (without the inner race) and start to position it by tightening the hub nut. Remove the nut, fit a spacer with an inside diameter of 37mm, and of 7mm thickness. Refit the nut and finally fit the bearing. Fit the inner race with the face 'b' of the nylon race to the inside. The faces 'b' Fig. 11.9 of the two races should face each other. Fit a new retaining nut with the threads greased and tighten to 35 to 40 kg f m (250 to 290 lb f ft). Bend the rim of the nut into the slot of the stub axle.
4   Grease both faces and thread of the ring nut and fit it. Tighten to

35 to 40 kg f m (250 to 290 lb f ft) or until the slots in the ring nut align with the marks made before removal, and lock by peening in two places.
5   Fit the brake caliper and complete the assembly as described in Chapter 8, Section 10.

9 Anti-roll bar - removal and replacement

Removal of the anti-roll bar necessitates the removal of both suspension arms, as described in Section 3, and the uncoupling of the height corrector from the bar. The anti-roll bar has a different number of splines at each end and can only be fitted the right way round.

10 Rear axle unit - removal

1   Position the rear of the car as described for the removal of the suspension arms, Section 3. Remove the battery earth strap from the negative terminal of the battery.
2   Remove the exhaust bracket and flexible supports. Remove the exhaust pipe and silencer. Empty the fuel tank, if necessary, and disconnect the filler pipe. Disconnect the manual control rods and remove the bolts securing the protective plate and the bolt holding the pipe bracket. Disconnect the union.
3   Slide the embellishers, on the rear shelf towards the rear to uncover the upper mounting bolts and remove the bolts. In the boot, lift the carpet at each side to give access to the suspension unit flexible mountings. Remove the inspection plate in the floor of the boot.
4   Place a jack with a cross beam under the suspension unit equidistant between the suspension cylinder spheres and the suspension arm swivels. Remove the nuts from the flexible mountings and with the jack lower the unit by no more than

Fig. 11.7. Rear hub ring nut (arrowed)

Fig. 11.8. Rear hub nut (arrowed)

Fig. 11.9. Rear hub, brake caliper and disc

1	Brake disc	5	Disc retaining bolt
2	Shim	6	Caliper inner half
3	Bearing	7	Caliper outer half
4	Nut		

100mm (4in) so that the pipes can be disconnected through the inspection plate aperture.

5   Remove the bolt securing the collar holding the pipes and disconnect the pipes from the corrector, the flexible pipe from the overflow return union, the flexible pipe from the tank gauge unit, the tank vent pipe, the pipe from the four-way union and the lead from the fuel gauge unit. Identify and mark each pipe as it is disconnected.

6   Make a check that all pipes have been disconnected and lower the unit, ensuring that it does not foul any of the pipes, and remove it from under the car.

11 Rear axle unit - dismantling and reassembly

1   For removal and replacement of the component parts of the axle unit refer to the relevant Chapters and Sections of the manual describing the different procedures. Do not remove more than is necessary to rectify the fault which required the removal of the unit.

2   Make sure the flexible mountings are in good condition. If new travel stops are being fitted use soapy water on their pegs (do not use oil or grease).

3   Preset the automatic height control and set the position of the manual height control rod as described in Chapter 6, Sections 24 and 27.

12 Rear axle unit - replacement

1   Replacement of the axle unit is the reverse of the removal sequence. Note that on the front mountings the spacer is fitted to the body location stud, whilst on the rear mountings the spacer is positioned underneath the retaining nut on the unit and the cap fitted between the body

and the mounting. When fitting the rear mounting spacer its large inside diameter must face the elastic mounting. Fit new seals in the pipe connections and tighten the unions to 0.8 to 0.9 kg f m (6 to 6.5 lb f ft). Tighten the flexible mounting nuts to 3.4 kg f m (25 lb f ft).

2   Start the engine, tighten the pressure regulator bleed screw and check that there are no leaks at the pipe connections. Bleed the brakes as described in Chapter 8, Section 19. Adjust the suspension heights as described in Chapter 6, Section 26.

13 Suspension arm support tube - removal and replacement

A Citroen tool set 2072-T is required for the removal and replacement of the support tube.

1   Remove the suspension arm, as described in Section 3. Remove the inspection plate on the floor of the boot. Slacken by two or three turns the automatic height control bolt on the anti-roll bar so that the bar can slide in the collar. The bolt must remain in place on the collar.

2   Measure the amount the support tube protrudes from the suspension unit for comparison with the new support tube. Push the anti-roll bar into the tube to allow the tool 2072-T to be fitted in the tube. Position the tool sleeve over the support tube and push the assembly into the support tube until the dogs of the tool can be heard to engage. Tighten on the extractor nut and remove the support tube from the housing.

3   Clean the support tube housing of the suspension unit. Fit the support tube in the suspension unit using the appropriate parts of tool 2072-T. The tightening torque of tool nut remains fairly high during the whole operation of fitting the support tube and becomes very high when the tube is in position.

4   Check that the tube protrudes approximately the same distance from the suspension unit as the one that was removed. Re-position the

Fig. 11.10 Rear axle pipe connections

1 Tank vent pipe
2 Flexible return pipe
3 Supply pipe
4 Corrector pipe
5 Corrector pipe
6 Bolt
7 Petrol pipe
8 Flexible corrector pipe
9 Petrol gauge lead

Fig. 11.11. Automatic height control bolt

Fig. 11.12. Tool for removing the support tube

Fig. 11.13. Tool for fitting the support tube

anti-roll bar. Fit the suspension arm and adjust the lateral play, as described in Sections 4 and 5.

5 Preset the automatic height control as described in Chapter 6, Section 24. Bleed the rear brakes. Fit the road wheels and lower the car. Check the rear height. Fit the inspection plate on the boot floor.

14 Wheel alignment check

1 Excessive tyre wear or vibration can be caused by incorrect wheel

alignment, especially if the car has been involved in an accident or the rear suspension has been subjected to abnormal stress.

2 The wheel alignment is not adjustable and if it is found to be incorrect, consult your Citroen agent.

3 Position the car on level ground and set the suspension to the 'normal' road position. Check the tyre pressures. Using a suitable track gauge, of which there are various types available, check that the rear wheels are parallel to within 4mm (0.16in) toe-in to 4mm toe-out for cars produced until September 1973. For cars produced after that date the toe-in must be 0 to 2mm (0 to 0.08in).

15 Fault diagnosis - rear axle and suspension

Before diagnosing faults from the following chart, check that any irregularities are not caused by:

1 - Incorrect tyre pressures, 2 - Incorrect 'mix' of tyres, 3 - Defects in the braking system.

Symptom	Reason/s	Remedy
Vibration and rattles	Loose suspension cylinder	Tighten the cylinder retaining collar.
	Suspension cylinder ball and socket worn	Renew the cylinder.
	Suspension arm hub bearing worn	Renew the bearing.
	Worn hub bearing	Renew the bearing.
	Axle unit flexible mountings loose or defective	Tighten or renew as necessary.
	Pipe clips and brackets loose	Tighten as necessary.
	Wheel alignment incorrect	Check alignment, if confirmed consult your Citroen agent.
Suspension bottoming	Fault in the hydraulic system	Check through the hydraulic system.
	Defective suspension cylinder/s	Renew as necessary.
	Suspension heights set incorrectly	Readjust the suspension height.
Excessive tyre wear	Incorrect wheel alignment	Check wheel alignment.

Chapter 12 Bodywork and fittings

For modifications, and information applicable to later models, see Supplement at end of manual

Contents

1 General description

The Citroen GS is of monocoque construction. The front and rear axle units being bolted directly to the rigid, sheet metal bodyshell. All the front panels are readily detachable for economy of replacement in the event of accident damage. Each one is rustproofed and dip-primed before being sprayed and stored.

The bumpers and all exterior bright parts are made of stainless steel.

The passenger rear doors are locked from the inside. The front doors are locked by key, but take care, because they can be locked, the key placed inside and the doors slammed locked!

Protection of the body is by electropheric priming to ensure an even coat and penetration of the paint into every cavity and potential rust-trap.

2 Maintenance - bodywork exterior

1 The general condition of a car's bodywork is the one thing that significantly affects its value. Maintenance is easy but needs to be regular and particular. Neglect, particularly after minor damage, can lead quickly to further deterioration and costly repair bills. It is important also to keep watch on those parts of the car not immediately visible, for instance the underside, inside all the wheel arches and the lower part of the engine compartment.

2 The basic maintenance routine for the bodywork is washing - preferably with a lot of water, from a hose. This will remove all the loose solids which may have stuck to the car. It is important to flush these off in such a way as to prevent grit from scratching the finish.

The wheel arches and underbody need washing in the same way to remove any accumulated mud which will retain moisture and tend to encourage rust. Paradoxically enough, the best time to clean the underbody and wheel arches is in wet weather when the mud is thoroughly wet and soft. In very wet weather the underbody is usually cleaned of large accumulations automatically and this is a good time for inspection.

3 Periodically it is a good idea to have the whole of the underside of the car steam cleaned, engine compartment included, so that a thorough inspection can be carried out to see what minor repairs and renovations are necessary. Steam cleaning is available at many garages and is necessary for removal of accumulation of oily grime which sometimes is allowed to cake thick in certain areas near the engine, gearbox and back axle. If steam facilities are not available, there are one or two excellent grease solvents available which can be brush applied. The dirt can then be simply hosed off.

4 After washing paintwork, wipe off with a chamois leather to give an unspotted clear finish. A coat of clear protective wax polish will give added protection against chemical pollutants in the air. If the paintwork sheen has dulled or oxidised, use a cleaner/polish combination to restore the brilliance of the shine. This requires a little effort, but is usually caused because regular washing has been neglected. Always check that the door and ventilator opening drain holes and pipes are completely clear so that water can drain out. Bright work should be treated the same way as paintwork. Windscreens and windows can be kept clear of the smeary film which often appears if a little ammonia is added to the water. If they are scratched, a good rub with a proprietary metal polish will often clear them. Never use any form of wax or other body or chromium polish on glass.

3 Maintenance - upholstery and carpets

1 Mats and carpets should be brushed or vacuum cleaned regularly to keep them free of grit. If they are badly stained removed them from the car for scrubbing or sponging and make quite sure they are dry before replacement. Seats and interior trim panels can be kept clean by a wipe over with a damp cloth. If they do become stained (which can be more apparent on light coloured upholstery) use a little liquid detergent and a soft nail brush to scour the grime out of the grain of the material. Do not forget to keep the head lining clean in the same way as the upholstery. When using liquid cleaners inside the car do not over-wet the surfaces being cleaned. Excessive damp could get into the seams and padded interior causing stains, offensive odours or even rot. If the inside of the car gets wet accidentally it is worthwhile taking some trouble to dry it out properly, particularly where carpets are involved. **Do not** leave oil or electrical heaters inside the car for this purpose.

4 Minor body repairs

The photographic sequences on pages 122 and 123 illustrate the operations detailed in the following sub-sections.

Note: *For more detailed information about bodywork repair, the Haynes Publishing Group publish a book by Lindsay Porter called The Car Bodywork Repair Manual. This incorporates information on such aspects as rust treatment, painting and glass fibre repairs, as well as details on more ambitious repairs involving welding and panel beating.*

Repair of minor scratches in the car's bodywork

If the scratch is very superficial, and does not penetrate to the metal of the bodywork, repair is very simple. Lightly rub the area of the scratch with a paintwork renovator, or a very fine cutting paste, to remove loose paint from the scratch and to clear the surrounding bodywork of wax polish. Rinse the area with clean water.

Apply touch-up paint to the scratch using a thin paint brush, continue to apply thin layers of paint until the surface of the paint in the scratch is level with the surrounding paintwork. Allow the new paint at least two weeks to harden; then, blend it into the surrounding paintwork by rubbing the paintwork, in the scratch area with a paintwork renovator, or a very fine cutting paste. Finally apply wax polish.

Where the scratch has penetrated right through to the metal of the bodywork, causing the metal to rust, a different repair technique is required. Remove any loose rust from the bottom of the scratch with a penknife, then apply rust inhibiting paint to prevent the formation of rust in the future. Using a rubber or nylon applicator fill the scratch with bodystopper paste. If required, this paste can be mixed with cellulose thinners to provide a very thin paste which is ideal for filling narrow scratches. Before the stopper-paste in the scratch hardens, wrap a piece of smooth cotton rag around the top of a finger. Dip the finger in cellulose thinners and then quickly sweep it across the surface of the stopper-paste in the scratch; this will ensure that the surface of the stopper-paste is slightly hollowed. The scratch can now be painted over as described earlier in this Section.

Repair of dents in the car's bodywork

When deep denting of the car's bodywork has taken place, the first task is to pull the dent out, until the affected bodywork almost attains its original shape. There is little point in trying to restore the original shape completely, as the metal in the damaged area will have stretched on impact and cannot be reshaped fully to its original contour. It is better to bring the level of the dent up to a point which is about 1/8 inch (3mm) below the level of the surrounding bodywork. In cases where the dent is very shallow anyway, it is not worth trying to pull it out at all.

If the underside of the dent is accessible, it can be hammered out gently from behind, using a mallet with a wooden or plastic head. Whilst doing this, hold a suitable block of wood firmly against the impact from the hammer blows and thus prevent a large area of bodywork from being 'belled-out'.

Should the dent be in a section of the bodywork which has a double skin or some other factor making it inaccessible from behind, a different technique is called for. Drill several small holes through the metal inside the dent area - particularly in the deeper sections. Then screw long self-tapping screws into the holes just sufficiently for them to gain a good purchase in the metal. Now the dent can be pulled out by pulling on the protruding heads of the screws with a pair of pliers.

The next stage of the repair is the removal of the paint from the damaged area, and from an inch or so of the surrounding 'sound' bodywork. This is accomplished most easily by using a wire brush or abrasive pad on a power drill, although it can be done just as effectively by hand using sheets of abrasive paper. To complete the preparations for filling, score the surface of the bare metal with a screwdriver or the tang of a file, or alternatively, drill small holes in the affected area. This will provide a really good 'key' for the filler paste.

To complete the repair see the Section on filling and respraying.

Repair of rust holes or gashes in the car's bodywork

Remove all paint from the affected area and from an inch or so of the surrounding 'sound' bodywork, using an abrasive pad or a wire brush on a power drill. If these are not available a few sheets of abrasive paper will do the job just as effectively. With the paint removed you will be able to gauge the severity of the corrosion and therefore decide whether to replace the whole panel (if this is possible) or to repair the affected area. Replacement body panels are not as expensive as most people think and it is often quicker and more satisfactory to fit a new panel than to attempt to repair large areas of corrosion.

Remove all fittings from the affected area except those which will act as a guide to the original shape of the damaged bodywork (eg; headlamp shells etc.,). Then, using tin snips or a hacksaw blade, remove all loose metal and any other metal badly affected by corrosion. Hammer the edges of the hole inwards in order to create a slight depression for the filler paste.

Wire brush the affected area to remove the powdery rust from the surface of the remaining metal. Paint the affected area with rust inhibiting paint; if the back of the rusted area is accessible treat this also.

Before filling can take place it will be necessary to block the hole in some way. This can be achieved by the use of aluminium or plastic mesh, or aluminium tape.

Aluminium or plastic mesh is probably the best material to use for a large hole. Cut a piece to the approximate size and shape of the hole to be filled, then position it in the hole so that its edges are below the level of the surrounding bodywork. It can be retained in position by several blobs of filler paste around its periphery.

Aluminium tape should be used for small or very narrow holes. Pull a piece off the roll and trim it to the approximate size and shape required, then pull off the backing paper (if used) and stick the tape over the hole; it can be overlapped if the thickness of one piece is insufficient. Burnish down the edges of the tape with the handle of a screwdriver or similar, to ensure that the tape is securely attached to the metal underneath.

Bodywork repairs - filling and respraying

Before using this Section, see the Sections on dent, deep scratch, rust hole, and gash repairs.

Many types of bodyfiller are available, but generally speaking those proprietary kits which contain a tin of filler paste and a tube of resin hardener are best for this type of repair. A wide, flexible plastic or nylon applicator will be found invaluable for imparting a smooth and well contoured finish to the surface of the filler.

Mix up a little filler on a clean piece of card or board - use the hardener sparingly (follow the maker's instructions on the packet) otherwise the filler will set very rapidly.

Using the applicator, apply the filler paste to the prepared area; draw the applicator across the surface of the filler to achieve the correct contour and to level the filler surface. As soon as a contour that approximates the correct one is achieved, stop working the paste - If you carry on too long the paste will become sticky and begin to 'pick-up' on the applicator. Continue to add thin layers of filler paste at twenty-minute intervals until the level of the filler is just 'proud' of the surrounding bodywork.

Once the filler has hardened, excess can be removed using a plane or metal file. From then on, progressively finer grades of abrasive paper should be used, starting with a 40 grade production paper and finishing with 400 grade 'wet or dry' paper. Always wrap the abrasive paper around a flat rubber, cork, or wooden block - otherwise the surface of the filler will not be completely flat. During the smoothing of the filler surface the 'wet-or-dry' paper should be periodically rinsed in water. This will ensure that a very smooth finish is imparted to the filler at the final stage.

At this stage the 'dent' should be surrounded by a ring of bare metal, which in turn should be encircled by the finely 'feathered' edge of the good paintwork. Rinse the repair area with clean water, until all of the dust produced by the rubbing-down operation is gone.

Spray the whole repair area with a light coat of grey primer - this will show up any imperfections in the surface of the filler. Repair these imperfections with fresh filler paste or bodystopper, and once more smooth the surface with abrasive paper. If bodystopper is used, it can be mixed with cellulose thinners to form a really thin paste which is ideal for filling small holes. Repeat this spray and repair procedure until you are satisfied that the surface of the filler, and the feathered edge of the paintwork are perfect. Clean the repair area with clean water and allow to dry fully.

The repair area is now ready for spraying. Paint spraying must be carried out in a warm, dry, windless and dust free atmosphere. This condition can be created artificially if you have access to a large indoor working area, but if you are forced to work in the open, you will have to pick your day very carefully. If you are working indoors, dousing the floor in the work area with water will 'lay' the dust which would otherwise be in the atmosphere. If the repair area is confined to one

This sequence of photographs deals with the repair of the dent and paintwork damage shown in this photo. The procedure will be similar for the repair of a hole. It should be noted that the procedures given here are simplified — more explicit instructions will be found in the text

In the case of a dent the first job — after removing surrounding trim — is to hammer out the dent where access is possible. This will minimise filling. Here, the large dent having been hammered out, the damaged area is being made slightly concave

Now all paint must be removed from the damaged area, by rubbing with coarse abrasive paper. Alternatively, a wire brush or abrasive pad can be used in a power drill. Where the repair area meets good paintwork, the edge of the paintwork should be 'feathered', using a finer grade of abrasive paper

In the case of a hole caused by rusting, all damaged sheet-metal should be cut away before proceeding to this stage. Here, the damaged area is being treated with rust remover and inhibitor before being filled

Mix the body filler according to its manufacturer's instructions. In the case of corrosion damage, it will be necessary to block off any large holes before filling — this can be done with aluminium or plastic mesh, or aluminium tape. Make sure the area is absolutely clean before ...

... applying the filler. Filler should be applied with a flexible applicator, as shown, for best results; the wooden spatula being used for confined areas. Apply thin layers of filler at 20-minute intervals, until the surface of the filler is slightly proud of the surrounding bodywork

Initial shaping can be done with a Surform plane or Dreadnought file. Then, using progressively finer grades of wet-and-dry paper, wrapped around a sanding block, and copious amounts of clean water, rub down the filler until really smooth and flat. Again, feather the edges of adjoining paintwork

The whole repair area can now be sprayed or brush-painted with primer. If spraying, ensure adjoining areas are protected from over-spray. Note that at least one inch of the surrounding sound paintwork should be coated with primer. Primer has a 'thick' consistency, so will find small imperfections

Again, using plenty of water, rub down the primer with a fine grade wet-and-dry paper (400 grade is probably best) until it is really smooth and well blended into the surrounding paintwork. Any remaining imperfections can now be filled by carefully applied knifing stopper paste

When the stopper has hardened, rub down the repair area again before applying the final coat of primer. Before rubbing down this last coat of primer, ensure the repair area is blemish-free – use more stopper if necessary. To ensure that the surface of the primer is really smooth use some finishing compound

The top coat can now be applied. When working out of doors, pick a dry, warm and wind-free day. Ensure surrounding areas are protected from over-spray. Agitate the aerosol thoroughly, then spray the centre of the repair area, working outwards with a circular motion. Apply the paint as several thin coats

After a period of about two weeks, which the paint needs to harden fully, the surface of the repaired area can be 'cut' with a mild cutting compound prior to wax polishing. When carrying out bodywork repairs, remember that the quality of the finished job is proportional to the time and effort expended body panel, mask off the surrounding panels; this will help to minimise the effects of a slight mis-match in paint colours. Bodywork fittings (eg; chrome strips, door handles etc.,) will also need to be masked off. Use genuine masking tape and several thicknesses of newspaper for the masking operation.

Before commencing to spray, agitate the aerosol can thoroughly, then spray a test area (an old tin, or similar) until the technique is mastered. Cover the repair area with a thick coat of primer; the thickness should be built up using several thin layers of paint rather than one thick one. Using 400 grade 'wet or dry' paper, rub down the surface of the primer until it is really smooth. While doing this the work area should be thoroughly doused with water, and the 'wet or dry' paper periodically rinsed in water. Allow to dry before spraying on more paint.

Spray on the top coat, again building up the thickness by using several thin layers of paint. Start spraying in the centre of the repair area and then, using a circular motion, work outwards until the whole repair area and about 2 inches of the surrounding original paintwork is covered. Remove all masking material 10 to 15 minutes after spraying on the final coat of paint.

Allow the new paint at least 2 weeks to harden fully; then, using a paintwork renovator or a very fine cutting paste, blend the edges of the new paint into the existing paintwork. Finally, apply wax polish.

5   Major body repairs

Where serious damage has occurred or large areas need renewal due to neglect, it means certainly that completely new sections or panels will need welding in and this is best left to professionals. If the damage is due to impact it will also be necessary to completely check the alignment of the bodyshell structure. Due to the principle of construction the strength and shape of the whole car can be affected by damage to a part. In such instances the services of a Citroen agent with specialist checking jigs are essential. If a body is left misaligned it is first of all dangerous as the car will not handle properly and secondly uneven stresses will be imposed on the steering, engine and transmission, causing abnormal wear or complete failure. Tyre wear may also be excessive.

6   Maintenance - hinges and locks

1   Oil the hinges of the bonnet, boot and doors with a drop or two of light oil periodically. A good time is after the car has been washed.
2   Oil the bonnet release catch mechanism and striker pin periodically.
3   Do not over lubricate door latches and strikers. Normally a little oil on the rotary cam spindle is sufficient.

7   Door rattles - tracing and rectification

Door rattles are due either to loose hinges, worn or maladjusted catches or loose components of the locking mechanism or window winding assembly inside the door. Loose hinges can be detected by opening the door and trying to lift. Any play will be felt. Worn or badly adjusted catches can be found by pushing and pulling on the outside handle when the door is closed. Once again any play will be felt. Readjust or replace the striker plate as necessary. To check the window winding mechanism open the door and shake it with the window open and then closed. If rattles are heard the mechanism is loose or worn, rectify as necessary.

8   Front wing - removal and replacement

1   To provide better access, jack-up the car and remove the relevant roadwheel.
2   With the front door open to give access to the upper and lower rear bracket attachment screws, loosen these screws by a few turns. Remove the lower screw from the cover at the rear of the wheel arch. Remove the screw, available through the circular aperture on the inner panel and

the two screws through the aperture at the front.
3   Remove the screws securing the wing to the upper edge of the inner panel and remove the front wing.
4   Replacement is the reverse of the removal sequence.

9   Bonnet catch - adjustment

1   Slacken the screw securing the safety catch to adjust the clearance; this must be between 0.5 and 2mm (0.02 and 0.08in).
2   Adjust the locking peg of the bonnet so that no play is present when attempting to lift the bonnet. Tighten the locking peg locknut.
3   Should the bonnet catch release cable break with the bonnet closed or should the bonnet be closed accidentally while the cable is disconnected, the catch can be released by inserting a wire hook into the gap existing between the headlamp, the front grille and the bonnet. Hook the end of the wire into the bonnet release and pull to operate the unlocking action. A light directed through the front grille will assist when hooking the wire on to the bonnet release.

10   Boot lid and tail door - removal and replacement

1   Disconnect the earth strap from the negative terminal of the battery. Disconnect the wiring from the number plate light and the interior light switch. Undo the wiring from the left-hand stay. Disconnect the lead from the heated rear window on the tail door.
2   Slacken the left-hand screw of each hinge by a few turns. Remove the right-hand screws. With the lid held firmly open, disconnect the bottom end of the stays and uncouple them by pushing them towards the centre of the car. Remove the screw from each hinge and lift off the lid. Collect any shims fitted and note to which hinge they are fitted.
3   Replacement is the reverse of the removal sequence. If necessary, adjust the thickness of shims behind the hinges. Adjust the lid lock by slackening the screws of the striker plate and positioning the striker plate so that when the boot lid is closed, there is no gap between the lid and its sealing strip. Tighten the securing screws.
4   The boot lid locks are fitted with two locking positions: 1st click is the safety catch; 2nd click is the locked position. Close the lid a few times to ensure that both these positions operate.

11   Windscreen glass - removal and replacement

1   When working on a windscreen or other glass fittings never use metal tools such as screwdrivers, hooks, etc., as these will scratch the glass and damage the rubber sealing strip and trimmings. Use the tapered down end of a piece of hard wood ('A' in Fig. 12.3).
2   After taking off the windscreen wiper arms, loosen the rubber sealing strip by running a hard wood tool round the aperture to break the seal between the moulding and the body aperture. If the windscreen has been shattered cover the facia air vents and stick adhesive sheeting on the windscreen then pull sections away. If the glass is intact press on the glass from inside the car and remove it complete with the moulding. Remove the embellisher strips, if fitted.
3   Before fitting a windscreen ensure that the rubber surround is completely free from old sealant, glass fragments and has not hardened or cracked. Clean the opening in the body in contact with the moulding, ensuring that there are no burrs or unevenness as these could lead to breakage of the new glass.
4   Fit the cleaned moulding to the replacement glass. Refit the embellisher strips. Cut a piece of cord greater in length than the periphery of the glass and insert it into the body flange locating channel of the rubber moulding.
5   Apply a thin bead of sealant to the face of the rubber channel which will eventually mate with the body. With the help of an assistant offer the windscreen to the body aperture and pass the ends of the cord, previously fitted and located at the bottom centre, into the vehicle interior.
6   From outside the vehicle press the windscreen into place and at the same time have an assistant pulling the cords to engage the lip of the rubber moulding over the body flange.
7   Check that the moulding fits snugly inside and outside all the way round. Remove any excess sealant with a cloth soaked in white spirit.

12 Side window and rear window - removal and replacement

The procedure for removing and replacing side windows and rear windows is the same as described for the windscreen in Section 11. When removing a heated rear window disconnect the wiring.

13 Door - removal and replacement

1   Remove the two screws securing the door check to the door. Support the door in the open position and remove either the roll pin holding the two halves of the hinge together or the screws securing the hinges to the pillar. Collect the shims, if fitted, from behind the hinge.
2   Replacement is the reverse of the removal sequence. The clearance between the door and the pillar is adjusted by the fitment of shims between the door hinge and the pillar. This clearance should be 6 ± 1 mm for the front door and $6 \pm \frac{2}{0.5}$ mm for the rear door.

14 Door windows and winding mechanism - removal and replacement

1   Although the shape of the windows in the front and rear doors are different, the winding mechanism is the same and the removal and replacement procedure is the same for all the doors.
2   Removal of the winding mechanism and window necessitates the removal of the door trim. Remove the door lock release by removing the two securing screws and unhooking them from the door lock release mechanism. Remove the window winding arm by pressing back the spring loaded retaining escutcheon and carefully levering the handle off the spindle. Remove the arm rest (photos).
3   Remove the door trim panel by levering its spring retaining clips out of their holes with a thin-bladed screwdriver or similar tool (photos).
4   Remove the four retaining screws of the winding gear and disengage the two locators from the guide at the lower edge of the glass. The winding gear can be withdrawn through the aperture in the door panel (photo).
5   Lower the glass by hand as far as possible and remove the inner and outer embellishers. Remove the screw retaining the glass guide and remove the glass upwards and out through the top. Because of the shape of the front door glass it has to be tilted forward to get it up and out (photo).
6   Replacement of the window, the winding mechanism and the door trim is the reverse of the removal sequence. The window winding handle should be fitted on its splines in the two o'clock position with the window closed.

15 Door lock - removal, replacement and adjustment

1   To remove the door lock mechanism it is necessary to remove the door trim as described in Section 14. Remove the lock assembly retaining screws, disconnect the remote control rods and withdraw the clock.
2   Replacement is the reverse of the removal sequence.
3   The door striker is secured by three screws to the pillar. Adjustment is made by fitting the required thickness of shims between the striker and the pillar to ensure correct engagement of the catch and adequate compression of the sealing strips. The rear edge of the front door and of the rear door must not stand proud by more than 2mm (0.08in).

16 Bumpers - removal and replacement

1   Remove the front grille by opening the bonnet and slackening the two bolts retaining the grille brackets. Pull the grille forward and lift out by pulling upwards.
2   Remove the screws retaining the bumper side pieces, two screws and one nut to each side piece. Remove the five screws from the top and the five screws from underneath which secure the bumper to the lower panel assembly.
3   The end pieces of the rear bumper are separate from the central part of the bumper, which is attached to the boot lid.
4   Open the boot lid and remove the screws securing the rear of the

side piece, the screw from the underneath and/or the screw(s) securing the front end from inside the car.
5   Remove the two screws at each end of the central bumper. Remove the two rubber joint sections and the two screws securing the bumper to the boot lid. Remove the bumper.
6   Replacement is the reverse of the removal sequence.

Fig. 12.1. Bonnet catch adjustment

1   Locknut   3   Safety catch
2   Locking peg

Fig. 12.2. Releasing the bonnet catch with a piece of wire

1   Wire hook

Fig. 12.3. Removing the windscreen

14.2 Door lock release lever

14.2a Door lock release retaining screws

14.2b Unhooking the lock release from the lock control

14.2c Removing the armrest retaining screws

14.2d Window winding spindle and spring

14.2e Fitting the window winding handle

14.3a Removing the door trim panel

14.3b Door with trim removed

14.4 Window winding mechanism retaining screws

14.5 Door window lifting channel

Chapter 13 Supplement:
Revisions and information on later models

Contents

1 Introduction

Since its introduction into the UK market in 1971, the Citroën GS range has undergone many modifications in order to keep up with continuous technical and servicing innovations.

This Chapter deals with information which primarily concerns the GSA range of models, but in many instances details are given concerning earlier models where additional information has subsequently been made available and where modifications were made.

Where no amendment is given in this Chapter, the original material should be considered applicable to all models.

2 Specifications

The Specifications here are revisions of, or supplementary to, the main Specifications at the beginning of the previous Chapters.

Engine – G Special – 1977 on
General

Type	Air-cooled, horizontally-opposed flat four
Bore	74 mm
Stroke	65.6 mm
Displacement	1129 cc (68.9 cu in)
Compression ratio	9 : 1
Horsepower (DIN)	56.5 bhp at 5750 rev/min
Torque (DIN)	58.6 lbf ft at 3500 rev/min

Engine – GS X3 – 1979 on
General

Type	Air-cooled, horizontally-opposed flat four
Bore	79.4 mm
Stroke	65.6 mm
Displacement	1299 cc (79.2 cu in)
Compression ratio	8.7 : 1
Horsepower (DIN)	65 bhp at 5500 rev/min
Maximum torque (DIN)	70 lbf ft at 3500 rev/min

Piston rings
Gap clearance:

Compression ring	0.10 to 0.25 mm
Scraper ring	0.10 to 0.25 mm
Oil control ring*	0.10 to 0.25 mm

* Except U-Flex type

Pistons
Fitting direction marks:

Right-hand	Arrow and D marking
Left-hand	Arrow and G marking

Valves
Inlet:

Head diameter	38 mm
Stem diameter	8 mm
Face angle	90°
Length	94.6 mm

Exhaust:

Head diameter	35.7 mm
Stem diameter	8.5 mm
Face angle	90°
Length	93.8 mm

Valve seat contact surface width:

Inlet	1 to 1.4 mm
Exhaust	1.4 to 1.8 mm

Valve guides
Valve guide bore:

Inlet	8 mm
Exhaust	8.5 mm

Valve timing
	As per G12/619 engine

Rocker clearance (cold)
Inlet and exhaust	0.20 to 0.25 mm (0.008 in to 0.010 in)

Rocker shaft – identification
Left inlet shaft and right exhaust shaft	No marking
Right inlet shaft and left exhaust shaft	Blind hole in middle of shaft

Drivebelt identification

Right-hand belt:
Length (total)	885.8 mm
Number of teeth	93 teeth

White timing mark positions – see Figure 13.6
A	43 teeth
D	50 teeth

Left-hand belt:
Length (total)	1000.1 mm
Number of teeth	105 teeth

Timing mark positions – see Figure 13.6
2 white marks – B	33 teeth
1 yellow mark – C	25 teeth
E	47 teeth

Camshaft identification

Right	A58 E60
Left	A57 E59

Torque wrench settings

	lbf ft	kgf m
Cylinder head nuts:		
Stage 1	6 to 7	0.8 to 1.0
Stage 2	15 to 18	2.0 to 2.5
Fan/starter dog nut	159 to 174	22 to 24
Manifold nuts and bolts	13	1.8

1299 cc 'ECO' engine (GSA from July 1981)
General

Details as for GS X3, except for the following:
Engine plate number	G13/646
Horsepower (DIN)	63.8 bhp at 5500 rev/min
Torque (DIN)	68.7 lbf ft at 3500 rev/min

Valve timing

Inlet opens	0° BTDC
Inlet closes	33° ABDC
Exhaust opens	38° BBDC
Exhaust closes	5° BTDC

Fuel system – alternative carburettors, 1974 on
Solex 28 CIC 4 – CIT 131$_5$ (1222 cc engine)

	Primary	Secondary
Venturi bore	19	19
Main jet	100	80
Air correction jet	1P3	2P4
Idling jet	50	–
Bypass jet	–	40
Constant richness idling jet	30	–
Econostat jet	–	130
Accelerator pump injector	50	–
Needle valve	1.8	
Float weight	11.4g	

Solex 34 PBIS (1015 cc engine)

	CIT 199	CIT 143*
Choke tube	25.5	25.5
Main jet	127.5	130
Air correction jet	EA	180 (EA)
Emulsion tube	3.4	–
Idling jet	42 ± 2	40 ± 2
Air correction jet	120	120
Constant richness idling jet	30	30
Air correction jet	140	140
Econostat jet	70	105
Pump injector	45	35
Needle valve	1.5	1.5
Float weight	5.7g	5.7g
Idle speed	90 to 950 rev/min	
CO level	2 to 3.5%	

Fitted to 1975 models only (in limited numbers)

Solex 28 CIC 4 – CIT 200 (1222 cc engine)

Idle speed:	
Manual transmission	900 to 950 rev/min
Automatic transmission	800 to 900 rev/min
CO level	2 to 3.5%

Weber 30 DGS 1/250 (W66.50) (1222 cc engine)

Idling speed:
    Manual transmission .... 900 to 950 rev/min
    Automatic transmission .... 800 to 900 rev/min
CO level .... 2 to 3.5%

Weber 30 DGS 2 (W58.01), 30 DGS 2/200 (W59.00 or 01) and 30 DGS 2/250 (W59.50)

	Primary	Secondary
As per Weber DGS 1 (W51.00) but with following differences:		
Venturi bore	21	21
Main jet	107	110
Emulsion tube	F71	F20

Weber 30 DGS/150 (W50.50) (1015 cc engine)

Idle speed .... 900 rev/min
CO level .... 2 to 3.5%

Weber 30 DGS 9/250 (W84.51) (1130 cc engines, April 1978 on)

	Primary	Secondary
Choke tube	20	20
Main jet	100	95
Air correction jet	195	195
Emulsion tube	F85	F20
Idling jet	45	45
Air correction jet	120	100
Econostat jet	–	100
Pump injector	45	–
Needle valve	1.5	
Float weight	11g	
Float level	6.5 mm (0.25 in)	
Idle speed	900 to 950 rev/min	
CO level	1 to 2.5%	
Primary throttle valve opening with choke valve plate closed	1.10 ± 0.05 mm	

*Measured between surface of cover joint gasket and float.
Carburettor cover should be in the vertical position without needle
valve ball bearing depressed.*

Fuel system – GS X3 (1300 cc) engine models

Solex 28 CIC 4 – Mark 185

	Primary	Secondary
Choke tube	20	22
Main jet	107.5	95
Air corrector jet	220	155
Emulsion tube	1S3	2TI
Idle jet	50	40
Air correction jet	100	100
Constant richness idle jet	30	–
Air correction jet	–	100
Econostat jet	–	95
Pump injector	55	–
Needle valve ball diameter	1.8 mm	
Float weight	11.4g ± 2	
Float setting	18 mm (0.70 in)	
Choke type	Flap	
Idle speed	850 rev/min (± 50)	
CO level	1.0 to 2.5%	
Choke flap opening (engine running)	4.0 ± 0.2 mm	
Fast idle throttle valve gap	1.30 ± 0.05 mm	

Weber 30 DGS 12/250 – Mark W92-50

	Primary	Secondary
Choke tube	21	21
Main jet	105	107
Air correction jet	200	155
Emulsion tube	F85	F20
Idle jet	45	45
Air correction jet	110	100
Econostat jet	–	65
Pump injector		45
Needle valve ball diameter	1.5 mm	
Float weight	11g ± 2	
Float setting	6.5 mm (0.25 in)	
Choke type	Flap	
Idle speed	850 rev/min (± 50)	
CO level	1.0 to 2.5%	
Choke flap opening (engine running)	5.25 ± 0.25 mm	
Fast idle throttle valve gap	1.35 ± 0.05 mm	

Fuel system – from November 1978 – 1130 cc engines

Solex 28 CIC 4 – Mark 217

	Primary	Secondary
Choke tube	20	21
Main jet	100	90
Air corrector jet	190	190
Emulsion tube	1P5	2P5
Idle jet	50	35
Idle air-bleed jet	100	100
Econostat jet	–	160
Econostat air-bleed jet	–	180
Pump injector	55	–
Needle valve ball diameter	1.8 mm	
Float weight	11.4g ± 2	
Float setting	18 mm/0.70 in	
Choke type	Flap	

Weber 30 DGS 14/250 (W93-50)

	Primary	Secondary
Choke tube	20	20
Main jet	100	95
Air corrector jet	195	195
Emulsion tube	F85	F20
Idle jet	45	45
Idle air-bleed jet	120	100
Econostat jet	–	100
Econostat air-bleed jet	–	150
Pump injector	45	–
Needle valve ball diameter	1.5 mm	
Float weight	11g ± 2	
Float setting	6.5 mm (0.25 in)	
Choke type	Flap	

Fuel system – from November 1978 – 1220 cc engine

Solex 28 CIC 4 – Mark 218

	Primary	Secondary
Choke tube	19	19
Main jet	100	80
Air corrector jet	230	170
Emulsion tube	1P3	2P4
Idle jet	50	40
Idle air-bleed jet	100	100
Econostat jet	–	130
Econostat air-bleed jet	–	220
Pump injector	50	–
Needle valve ball diameter	1.8 mm	
Float weight	11.4g ± 2	
Float setting	18 mm (0.70 in)	
Choke type	Flap	

Weber 30 DGS 11/250 (W90-50)

	Primary	Secondary
Choke tube	20	20
Main jet	100	107
Air corrector jet	190	190
Emulsion tube	F71	F20
Idle jet	45	45
Idle air-bleed jet	110	100
Econostat jet	–	65
Econostat air-bleed jet	–	150
Pump injector	50	–
Needle valve ball diameter	1.5 mm	
Float weight	11g ± 2	
Float setting	6.5 mm (0.25 in)	
Choke type	Flap	

Fuel system – from 1979 – 1129 cc engine models

Solex 28 CIC 4 – Mark CIT 213

	Primary	Secondary
Choke tube	20	21
Main jet	100	90
Air correction jet	200 (1P5)	180 (2P5)
Idle jet	50	–
Air correction jet	100	–
Bypass jet	–	35
Air correction jet	120	
Econostat jet	–	160
Acceleration pump injector	55	–
Needle valve ball diameter	1.8 mm	
Float weight	11g	
Float level setting	18 mm (0.70 in)	

Fuel system – from January 1980 – GSA models with manual gearbox
Weber 30 DGS 12/250 – Mark W92-50
Details as per GS X3 engine models

Fuel system – from January 1980 – GSA models with semi-automatic gearbox
Weber 30 DGS 19/250 Mark W99-50
Details as per Weber 30 DGS 12/250 Mark W92-50

Fuel system – from March 1980 – GSA 1300
Solex 28 CIC 4 – Mark 230

	Primary	Secondary
Venturi bore	20	22
Main jet	107.5	95
Air correction jet	210	200
Emulsion tube	Y3	T1
Idling jet	50	40
Idling air correction jet	100	–
Constant CO idling jet	30	–
Constant CO ventilation	120	–
Econostat jet	–	90
Cold start device jet	50	–
Cold start device vacuum setting	35	–
Pump injector	55	–
Acceleration pump cam	12	
Needle ball valve diameter	1.8 mm	
Float weight	11.4 ± 2g	
Float setting	18 mm	
Choke type	Flap	
Idle speed	850 to 900 rev/min	
CO level	1.0 to 2.5%	
Choke flap opening (engine running):		
Mark 229	3.6 ± 0.3 mm	
Mark 230	4.0 ± 0.3 mm	
Fast idle throttle valve gap:		
Mark 229	1.25 ± 0.05 mm	
Mark 230	1.30 ± 0.05 mm	

Fuel system – from September 1980 – GSA Special – 1130 cc engine
Weber 30 DGS 17/250 – Mark W97-50

	Primary	Secondary
Choke tube	20	20
Main jet	100	90
Air correction jet	230	215
Emulsion tube	F74	F74
Idle jet	45	45
Idle speed air jet	120	100
Econostat jet	–	100
Econostat air jet	–	150
Idle compensation jet	195	–
Pump injector	45	–
Accelerator pump cam	No 176	
Needle valve ball diameter	1.5 mm	
Float weight	11g ± 2	
Float setting	6.5 mm (0.25 in)	
Choke type	Flap	
Idle speed	850 to 900 rev/min	
CO level	1.0 to 2.5%	
Choke flap opening (engine running)	3.50 ± 0.25 mm	
Fast idle throttle valve gap	1.15 ± 0.05 mm	

Fuel system – from September 1980 – GSA Club and Pallas – 1299 cc engine
Manual transmission – Weber 30 DGS 16/250 – Mark W96-50

	Primary	Secondary
Choke tube	21	21
Main jet	103	103
Air corrector jet	230	175
Emulsion tube	F74	F74
Idle jet	45	45
Idle speed air jet	110	110
Econostat jet	–	65
Econostat air jet	–	150
Idle compensation jet	195	–
Pump injector	45	–
Accelerator pump cam	No 176	
Needle valve ball diameter	1.5 mm	
Float weight	11g ± 2	

Float setting	6.5 mm (0.25 in)	
Choke type	Flap	
Idle speed	850 to 900 rev/min	
CO level	1.0 to 2.5%	
Choke flap opening (engine running)	3.25 ± 0.25 mm	
Fast idle throttle valve gap	1.35 ± 0.05 mm	

Semi-automatic transmission – Weber 30 DGS 18/250 – Mark W98-50

Details as per Weber 30 DGS 16/250 (W96-50) but with following differences

	Primary	Secondary
Idle speed air jet	100	110

Fuel system – from July 1981 – GSA 1299 cc ECO engine
Manual transmission – Weber 30 DGS 25/250 – Mark W115-50

	Primary	Secondary
Choke tube	22	22
Main jet	97	100
Air correction jet	205	140
Emulsion tube	F74	F20
Idle jet	40	40
Idle air-bleed jet	110	100
Enrichment device air jet	180	–
Econostat jet	–	65
Pump injector	55	–
Accelerator pump cam	Position number 1	
Needle valve ball diameter	1.5 mm	
Float weight	11g ± 2	
Float setting	6.5 mm (0.25 in)	
Choke type	Flap	
Idle speed	650 to 700 rev/min	
CO level	0.5 to 1.5%	
Choke flap opening (engine running)	3.70 ± 0.30 mm	
Fast idle throttle valve gap	1.35 ± 0.05 mm	

Semi-automatic transmission – Weber 30 DGS 26/250 – Mark W116-50

Details as per Weber 30 DGS 25/250 – Mark W115-50

Solex 28 CIC 5 – Mark 247

	Primary	Secondary
Venturi bore	20 mm	22 mm
Main jet	95	95
Air correction jet	210	160
Emulsion tube	53	T1
Idle jet	55	–
Bypass jet	–	40
Econostat jet	–	90
Pump injector	55	–
Enrichment jet	50	–
Needle valve	1.8 mm	
Float weight	11.7g	
Float setting	18 mm (estimated)	
Dashpot closing time (4500 to 1200 rpm)	2.0 to 4.5 seconds	
Idle speed	650 to 700 rev/min	
CO level	0.5 to 1.5%	
Choke flap opening (engine running)	2.5 ± 0.3 mm	
Fast idle throttle valve gap	1.30 ± 0.05 mm	

Ignition System
Spark plugs

	1130 cc engine	1300 cc engine
AC	42 XLS	41.4 XLS
Bosch	W6D	W6D
Champion	N7YC	N7YC
Marchal	GT 34-2H	GT 34-2H
Marelli	GW 78 LP	–

Distributor

1130 cc engine	SEV Marchal 41 301 802
1300 cc engine	SEV Marchal 41 301 502 or Ducellier 525 073

Ignition timing

Static or idle setting	10° BTDC
Advance (vacuum disconnected) – dynamic timing:	
1130 cc engine	27° at 3000 rev/min
1015 cc and 1220 cc engines	33° at 2500 rev/min
1299 cc engine	24° at 2500 rev/min

Dwell adjustment
Dwell angle .... 57 ± 2°
Dwell ratio .... 63 ± 3%

Coil .... Ducellier 2777C or SEV-Marchal E44 910 312 or Marelli BZR 206 A or Femsa B1 12 R70

Transistorised ignition system – 1300 cc engine GSA models – from July 1981 on
Spark plugs
AC .... 41.4 XLS
Bosch W6D
Champion N7YC
Marchal .... GT 34-2H
Eyquem .... 800 LS
Electrode gap .... 0.6 to 0.7 mm (0.023 to 0.027 in)

Distributor
Make/type .... Ducellier/525 332 A or SEV-Marchal /417-10002 A 497
Advance (vacuum disconnected) at 3000 rev/min .... 27°

Coil
Make/type .... Ducellier/520 015 A or Bosch/0221 122 317

Module
Make/type .... Ducellier/521 007 A or Bosch/0227 100 111

Clutch (from January 1980)
Type .... Diaphragm reference 180 DBR 285

Pedal free movement .... 15 to 20 mm (0.59 to 0.78 in)

Driven plate .... 3 black springs – 3 red springs

Manual gearbox – 4-speed
G Special 1129 cc engine, 1978
Ratios:
    1st .... 3.83 : 1
    2nd .... 2.29 : 1
    3rd .... 1.50 : 1
    4th .... 1.03 : 1
    Reverse .... 4.18 : 1
Overall ratio (top gear) .... 4.25 : 1

G Special – from November 1979
Ratios as given above but 1st gear changed to 3.81 : 1

GS X3 (1300 cc engine) from July 1978
Ratios:
    1st .... 3.81 : 1
    2nd .... 2.29 : 1
    3rd .... 1.50 : 1
    4th .... 1.09 : 1
    Reverse .... 4.18 : 1
Overall ratio (top gear) .... 4.52 : 1

GSA models from March 1980
1130 cc engine model – ratios same as for GS X3 above but with following differences:
    4th .... 1.03 : 1
    Overall ratio (top gear) .... 4.25 : 1

Manual gearbox – 5-speed
General
Ratios:
    1st .... 3.81 to 1
    2nd .... 2.29 to 1
    3rd .... 1.50 to 1
    4th .... 1.13 to 1
    5th .... 0.91 to 1
    Reverse .... 4.18 to 1
Overall ratio – 5th gear (long ratio gearbox*) .... 3.76 to 1
Overall ratio – 5th gear (short ratio gearbox**) .... 3.99 to 1
*Long ratio gearbox type number 453

**Short ratio gearbox type number 456
Speedometer drive ratio .... 1.91 to 1

Gearbox lubrication
Oil type .... EP 80
Oil capacity .... 1.5 litres (2.63 Imp. pts)

Tolerances
1st/2nd synchro hub endfloat (maximum) .... 0.05 mm
3rd/4th synchro hub endfloat (maximum) .... 0.05 mm
Halfwasher clearances (between 2nd and 3rd gears) .... 0.05 mm

Speedometer ratio .... 2.16 to 1

Torque wrench settings

	lbf ft	kgf m
From December 1978		
Primary shaft nut	43 to 50	6 to 7
Secondary shaft nut (for new bearing type only)	72 to 86	10 to 12
Speedometer drive nut on pinion shaft	159 to 180	22 to 25
5-speed gearbox		
Rear cover bolts (6 off)	14 to 17	1.9 to 2.3
Rear cover bolts (2 off)	2.1 to 3.6	0.3 to 0.5
Half casing bolts	10.1 to 10.8	1.4 to 1.5
Thrust plate bolts	18 to 21	2.5 to 3
Clutch housing	10.1 to 10.8	1.4 to 1.5
Driveshaft ring nuts	43 to 54	6.0 to 7.5
Drain and level plug	25 to 32	3.5 to 4.5
Secondary shaft nut	159 to 180	22 to 25
Primary shaft nut	43 to 50	6 to 7
Reverse gear reversing lever shaft	19.5 to 21	2.7 to 3
Bearing thrust plate attachment screws	18 to 21	2.5 to 3

Semi-automatic gearbox
General
Ratios – September 1979 to February 1980:

1st	2.73 : 1
2nd	1.70 : 1
3rd	1.03 : 1
Reverse	2.5 : 1
Overall ratio (top gear)	4.25 : 1
Speedometer drive ratio	2.16 : 1

Ratios – from 1980:
Same as given above but gearbox fitted with parking lock.

Tolerances
1st/reverse synchro hub endfloat (maximum) .... 0.05 mm
2nd/3rd synchro hub endfloat (maximum) .... 0.05 mm
Half washers clearance 1st/2nd gear pinions (maximum) .... 0.05 mm

Electro-valve switch contact gap (GSA)
1st and reverse gears .... 1.45 ± 0.20 mm
2nd and 3rd gears .... 1.60 ± 0.20 mm

Torque wrench settings

	lbf ft	kgf m
Drain plug	25 to 33	3.5 to 4.5
Level plug	25 to 33	3.5 to 4.5
Reversing lamp switch	9 to 11	1.2 to 1.5
Gearbox casing nuts and bolts	9 to 11	1.2 to 1.5
Rear cover screws	18 to 22	2.5 to 3.0
Pipe coupling screws	25 to 33	3.5 to 4.5
Strainer plug	7 to 11	1.0 to 1.5
Pinion nut	72 to 87	10 to 12
Primary shaft nut	43 to 51	6.0 to 7.0
Crownwheel bolts	58 to 65	8.0 to 9.0
Output shaft bush nuts	43 to 54	6.0 to 7.5

Hydraulic system
General
Fluid type .... LHM (green)
Capacity:
    Early models .... 3.3 litres (6.0 pints)
    As at July 1977 .... 2.9 litres (5.1 pints)
    1980 models .... 4.2 litres (7.3 pints)
Safety valve calibration pressure .... 70 to 90 bar (1015 to 1305 lbf/in²)

Torque wrench settings

	lbf ft	kgf m
Pressure regulator screws	13	1.8
Safety valve screws	8 to 9.4	1.1 to 1.3
HP pump nuts	8.6 to 10	1.2 to 1.4

Front axle and suspension (GSA)
Torque wrench settings

	lbf ft	kgf m
Hub-to-driveshaft nut (greased)	253 to 289	35 to 40
Driveshaft-to-gearbox flange nuts	36 to 40	5.0 to 5.5

Braking system (GSA)
General

	Front	Rear
Disc diameter	270 mm	178 mm
Disc thickness:		
New	9.0 mm	7.0 mm
Wear limit	7.0 mm	5.0 mm
Piston diameter	45.0 mm	30.0 mm

Torque wrench settings

	lbf ft	kgf m
Front brake unit attachment bolts	43	6.0
Brake valve attachment screws	12 to 13	1.7 to 1.8
Pedal unit attachment screws	14	1.9
Handbrake cable locknut	11	1.5

Wheels and tyres
Tyres – Saloon and Estate

Standard wheel	145 SR XZX
Optional light alloy wheel	145 HR 15 XVX

Tyre pressures

	Front	Rear
Standard wheel	1.8 kgf/cm² (26 lbf/in²)	1.9 kgf/cm² (27.5 lbf/in²)
Light alloy wheel	1.7 kgf/cm² (24 lbf/in²)	1.8 kgf/cm² (26 lbf/in²)

Torque wrench settings

	lbf ft	kgf m
Wheel nuts:		
Light alloy wheel	54 to 61	7.5 to 8.5
Steel wheel	40 to 54	5.5 to 7.5

Electrical system
Battery

GSA X3 and GS X3	12V 225/45 amp hour
Other GSA models	12V 200/49 amp hour

Alternator (GSA models)

Paris-Rhone	A 12R 38 or A 12R 46
Ducellier	514 006
Motorola	9 AR 2748 G
Rated current/voltage	40A/12V

Regulator (integral with alternator)

Paris-Rhone	YL 131
Ducellier	511 007
Motorola	9 RC 7053

Starter motor – GS and GS X3 models from 1978 and all GSA models

Type	Ducellier 532016 or Paris-Rhone D8E 155
Power	0.90 kW

Torque wrench settings

	lbf ft	kgf m
Alternator pulley nut	40	5.5

Rear axle and suspension
Rear wheel alignment (GSA)

Toe-in	0 to 5 mm (0 to 0.2 in)
Camber	0° 00' ± 0° 40'

3   Routine maintenance

Maintenance intervals (all models)

1   Over the years the basic maintenance interval has been extended from 3000 miles, first to 5000 and then to 6000 miles. The home mechanic may prefer to observe shorter intervals, especially on older or high-mileage vehicles.

2   The makers recommend that vehicles used in 'hard conditions' be serviced every 5000 miles. 'Hard conditions' include: exclusively stop-start operation; dusty environments; extremes of heat or cold;

full-time trailer towing.

3   On vehicles covering less than 6000 miles per year, the engine oil must be changed at least once a year, and the gearbox oil and hydraulic system fluid changed every two years.

Maintenance schedule (later models)

4   This schedule applies specifically to 1985 model year vehicles, but may be used as a guide for all later models. The frequency of some tasks may be modified according to experience or operating conditions.

Under-bonnet view of a 1983 model GSA – spare wheel removed

1 Heater blower motor	10 Econoscope sensor	19 Engine oil dipstick	28 Headlamps
2 Handbrake lever	11 Speedometer cable	20 Inlet manifold (LH)	29 Windscreen washer reservoir
3 Gearchange lever	12 Heater hose	21 Throttle return spring	30 Windscreen washer pump
4 Choke cable	13 Distributor vacuum capsule	22 Alternator	31 LHM reservoir
5 Throttle cable	14 Diagnostic socket	23 Carburettor	32 LHM level indicator
6 Handbrake cables	15 Ignition coil	24 Fuel supply hose	33 LHM filler cap
7 Fusebox	16 Ignition module	25 Fuel return hose	34 Wheelbrace/starting handle
8 Battery	17 Engine oil filler cap	26 Breather hose	35 Hydraulic pressure regulator
9 Front suspension spheres	18 Preheater pipe (LH)	27 Air cleaner	36 Oil filter

Weekly, before a long journey, or at least every 600 miles (1000 km)

Check the engine oil level
Check the hydraulic fluid level
Top up the washer reservoir(s)
Check the tyre pressures
Check the operation of the lights, indicators and horn

Every 6000 miles (10 000 km)

Change the engine oil
Check the gearbox oil level
Check the battery electrolyte level (when possible)
Check suspension units, pipes, etc, for leaks
Check condition of driveshaft and steering rack gaiters
Check condition of steering and suspension balljoints
Inspect tyres thoroughly, investigate abnormal wear
Inspect front brake pads

Every 12 000 miles (20 000 km) – additional work

Renew engine oil filter
Inspect spark plugs, clean and regap or renew
Check clutch adjustment
Check condition and tension of alternator drivebelt
Check handbrake adjustment
Renew in-line fuel filter
Grease clutch cable and linkage
Check engine valve (rocker) clearances

Every 18 000 miles (30 000 km) – additional work

Renew air cleaner element
Clean hydraulic system suction and return filters
Lubricate door hinges, check straps, latches, etc

Every 24 000 miles (40 000 km) – additional work

Change manual gearbox oil
Inspect rear brake pads

Every 30 000 miles (50 000 km) – additional work

Change semi-automatic gearbox fluid

Every 36 000 miles (60 000 km) – additional work

Change hydraulic fluid
Renew timing belts (if wished)

4   Engine

Part A – Further operations to those given in Chapter 1.

1   The following operations are in addition to those given in Chapter 1.
2   When referring to operations in Chapter 1 or to those given below, further references should be made to Part C of this Section.

Rocker shaft and rockers – removal and refitting (engine in vehicle)

3   To remove the intake valve rocker shaft, first remove the air

intake grille, then the headlamps. Disconnect the bonnet-lock cable, and unbolt the fan panel.
4   To remove the exhaust valve rocker shaft, extract the bolt which holds the engine front flexible mountings and raise the engine/gearbox slightly.
5   The upper cylinder head holds the inlet valves while the lower cylinder head holds the exhaust valves. This arrangement is repeated on both sides of the crankcase.
6   Remove the starter dog. To do this, unscrew the starter dog locknut using a 42 mm socket with a long knuckle bar. In order to prevent the crankshaft turning as the nut is unscrewed, jam the flywheel starter ring gear by inserting a cold chisel or piece of flat metal into the exposed part of the ring gear just behind the engine oil dipstick. Unscrew and remove the starter dog. Pass a socket through the fan blades, and release the alternator mounting and adjuster link bolts then push the alternator to slacken the drivebelt. Remove the fan and disengage the alternator drivebelt from its pulley groove.
7   Temporarily refit the starting handle dog then, using the starting handle, turn the crankshaft until the mark (b) on the crankshaft sprocket intermediate flange is at its highest point, and the camshaft sprocket marks (a and c) are at their highest and lowest points as shown (Fig. 13.1). Ignore any marks on the timing belts themselves.
8   Slacken the belt tensioner nut, compress the tensioner to slacken the timing belt and with it still compressed, re-tighten the nut.
9   Slip the belt from the camshaft sprocket.
10   You will now need special Citroën tool number MR630-11/26 which is a camshaft retaining bar. If not available make one up referring to Fig. 13.2. Bolt the lever to the camshaft sprocket and, holding the sprocket quite still, unscrew and remove the camshaft sprocket nut.
11   With the timing belt(s) disconnected, do not turn the crankshaft from its originally set position.
12   Unbolt and remove the appropriate rocker cover then seal the oil return hole with a piece of rag or a plug to prevent anything falling in during the following operation.
13   Turn the camshaft as necessary to relieve the tension on the rockers, then release the adjuster screw locknuts and screws taking care not to let the valve caps (if fitted) drop.
14   Unscrew and remove the plug from each end of the rocker shaft.
15   Using a 3 mm Allen key, extract the grub screw.
16   Remove the stud. This can be done without damaging the stud if two nuts are locked together on the stud threads and the stud unscrewed with a spanner.
17   Unscrew the hollow bolt from the banjo union.
18   Using a suitably threaded length of studding and tubular distance pieces, draw out the rocker shaft so that it emerges from the front end of the cylinder head. A special tool is available for this operation (MR 630-25/8). As the rocker shaft is withdrawn, remove

Fig. 13.1 Engine front end (Sec 4A)

1 Belt tensioner nut	b Timing mark
2 Camshaft sprocket nut	c Timing mark
a Timing mark	

MATERIAL steel strip 50 ×10 mm,
steel rod Ø=22

Fig. 13.2 Camshaft sprocket retaining lever, special tool MR 630-11/26. Dimensions shown in mm. Inset shows lever in position (Sec 4A)

the O-ring seals, caps, copper washers, rockers arms and springs.
19 To reassemble, first stick the caps (where fitted) to the rocker arm adjuster screws using thick grease.
20 Install the rocker shaft, picking up the rocker arms and springs, the latter being against the outer faces of the shaft bearing webs. Turn the rocker shaft as it is fitted so that the groove for the pin, and the dimple for the grub screw, are correctly aligned. Fully insert the shaft by tapping it with a copper or plastic faced mallet.
21 Screw in the rocker cover stud so that the shorter length of its thread is into the cylinder head.
22 Smear the threads of the grub screw with a thread locking compound and screw it into position.

23 Fit and tighten the end plugs together with the O-rings, caps and copper washers as shown in Figure 1.24. Tighten the plugs to the specified torque.
24 Refit the banjo union bolt, using new sealing washers if necessary.
25 Fit the camshaft sprocket and tighten the nut to the specified torque while holding the sprocket with the lever (MR 630-11/26).
26 With the three sprocket timing marks positioned as described in paragraph 7, the timing belts can now be refitted. Fit the shorter right-hand (as viewed from the driver's seat) belt first, positioning it over the sprockets so that the white paint marks on the belt align with the marks on the sprockets.

Fig. 13.3 Rocker shaft extraction method (Sec 4A)

(D) Oil return hole

Fig. 13.4 Rocker shaft arrangement (Sec 4A)

5 Cap	8 End plugs
6 Cover stud	9 Hollow bolt
7 Grub screw	10 Coil springs

27 When correctly fitted, the belt tooth spacing should conform to the following (see Fig. 13.5).

   Marks 'a' to 'd' (1015 cc engine) 42 teeth
   Marks 'a' to 'd' (1130 & 1222 cc engines) 43 teeth
   For 1299 cc engine refer to the Specifications of this Chapter and Fig. 13.6

Count the number of teeth on the length of belt which runs over the tensioner pulley, not the top run of the belt as is the case with the left-hand belt.

28 Check the position of the sprocket marks and then refit the longer left-hand belt, aligning the white paint marks on the belt with the sprocket marks. If correct, the yellow paint mark on the belt should be aligned with the mark on the oil pump drive sprocket. If necessary, turn the oil pump sprocket to achieve this.

29 When correctly fitted, the belt tooth spacing should conform to the following, measured along the top run of the belt (see Fig. 13.5):

   Marks 'a' to 'b' (1015 engine) 32 teeth
   Marks 'a' to 'b' (1130 & 1222 cc engines) 33 teeth
   For 1299 cc engine refer to the Specifications of this Chapter and Fig. 13.6

30 Release the tensioner pulley nuts and allow them to tension the belts, and then retighten the nuts.

31 Adjust the valve clearances to the specified tolerance (see Part B of this Section). Do this individually with each rocker pad opposite the lowest profile (base circle) of the cam lobe.

32 At this stage the timing belts should be finally re-tensioned. To do this, turn the crankshaft to set up the timing marks as described in paragraph 7 of this Section. Now turn the crankshaft through a further 90° clockwise. Slacken the tensioner nut on the left-hand belt, and then re-tighten it to the specified torque.

33 Turn the crankshaft through one complete turn clockwise and carry out similar operations on the right-hand tensioner.

34 Apply engine oil to the rocker gear, remove the rag or plug used to cover the oil return hole, and fit the rocker covers.

35 Lower the engine and tighten the flexible mountings.

36 Loosen the engine cooling fan cowling bolts and leave them loose.

37 Fit the spacer and the fan, making sure to engage the alternator drivebelt in the fan pulley groove. Apply grease to the starter dog threads, screw it into position and tighten the locknut when the starter dog cutouts are horizontal with the engine at TDC. Adjust its position by means of the locknut, if necessary, so that about 0.13 in (5.0 mm) of thread is visible. The starter ring gear on the flywheel

Fig. 13.5 Timing belts alignment mark locations (Sec 4A)

   a   Crankshaft mark
   b   Left-hand camshaft sprocket mark
   c   Oil pump drive sprocket mark
   d   Right-hand camshaft sprocket mark
   1 and 2 Tensioner pulley retaining nuts
   4   Crankshaft sprocket outer flange

Note: *For 1299 cc engine refer to Fig. 13.6*

Fig. 13.6 Camshaft belt refitting positions for the 1299 cc engine – see Specifications (Chapter 13) for details (Sec 4A)

P = 1 tooth

Fig. 13.7 Fan spacer (6) and alternator drivebelt (7) (Sec 4A)

will again have to be jammed when tightening the locknut. The shoulder on the locknut must always be towards the fan.

38 With the fan now fitted, move the fan cowling in relation to the fan to provide an even clearance all round the fan blades. Tighten the cowling nuts. Install the fan panel.

39 Stick the cowling sealing strip in position, if necessary, using a suitable adhesive.

40 Fit the headlamps and have the beam alignment checked as soon as possible.

41 Check and top-up the engine oil.

42 Tension the alternator drivebelt (see Part B of this Section).

43 Refit the air intake grille.

Timing belt, tensioner and sprocket – removal and refitting (engine in vehicle)

44 The operations involved are essentially those described in the preceding paragraphs, but the following points must be noted.

45 The right-hand belt cannot be completely removed without first having removed the left-hand belt.

46 The belt tensioners can be unbolted and removed without having to disturb the timing belts themselves.

47 When removing the intermediate flange from the crankshaft, do not burr or lose the Woodruff key.

48 When refitting the camshaft sprockets, fit the inner one so that its groove is nearer the crankcase and the outer one is facing outwards. Don't forget the intermediate flange between them and the Woodruff key.

49 Make sure that the tensioner roll pins are in position.

Camshaft – removal and refitting (engine in vehicle)

50 Unbolt and remove the air intake grille and fan panel as described in paragraph 3.

51 Disconnect the engine front mountings.

52 Remove the starter dog, the fan and the engine cooling fan cowling. Remove the oil filter (where applicable).

53 Unbolt and remove the rocker covers.

54 Disconnect and remove the spark plug leads.

55 If the right-hand camshaft is to be removed, unbolt and remove the fuel pump, spacer and its mounting studs. Unscrew the studs by tightening two locknuts on the stud threads and then unscrew them. Remove the pre-heater pipe from the air intake box.

56 If the left-hand camshaft is to be removed, remove the distributor as described in Chapter 3.

57 Temporarily refit the starter dog and set the engine timing marks as described in paragraph 7.

58 Carry out the operations described in paragraphs 8, 9, 10 and 11.

59 Fully release the rocker arm adjuster screws on the side of the engine from which the camshaft is to be withdrawn.

60 Unscrew and remove the camshaft bearing nuts.

61 Tap off the bearing then withdraw the camshaft, taking care not

to damage the cam lobes or adjacent components. If a right-hand camshaft is being removed, push the engine to the left as far as it will go so that the camshaft will pass between the heater duct and the final drive housing. The camshafts are removed towards the rear of the vehicle; they are complete assemblies with their rear bearings, and cannot be dismantled.

62 Extract the camshaft oil seal.

63 Commence refitting by locating a new paper gasket between the camshaft rear housing and the cylinder head. Make sure that the cut-out in the gasket aligns with the oil return groove in the cylinder head. Do not use gasket cement.

64 Install the camshaft into the cylinder head.

65 Locate a left-hand rear bearing so that the oil return boss aligns with the groove in the cylinder head. When this is correct it will be facing the exhaust ports. On the right-hand cylinder head the camshaft rear bearing must be fitted so that the fuel pump mounting stud holes are directly upwards.

66 Tighten the camshaft bearing nuts to the specified torque.

67 Grease the oil seal lips and fit it to the front of the camshaft.

68 Fit the camshaft sprocket and timing belt as described in paragraphs 25, 26, 27 and 28.

69 Adjust the valve clearances as described in Part B of this Section, then adjust the belt tension as described in paragraph 32.

70 Fit the fuel pump or distributor, according to which side of the engine the unit was removed.

71 Refit the fan, starter dog, fan cowling and the fan panel all as described in paragraphs 36 to 39.

72 Fit the accessory support plate.

73 Refit the engine front mounting bolts.

74 Refit the oil filter, and top-up the engine with oil.

75 Check the ignition timing (see Chapter 3) if the distributor was removed and refitted.

Oil pump components – removal and refitting (engine in vehicle)

76 Remove the fan panel, the starter dog and fan, and the engine cooling fan cowling all as described earlier in this Section.

77 Slacken the hydraulic system pressure regulator bleed screw (see Chapter 6).

78 Remove the left-hand timing belt as described earlier in this Section.

79 Extract the five bolts from the oil pump drive sprocket, and carefully lever off the sprocket using two levers at opposite points on its outer edge.

80 Release the clips on the oil pump pressure line by extracting the two screws.

81 Unscrew the oil pump mounting nuts, then move the pump just enough to be able to push out the spindle and release the rod.

82 Extract the oil pump gears and closing plate (refer to Fig. 1.35 in Chapter 1).

83 Reassemble the oil pump. If a guide stud is not fitted to your engine, temporarily screw one in to assist in aligning the pump drive.

84 Fit the closing plate so that its recessed parts are inside and the smallest hole is at the top.

85 Fit the pump connecting rod and drive components as described in Chapter 1, Section 18, paragraph 9.

86 Renew the O-ring seal; fit the oil pump, at the same time connecting the piston spindle. Tighten nuts to the specified torque.

87 Fit the clips which secure the oil pump.

88 Refit the left-hand timing belt as described in paragraphs 26 and 27. Adjust the final belt tension as described in paragraph 32.

89 Fit the engine cooling fan cowling, fan and starter dog as described in paragraphs 36, 37 and 38.

Oil cooler – cleaning

90 Remove the air cleaner occasionally and clean the oil cooler fins by blowing through with compressed air, or using a soft brush and detergent. Do not use a wire brush, nor poke the fins with wire etc, as the matrix is easily damaged.

91 After high mileage, or if the oil changing has been neglected, the cooler may become blocked internally. Remove the air cleaner, carburettor and right-hand inlet manifold, then disconnect the oil cooler pipes, remove its two securing bolts and remove the cooler for flushing.

92 Flush the oil cooler with cellulose thinners or a similar solvent. Make sure that all traces of the solvent are blown out afterwards.

Fig. 13.8 Detach the oil pump rod (10) (Sec 4A)

93 When bearing failure has occurred and the oil cooler is found to contain metallic debris, it is probably best to renew it.
94 Use new sealing washers on the unions when refitting the oil cooler.

Part B – Adjustments and renewals

Rocker arm adjustments – engine in vehicle

1 The rocker arm adjustments must only be checked/adjusted when the engine is cold. Start by disconnecting the spark plug leads to cylinders 2 and 4.
2 Unbolt and remove the rocker covers from each side of the engine. Before removing the bottom covers, cover the manifold with rag as oil will run on to them as soon as the covers are released. (In fact it is not necessary to remove the bottom covers for checking, only for adjustment, so if preferred they can be left in place until a check of the clearances has been made).
3 Insert the starting handle and turn the crankshaft until the first valve to be checked is fully closed and the pointed end (peak) of the cam lobe is furthest from the rocker arm pad.
4 Check the gap between the cam base and the rocker arm pad with a feeler blade 0.008 in (0.20 mm) thick. It should be a stiff sliding fit. If it is not, release the rocker arm adjuster screw locknut and turn the screw in or out as necessary to achieve the correct gap.
5 When the gap is as specified, hold the screw from moving and tighten the locknut.
6 Repeat the operation on all the remaining rocker arms in turn. Less turning of the crankshaft will be needed if the engine firing order is followed – 1, 4, 3, 2. Number 1 cylinder is at the left rear, No 2 is left front, No 3 is right rear and No 4 is right front. *Do not be tempted to check and adjust both valves in the same cylinder head at the same time just because they are closed – the position of the cam lobe will not be correct for both valves at the same crankshaft setting.*
7 When checking and adjusting the lower rocker arm clearances, a mirror and a cranked screwdriver will be required.
8 When refitting the rocker covers, check that the gaskets are in good condition, and do not tighten the nuts beyond the specified torque.

Alternator drivebelt – adjusting tension

9 Remove the air intake grille from the front of the car.
10 Turn the crankshaft with the starting handle until the drivebelt tension can be checked by inserting the fingers through the fan blades.
11 The correct tension is when the total deflection at the mid-point of the longest run of the belt is 0.4 in (10 mm).
12 Adjust, if necessary, by passing a sprocket and extension through the fan blades, and releasing the alternator mounting bolts and adjuster link bolt. Move the alternator as necessary to achieve the correct tension, then retighten the bolts.

Fig. 13.9 Lower rocker arm adjustment using a feeler gauge (a) and cranked screwdriver (A) – engine in vehicle (Sec 4B)

Alternator drivebelt – renewal

13 Drivebelt renewal is a lengthier business than on some other vehicles; it is recommended that the belt be renewed every couple of years as a precautionary measure.

14 If a drivebelt breaks in service, provided that the fan is not damaged the vehicle can continue to be driven so long as the battery charge holds out.

15 To renew the drivebelt, first disconnect the battery earth lead.

16 Remove the alternator as described in Chapter 10, Section 8. Access to the pivot nut and bolt may be improved by removing the air cleaner.

17 With patience, the drivebelt can now be worked past the fan blades and removed. Be careful not to damage the fan blades.

18 Thread the new belt past the fan blades and onto the pulley. Hook the belt up with an old coat hanger or similar piece of wire and refit the alternator.

19 Tension the drivebelt as just described, then refit the displaced trim and reconnect the battery earth lead.

20 Recheck the tension of a new belt after a few hundred miles.

Timing belt tension – adjusting at routine maintenance intervals

21 Remove the air intake grille.

22 Unscrew the starter dog locknut as described in Part A of this Section (paragraph 6).

23 Unscrew and remove the starter dog, then release the alternator bolts and slacken the drivebelt. Remove the fan.

24 The timing belt tensioner pulley nuts are now exposed.

25 Temporarily screw in the starter dog and turn the crankshaft with the starting handle until the mark on the crankshaft sprocket intermediate flange is at the highest point. Now turn the crankshaft through a further 90° clockwise, loosen the nut on the left-hand belt tensioner, then retighten it to the specified torque.

26 Turn the crankshaft through one complete revolution clockwise, then release the nut on the right-hand belt tensioner and retighten the nut to the specified torque.

27 When carrying out these operations, make sure that the nuts on the tensioner pulleys are sufficiently unscrewed to allow the tensioner to apply pressure to the belts before retightening them.

28 Refit the fan and starter dog as described in Part A of this Section, paragraph 37 onwards.

29 Refit the air intake grille.

Valve timing – checking

30 This is not a routine operation. It may be necessary if the camshaft drivebelts are suspected of having slipped or having been incorrectly fitted.

31 With the engine cold, remove the upper rocker covers on each side.

32 Turn the engine with the starting handle until the valves of No 1 cylinder are 'rocking' – ie the exhaust is closing and the inlet is opening.

33 On very early models, insert a 5 mm gauge rod into the timing hole and turn the engine until the rod enters the reference hole in the flywheel – see Chapter 3. On later models, align the flywheel timing mark with the graduated sector as follows:

Engine codes G10, G11, G12/611 and G12/612 – 10° BTDC
Engine codes G12/619 and G12/625 – 15° BTDC

34 Slacken the rocker adjuster locknut on No 1 inlet valve. Back off the adjuster screw until the clearance between the valve stem and the screw is zero, then tighten the locknut without altering the position of the screw.

35 Withdraw the gauge rod (early models). Turn the crankshaft 360° (one full turn) so that the timing marks are again aligned or the gauge rod will again enter the hole, but this time No 1 cylinder is on compression.

36 Measure the clearance between the rocker arm adjuster screw and the valve stem on No 1 inlet valve. It should be 0.5 to 1.0 mm (0.020 to 0.039 in) – if so, the left-hand camshaft is correctly timed.

37 To check the right-hand camshaft timing, repeat the procedure on No 3 cylinder inlet valve.

38 Reset the rocker arm clearances to their normal values on completion, then refit the upper rocker covers.

39 If the valve timing is found to be incorrect, the front of the engine will have to be dismantled for inspection of the timing marks. See Figs. 13.5 and 13.6.

Cylinder head stud location

40 Four different lengths of cylinder head stud are fitted. Refer to Figs. 13.12 and 13.13 for their correct location.

41 When fitting or refitting a stud, the ends which screw into the right-hand crankcase must be coated with Loctite Formetanch or equivalent sealing compound.

Engine/gearbox mountings – removal and refitting
Front

42 Raise and support the front of the vehicle.

43 Undo the two mounting-to-crossmember bolts.

44 Place a jack and a block of wood under the engine. Raise the jack, with the wood spreading the load on the engine, to relieve the weight on the front mountings.

45 Undo the four mounting-to-engine bolts and remove the mountings. Access to these bolts is not good.

46 If new mountings are being fitted, make sure that they are both of the same type and manufacture.

47 Refit in the reverse order to removal.

Fig. 13.10 Flywheel notch (A) and timing mark (B) – GS semi-automatic models. For GSA see Fig. 13.39 (Sec 4B)

Fig. 13.11 Checking the valve stem-to-rocker arm clearance – this is only done when checking the valve timing (Sec 4B)

1 Adjuster screw and locknut

Fig. 13.12 Cylinder head stud identification. For fitted positions of lengths A to D see Fig. 13.13 (Sec 4B)

e   Crankcase end

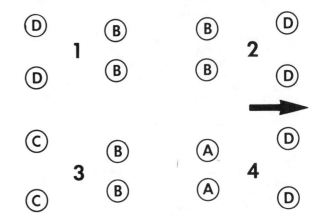

Fig. 13.13 Location of stud lengths A to D. Numbers are cylinder numbers, arrow shows front of engine (Sec 4B)

Rear

48 Open the bonnet and remove the spare wheel.
49 On 3-speed and 4-speed gearboxes, disconnect the speedometer cable from the gearbox.
50 Raise and support the front of the vehicle.
51 Drain the gearbox oil.
52 Remove the exhaust system Y-shaped pipe union and support the main exhaust pipe.
53 Remove the nut and bolt which secure the rubber mounting to the subframe.
54 Remove the eight bolts which secure the gearbox rear cover. (Two of these bolts enter the cover from the front).

55 Remove the rear cover and rear mounting together. It would appear that the cover and mounting are only available as an assembly.
56 When refitting, clean the gearbox and cover mating faces and apply jointing compound. Bolt up the cover and then fit the mounting nut and bolt.
57 Refit the exhaust system union.
58 Refit the speedometer cable (when applicable).
59 Refill the gearbox with oil.
60 Refit the spare wheel.
61 Road test the vehicle and then check that there are no oil leaks from the gearbox rear cover.

Fig. 13.14 Engine/gearbox front mountings (Sec 4B)

1   Mounting-to-engine bolts   2   Mounting-to-crossmember bolts

Fig. 13.15 Engine/gearbox rear mounting (Sec 4B)

4   *Gearbox rear cover bolt*   5   *Mounting-to-subframe bolt*

Fig. 13.16 One of the gearbox rear cover bolts (6) which enters from the front (Sec 4B)

Part C – Modifications

G Special (1129 cc) – from 1978
1   The 1978 G Special is fitted with an 1129 cc engine. This increased capacity is achieved by increasing the stroke to match that of the 1222 cc engine.
2   The only major difference noticeable from other power units in the range is a rubber-covered telescopic section incorporated in the intake pipes between the carburettor intake manifold and the right-hand cylinder head.

G13 (X3 engine) (1299 cc) – from 1979
3   This engine differs from that of the G12 type in the following respects: crankcase, cylinder heads, pistons, rings and cylinders, crankshaft, bearing bushes, flywheel and flywheel fixing method.
4   There are dimensional differences on all of the above items and they are not interchangeable with their corresponding components on the G12 engine type.
5   In the case of the crankshaft bearing bushes, these have been changed in design and have reduced clearances. A reference letter denoting bearing size is stamped into the crankshaft web next to the

Fig. 13.17 Reference letter positions for bearing size – G13 (X3) engine (Sec 4C)

H16223

Fig. 13.18 Bearing bush identification marks (Sec 4C)

H16224

Fig. 13.19 Piston orientation – G13 (X3) engine (Sec 4C)

bearing in question, the letter being A or B as applicable. The two bearing types allow for the necessary clearance reduction. With the type A bearing the bush bearing will not be marked, but with type B bearing the bush bearing will have a yellow mark.

Pistons (up to October 1981)
6   The pistons fitted to the G13 engine have offset gudgeon pins, locked oil scraper rings and the compression ratio marking (8.7) is stamped into their crown. They are also marked with the letter D for right-hand and G for left-hand cylinder identification. When the pistons have been fitted to their connecting rods their orientation must be with the stop pin upwards and the arrow marks pointing towards the timing belts when fitted as with all G engines, see Figure 13.19. Reference to Figure 13.20 will show the correct orientiation of the piston rings when fitted.

Crankshaft
7   The primary shaft bush in the end of the crankshaft differs according to the type and the corresponding seal also differs in diameter – see Fig. 13.21.

Flywheel
8   The G13 engine flywheel has a machined rebate for the different clutch hub fitted to this model and the securing screws have a shoulder under the head. When fitting this flywheel, apply Loctite Formetanch to three points between the flywheel and the crankshaft. The securing screw threads and shoulder face must be

smeared with grease when fitting and tightened to the specified torque wrench setting given for other engine types (see page 11).

All GS models (except GS X2 and GS X3) from December 1978
Miofiltre oil trap
9   This device is a plastic oil trap and is located between the breather and the air filter by rubber pipes. It is also connected to the dipstick guide tube by a smaller diameter nylon pipe so that any collected oil can be returned to the sump. The layout of the system is shown in Fig. 13.22.

Valve timing
10 Minor changes have been made to the valve timing. The checking procedure remains unchanged.

1130-1220-X2
fitting

X3 fitting

Fig. 13.21 Old and new type crankshaft bushes (Sec 4C)

Fig. 13.20 Piston ring profiles (Sec 4C)

Fig. 13.22 The revised crankcase emission control system
incorporating the Miofiltre (1) fitted to later models
(Sec 4C)

2 Breather pipe to air filter
3 Breather pipe from crankcase breather pipe connector
4 Nylon pipe
5 Nylon pipe connectors
6 Dipstick tube
7 Breather pipe connector

GSA 1300 cc ECO engine

11 Introduced into the British market in July of 1981, this engine
was fitted into the Special, Club and Pallas variants. The main
differences for this engine are:

(a) Cylinder head: modified to take rockers having trapezium
    shape ends.
(b) Camshafts: revised cam profiles to change the lift
    characteristics. These camshafts can be identified by having
    two grooves machined in the central bearing journal.
(c) Flywheel: this is lightened but is otherwise unchanged.
(d) Valve timing: changed to improve fuel economy – see
    Specifications. Checking procedure unchanged.

GSA 1300 engines from October 1981

Pistons

12 From the above date new type pistons were fitted to all 1300 cc
models, the main difference to the earlier types being that the offset
gudgeon pin axis was eliminated. Whilst the right- and left-hand
pistons became the same, it is still important when reassembling this
type to ensure that the stop pin faces upwards and the piston itself
is located the correct way round when assembled onto the
connecting rod.

Bypass valve

13 From November of 1981 the cooler bypass valve was modified.
Sectional views of the old and new type bypass valve assemblies
are shown in Figure 13.23. The two are not interchangeable.

All GSA engines from June 1982 (and where applicable all earlier engine types)

14 From the above date new type front and rear crankshaft oil seals
were fitted incorporating a micro turbine on their inner lip. They are
identified as follows:

The front seal has a red inner lip and is marked 'Cote
distribution' (at the timing end).

The rear seal has a brown inner lip and is marked 'Cote volant'
(flywheel end).

15 It is important that earlier type seals are not fitted to engines
produced from this date, but the later 'turbine' type seals can be
fitted to engines produced previous to this date.

16 When fitting these seals, apart from checking that they are
correctly orientated at their respective ends, lubricate the crankshaft
bearing surface with engine oil. When fitting do not distort or
damage the seal lips.

Engine and gearbox – removal and refitting on later models

17 The procedure is essentially still as described in Chapter 1,
Section 5, but allowance must be made for additional wiring which
must be disconnected. This includes:

(a) Brake pad wear indicators
(b) Diagnostic socket
(c) Idle cut-off
(d) Heater blower motor

18 When disconnecting the speedometer drive cable on those
models fitted with the five-speed gearbox, note that the cable
connection is in the clutch housing and not on the rear cover as for
the four-speed models.

---

5 Fuel and exhaust systems

Idle adjustments (later models) – tamperproofing

1 The idle mixture adjustment screw on all later models is covered
by a tamperproof plug. The purpose of this is to discourage, and to
detect, adjustment by unqualified operators.

2 Adjustment should normally be confined to the idle speed

Fig. 13.23 Sectional views of oil cooler bypass valves – old type (left) and new type (right) (Sec 4C)

Fig. 13.24 Crankshaft oil seals. Microturbine face on new seal is shown by a heavy arrow (Sec 4C)

adjusting screw. If adjustment of the idle mixture becomes necessary – for instance after carburettor overhaul – the tamperproof plug must be prised out for access to the mixture adjustment screw. Adjustment should then be carried out using an exhaust gas analyser (CO meter).

3   On completion of adjustment a new tamperproof plug must be fitted when this is required by law. In some EEC countries (though not yet in the UK) it is an offence to use a vehicle with missing tamperproof plugs.

Solex 28 CIC 4 series carburettor – idle adjustments

4   Before attempting to adjust the idle speed, the engine must be at operating temperature and the ignition system adjustments must be correct.

5   Connect a tachometer (rev counter) to the engine in accordance with the maker's instructions.

6   Run the engine and turn the idle speed adjustment screw as necessary to obtain the desired speed.

7   If idle mixture adjustment is necessary, refer to paragraphs 1 to 3 of this Section.

8   On carburettors fitted with an idle cut-off solenoid, note that, if the solenoid is defective or becomes disconnected, the engine will idle very roughly or not at all. Test the solenoid by substitution of a known good unit; a functioning solenoid will normally produce an audible 'click' when energised.

9   When idle adjustment is complete, stop the engine and disconnect the tachometer.

Solex 34 PBIS carburettor – idle adjustments

10 Proceed as described for the 28 CIC 4 series, but refer to Fig. 13.26 for the location of the adjustment screws.

Solex 28 CIC 5 series carburettor – idle adjustments

11 Proceed as described for the 28 CIC 4 series. Note that on this carburettor the idle speed adjustment screw acts directly on the primary throttle butterfly. Refer to Figs. 13.27 and 13.28.

Fig. 13.25 Adjustment points – Solex 28 CIC 4 carburettor (Sec 5)

1 Idle speed adjustment screw   3 Idle mixture adjustment screw   b Choke opener link rod
2 Dashpot   a Fast idle link rod

Fig. 13.26 Adjustment points – Solex 34
PBIS carburettor (Sec 5)

1 Idle speed adjustment screw
2 Idle mixture adjustment
   screw

Fig. 13.27 Adjustment points – Solex 28 CIC 5 carburettor
(Sec 5)

1 Idle speed adjustment screw   3 Dashpot bracket
2 Secondary throttle   4 Dashpot end
   adjustment screw (sealed)   5 Dashpot

Fig. 13.28 Idle mixture adjustment screw (6) – Solex 28 CIC 5 carburettor (Sec 5)

Fig. 13.29 Adjustment points – Weber 30 DGS carburettor (Sec 5)

1   Idle mixture adjustment screw
2   Fast idle adjustment screw
3   Choke opener adjustment screw

Weber 30 DGS series carburettor – idle adjustments
12 Proceed as described for the 28 CIC 4 series. Again, the idle speed adjustment screw acts on the throttle butterfly (photo).
13 On models with semi-automatic transmission, adjust the compensated idle speed as follows.
All except carburettor type W 116-50
14 Chock the wheels and apply the handbrake. With the engine running, select first gear and check that the idle speed is maintained at 850 to 900 rev/min. Adjust if necessary by turning the idle compensation screw.
Carburettor type W 116-50
15 Idle compensation is applied full-time when the engine is cold (oil temperature below 60°C/140°F approx), whether or not a gear is engaged. Additionally, the basic idle speed is lower.
16 With the engine idling at normal operating temperature, disconnect the idle compensator vacuum hose. Disconnect the carburettor-to-electrovalve vacuum hose at the electrovalve and connect it to the idle compensator instead. The idle speed should rise to 850 to 900 rev/min. Adjust if necessary by turning the idle compensation screw.
17 Remake the original vacuum connections and stop the engine.
18 Malfunction of this system may be due to a fault in the thermal switch (located under the alternator). The switch should be closed, thus earthing the electrovalve and completing its circuit, at temperatures of 60°C/140°F and above. The electrovalve blocks the vacuum when it is energised (thermal switch closed and gearbox in

5.12 Idle speed adjustment – Weber carburettor

Fig. 13.30 Adjustment points – Weber 30 DGS carburettor fitted to models with semi-automatic transmission (Sec 5)

2 *Fast idle adjustment screw*
4 *Idle compensation screw*
5 *Idle speed adjustment screw*
6 *Fast idle screw locknut*
7 *Secondary throttle adjustment screw (sealed)*

neutral), and allows vacuum to pass to the idle compensator when de-energised.

Choke flap opening adjustment (all GSA)
19 Remove the air cleaner connector from the top of the carburettor.
20 Allow the engine to idle. Pull the choke control out fully and measure the opening of the choke flap with a gauge rod or twist drill. The desired opening is given in the Specifications.
21 If adjustment is necessary, bend the link rod which connects the choke opener vacuum capsule to the choke flap lever (Solex) or turn the choke opener adjusting screw (Weber).
22 Stop the engine and refit the air cleaner connector.

Fast idle throttle valve gap (all GSA)
23 This is not a routine adjustment and should only be necessary after overhaul. The carburettor must be removed from the engine.

24 Close the choke flap valve completely and measure the opening of the primary throttle valve, using a gauge rod or twist drill. The desired opening is given in the Specifications.
25 If adjustment is necessary, act on the fast idle adjusting screw (Weber) or bend the fast idle link rod (Solex).

Dashpot adjustment (all GSA with manual gearbox)
26 A tachometer and a watch capable of displaying seconds will be needed for this operation.
27 Connect the tachometer. Run the engine at 4250 rev/min and verify that the dashpot (throttle closing damper) is neither compressed nor slack. Release its locknut and adjust it if necessary.
28 Increase the engine speed to 5000 rev/min. Release the throttle and record the time taken for the speed to drop from 4500 to 1200 rev/min. The desired time is between 2.0 and 4.5 seconds.
29 Adjust the closing rate of the dashpot by varying the position of the throttle return spring. If the time taken for the engine speed to

Fig. 13.31 Choke flap opening dimension (b). Solex shown, others similar (Sec 5)

Fig. 13.32 Fast idle throttle valve gap (a). Solex shown, others similar (Sec 5)

drop is always less than 2 seconds regardless of the spring position, renew the dashpot.

Carburettor – removal and refitting (all later models)

30 Proceed as described in Chapter 2, Section 9, but make allowance for the additional electrical and/or vacuum connections on later model carburettors.

31 Most later carburettors have a fuel return connection as well as fuel supply. The direction of fuel flow is shown by arrows cast into the carburettor cover. Normally the supply and return hoses are different sizes to avoid confusion; if not, label them.

Econoscope (GSA models) – general

32 This device is fitted to all GSA models with manual transmission from July 1981. Its function is to assist economical driving by illuminating warning lights in response to decreasing manifold vacuum.

33 The main component of the Econoscope is the vacuum sensor and switching device, which is attached to the diagnostic socket in the engine bay (photo).

34 The circuit diagram and operating conditions of the Econoscope are shown in Fig. 13.33. The system can be switched on and off by a switch on the right-hand control keyboard.

5.33 Econoscope vacuum sensor/switching unit

Display key :

- Ignition on
- Engine not running
- Econoscope switch on

Lamp	
Yellow	Orange
●	○

Engine running - Switch on			
Lamp		Vacuum in mb	Consumption
Yellow	Orange		
○	○	> 275	Low
☼	○	250 ± 25	Normal
⊛	○	200 ± 50	Increasing
●	○	150 ± 50	High
○	●	< 100	Excessive

Fig. 13.33 Circuit diagram and operating conditions of the Econoscope (Sec 5)

Inlet manifolds – all models from July 1981

35 Rigid inlet manifolds were fitted from the above date. The inlet housing bracket and associated support components are no longer fitted.

36 When refitting rigid type manifolds, tighten the flange bolts in the usual way with the engine cold. When reassembly is complete, run the engine up to operating temperature, then allow it to cool. Slacken all the inlet manifold-to-cylinder head bolts by half a turn or so, then retighten them to the specified torque.

Air cleaner element – all models from May 1980

37 The washable air cleaner element has been superseded by a disposable paper element (photo). The element must be renewed at the specified intervals, or more frequently in very dusty conditions.

Exhaust system (all models) – component renewal

38 The exhaust system consists of two front pipes, a Y-shaped union and a main exhaust pipe/silencer assembly. Preheater pipes run from the right-hand front pipe and the left-hand manifold to the inlet housing.

39 When purchasing exhaust system components, bear in mind that although proprietary parts may be cheaper than those of Citroën manufacture, they will not necessarily be a good fit. This is particularly important when dealing with the front pipes.

Main exhaust pipe/silencer

40 Raise and support the rear of the vehicle. Release the clamp which secures the main pipe to the Y-pipe, unhook the silencer from its mountings and remove the pipe and silencer together.

41 Refit in the reverse order to removal, using new mountings and clamps if necessary. Run the engine and check for leaks, and finally tighten the clamps when the system has warmed up.

Front pipes

42 The front pipe sections are notoriously difficult to deal with, and it is worth renewing them on a precautionary basis if the engine is removed for any other reason.

43 It is not in fact necessary to remove the engine in order to renew the front pipes, but it may be necessary to disconnect the engine front mountings and raise the engine in order to fit the right-hand pipe.

44 Citroën now supply a right-hand pipe fitting kit which includes a separate preheater branch pipe (the original branch pipe was fixed to the exhaust pipe). The maker's instructions for fitting this pipe are as follows.

45 Remove the front grille and fan panel, as described for engine removal (Chapter 1, Section 5). Also remove the air cleaner, the hot air pick-up pipe and the heater unit.

46 Undo the flanged joint which secures the right-hand preheater pipe to the inlet housing.

5.37 Removing a disposable type air cleaner element

47 Raise and support the front of the vehicle. Unclip the heat exchanger lower section and release its seals.

48 Saw off the preheater branch pipe as close as possible to the main exhaust pipe. Access for the saw is not good: a padsaw, or a hacksaw blade alone, will have to be used. Take care not to cut into any hydraulic pipes or other nearby components.

49 Remove the right-hand preheater pipe and separate it from the branch pipe on the bench. (This is a sliding joint which would almost certainly be impossible to separate when installed).

50 Remove the clamps which secure the right-hand exhaust pipe to the manifold and to the Y-pipe. Recover the heat exchanger seals, if not already done, noting their position and direction of fitting – they are not interchangeable.

51 In theory, the right-hand exhaust pipe can now be withdrawn from the front of the vehicle. If this proves difficult the old pipe can easily be sawn into more manageable sections, but this technique can hardly be used to fit the new pipe.

52 Manoeuvre the new pipe into position, if necessary raising the

Fig. 13.34 Right-hand exhaust pipe and fitting kit (Sec 5)

engine to provide adequate clearance. Loosely fit the heat
exchanger seals, heat exchanger and clamps.
53 Fit the new preheater branch pipe and clamp to the exhaust
pipe. Use plenty of anti-seize compound on the sliding joint.
54 Refit the preheater pipe to the inlet housing, but do not tighten
the flanged joint yet. Use plenty of anti-seize compound and mate
the preheater pipe to the new branch pipe.
55 Apply exhaust jointing compound to the manifold and Y-pipe
joints.
56 When satisfied that the new pipes are correctly routed and free
of stress, tighten all four clamps and the flanged joint.
57 Run the engine and check for leaks; retighten the clamps after
the system has warmed up.
58 The left-hand pipe poses fewer problems since the preheater
pipe is attached to the left-hand manifold instead of to the exhaust
pipe.
59 When satisfied that the new pipes are correctly fitted, refit the
front grille, fan panel and other disturbed components.

Fuel cut-off ('Decel') system – general

60 Fitted to some 1983 and later models, the Decel system
improves fuel economy by cutting off the power supply to the idle
cut-off solenoid when the vehicle is decelerating in gear.
61 A circuit diagram of the system will be found with the other
wiring diagrams (Fig. 13.105).
62 If the system malfunctions, disconnect the Decel harness
connector from the idle cut-off solenoid and in its place connect the
black connector from the front wiring harness adjacent. If
malfunction continues, it is probably the solenoid which is at fault.

Fig. 13.35 Fitting the right-hand exhaust pipe (Sec 5)

Fig. 13.36 SEV-Marchal cassette points adjustment (Sec 6)

1 Adjuster notch   2 Clamp screw

6 Ignition system

Cassette-type contact breaker points – renewal

1 Remove the distributor cap and move it to one side with the
spark plug leads still attached.
2 Remove the distributor, as described in Chapter 3, making sure
that the lead from the lower tag on the condenser and the vacuum
pipe from the distributor vacuum capsule have been disconnected.
3 Carefully pull the complete vacuum capsule and cassette points
assembly upwards until the connectors at the top of the condenser
can be pulled off.
4 Continue withdrawing the cassette and vacuum unit from the
distributor body.
5 Refit the new cassette, making sure that the lugs on the vacuum
unit arm engage in the cutout of the cassette. In order to avoid
damage to the contact points cam follower, turn the distributor shaft
so that the cam follower will *not* be in alignment with either the
rotor slot in the cam or a cam peak.
6 Push the connectors onto the tags at the top of the condenser,
then push the vacuum unit and cassette assembly fully downwards.
Check that the sides of the top plastic connector to the condenser
are fully seated in the recess, and the locating grooves at the sides
of the vacuum unit are correctly engaged with the distributor body.
7 Turn the distributor shaft to open the points fully, then check the
gap which should be as specified. If it is not, insert a screwdriver in
the small notch provided and adjust the gap. Do not loosen the
domed points clamp screw but just lever the notch in the
appropriate direction.
8 On some types of distributor, the points are adjustable by means
of a socket screw which can be turned by inserting a 3 mm Allen
key from outside the distributor body.
9 Refit the distributor as described in Chapter 3, refit the rotor and
connect the lead to the tag on the base of the condenser; reconnect
the vacuum pipe.
10 Refit the distributor cap.
11 The points setting using a feeler blade must only be regarded as
a basic adjustment to get the engine started. A dwell meter should

H.8410

Fig. 13.37 Cassette points distributor with external
adjustment (Sec 6)

A Hole for Allen key

be connected to the engine in accordance with the manufacturer's instructions and the dwell angle checked. The dwell angle is the number of degrees through which the distributor cam turns between the instants of closure and opening of the contact breaker points. The correct dwell (cam) angle is between 55 and 59°. If the angle is too large, increase the points gap; if it is too small, reduce the gap.
12 To vary the points gap, either insert a screwdriver in the small V-notch on the top surface of the cassette and lever towards or away from the domed screw, or on distributors which have external access to the socket type adjuster screw, turn the screw with a 3 mm Allen key.
13 With the former type of distributor, the distributor cap and rotor will have to be removed before the points can be adjusted. Adjust only by fractional increments before rechecking the dwell angle. With the latter type of distributor, the engine can be kept running while the adjuster screw is turned and the reading on the dwell meter observed.
14 On completion of adjustment, check the dynamic timing as described later in this Section.

Rotor arm modification – from July 1978
15 A strengthened rotor arm was fitted to Ducellier distributors from 1978 on and the location groove of the rotor arm stud on the shaft was widened accordingly to 4 mm (0.157 in). The rotor arm securing circlip was replaced by a spring blade located within the bore of the rotor arm.
16 The two types are not interchangeable.

Transistorised ignition system – description
17 A transistorised ignition system is fitted to GSA 1300 models produced from July of 1981. The main advantage of this system is that it requires no routine maintenance except for checking the ignition timing at the specified intervals.
18 An impulse goes from the distributor to the control unit. This makes and breaks the current to the ignition coil with the help of impulses from the impulse sender. The dwell angle is regulated electronically. From the ignition coil, the high tension impulse goes as usual to the spark plugs via the distributor rotor arm.
19 The ignition advance is still controlled by means of centrifugal weights and a vacuum chamber.
20 The impulse sender opens and closes a magnet, as opposed to an electrical circuit. This induces impulses in the magnetic pick-up or coil. The impulse sender is made up of four main parts: the stator, the magnetic pick-up (or coil), the rotor and the magnet. Whilst the stator, pick-up and magnet are connected to the distributor housing, the rotor is connected to, and rotated with, the distributor shaft.
21 The control unit, or electronic module, is of a solid state design employing transistors. It converts and amplifies the impulses from the impulse sender and sends them on to the coil, next to which it is located (photo). It also performs a second function; control of the dwell angle.

22 The magnet creates a magnetic field which passes through a stator. When the pole teeth are opposite each other, the magnetic circuit is closed; when the teeth are apart, the circuit is open. In this way the rotor opens and closes the magnetic field as it rotates; this generates the current pulses in the magnetic pick-up. The pole teeth have in effect a similar function to that of the cam lobe in a conventional distributor.

Transistorised ignition system – fault diagnosis and precautions
23 As with the conventional mechanical contact breaker ignition system, should faults occur, basic checks should be made of the HT and LT circuits. However it is most important that the following precautionary notes be observed to avoid causing damage to the transistorised system.

    (a) *When an HT lead is disconnected for testing ensure that it is earthed before starting the engine*
    (b) *Do not disconnect an HT lead whilst the engine is running*
    (c) *Due to the relatively high current which it draws, a test light should not be used for checks*
    (d) *For dynamic timing checks use only a timing light (strobe) with an induction clamp*

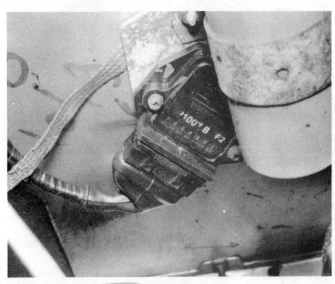

6.21 Transistorised ignition control unit

Fig. 13.38 Transistorised ignition system circuit diagram (Sec 6)

1 Ignition switch
2 Condenser (radio interference suppression)
3 Ignition coil
4 Distributor
5 Control unit

(e) A quick-action booster should never be used to start the engine and if any arc-welding is to be undertaken on the bodywork the battery leads must be disconnected

(f) The voltage produced from the HT circuit on an electronic ignition system is considerably greater than that from a conventional system. In consequence, take extra precautions when handling the HT leads with the engine running. Although not lethal, the shock experience could be severe

24 Apart from the basic checks mentioned above, more detailed checks of the transistorised ignition system will need to be carried out by your Citroën dealer or local automotive electrician, due to the specialised equipment required.

Transistorised ignition distributor – general information and overhaul

25 The main difference between this distributor type and the conventional contact breaker points type given in Chapter 3 is that the contact breaker points are replaced by a reluctor and magnetic pick-up (photo).

26 The air gap between the reluctor and magnetic pick-up is pre-set during manufacture and requires no adjustment in service. With this system the ignition timing can only be checked using a strobe light and an auxiliary revolution counter (tachometer), a static timing check not being possible. Only use a 'high tension' rev counter with an induction clamp. The advance characteristics also differ, the vacuum advance setting for checking the timing being given in the Specifications in this Chapter.

27 Testing of individual distributor components is not within the scope of the home mechanic, but the accompanying photo sequences of the Ducellier breakerless type distributor show the dismantling procedure. Renew any worn components or any items which are proved faulty by an authorised auto electrician.

28 Before removing the distributor, take off the cap and place to one side complete with leads. Disconnect the vacuum pipe, then mark the relative position of the distributor and clamping flange. The distributor can then be unbolted and removed.

29 When refitting the distributor align the relative position markings of the clamp flanges made during removal before fully tightening the clamp bolts.

30 Reconnect the cap and leads and then check the ignition timing as described in the next sub-Section.

6.25 Transistorised ignition distributor – Ducellier type

6.27A Separating distributor upper and lower bodies

6.27B Detach the earth lead and free the plug retainer ...

6.27C ... then detach the plug

6.27D Remove the plastic ring ...

6.27E ... and lift out the reluctor

6.27F The advance plate is now accessible ...

6.27G ... and can be removed

6.27H Removing the vacuum advance capsule

6.27J Lower body and advance springs

Dynamic timing using stroboscope – contact breaker ignition

31 Before commencing this timing check method on engines fitted to semi-automatic transmission models, you will first need to check and identify the correct ignition timing mark on the periphery of the torque converter driveplate. Rotate the engine and locate the larger of the two slots – B in Fig. 13.39. Now count five starter ring teeth (GS) or ten teeth (GSA) in front of this slot as indicated by the arrow and check if there is a timing index mark as shown at 'a'. If not, paint a mark accordingly.

32 On all models highlight the timing marks on the flywheel/driveplate and the relevant graduations on the timing scale with quick-drying white paint. Typist's correcting fluid is ideal.

33 The engine must be at normal operating temperature and (where applicable) the contact breaker points must be correctly adjusted and in good condition. Disconnect and plug the distributor vacuum pipe.

34 Connect a timing light (strobe) to No 1 spark plug HT lead in accordance with the maker's instructions. Some timing lights connect in series with the spark plug; others require additional connections to a 12 volt battery or to an external power supply. Position all leads clear of moving parts, and make sure that you do not get articles of clothing, long hair etc caught in engine moving parts during subsequent operations.

35 Start the engine and allow it to idle. Point the strobe at the timing marks. The flywheel/driveplate mark will appear stationary and (if the timing is correct) in alignment with the static/idle mark on the timing scale. If not, stop the engine, slacken the distributor mounting bolts and turn the distributor slightly one way or the other. Turn the distributor clockwise to retard the timing, or anti-clockwise to advance it. Tighten the mounting bolts and recheck the timing.

36 When the static/idle timing is correct, run the engine up to the specified advance check speed. Point the strobe at the timing marks and check that the flywheel/driveplate mark is aligned with the appropriate mark on the timing scale.

37 If the marks are not aligned, do not alter the distributor static timing position to align the marks, but remove the distributor and have its advance curve mechanism and characteristics checked by your Citroën dealer. This is necessary since accurate checking of the centrifugal and vacuum advance mechanisms is beyond the scope of the DIY mechanic. A rough check may be made by increasing engine speed and checking that the timing mark appears to move away from the pointer on the timing scale. If the vacuum pipe is reconnected, a further advance should be observed. Jerky movement of the timing mark, or flutter, suggests that the automatic advance mechanisms are worn or sticking.

38 When adjustment is complete, switch off the engine, disconnect the timing light and remake the original connections.

Dynamic timing using a stoboscope – transistorised ignition

39 Proceed as described above, but note that no static/idle timing is specified. Alter the distributor position if necessary to obtain the specified advance at the correct engine speed – see Specifications.

Spark plugs – removal and refitting

40 Open the bonnet. Remove the air cleaner end cover and element to improve access on the right-hand side. Also remove the air cleaner hot air pick-up tube (photo).

41 Pull the plug caps off the plugs; pulling on the cap itself, not on the HT lead. Label the leads if there is any possibility of confusion when refitting.

42 Brush or blow any dirt from around the seats of the plugs. A bicycle pump works well for this.

43 Unscrew and remove the plugs. A 3/8 in drive socket spanner, with a short extension and a ratchet handle, can be used for all four plugs (photo). A box spanner can also be used, but there is limited access for applying pressure to the tommy bar. Some other patterns of plug spanner cannot be used in some or all positions.

44 Inspect the plugs as described in Chapter 3, Section 5. Either clean them and reset the gap, or renew them. The gap on new plugs must be checked before fitting.

45 Apply a smear of copper-based anti-seize compound to the threads of each plug before fitting. Screw each plug into its hole by hand to avoid cross-threading, using a piece of tubing if wished, as suggested in Chapter 3, Section 5.

46 Final tightening of the plugs should ideally be carried out using a torque wrench. In the absence of a torque wrench, tighten each plug by no more than a quarter of a turn beyond the point where the washer contacts the plug seat.

47 Refit the plug caps, pushing them fully home onto their plugs. Note that the plug caps serve to keep any moisture in the airflow off

Fig. 13.39 Timing mark (a) on GSA with semi-automatic gearbox (Sec 6)

B   Slot in torque converter

6.40 Removing the hot air pick-up tube

6.43 Removing a spark plug

the plug connections, and also act as bungs preventing the premature escape of cooling air. Non-standard caps should not therefore be fitted.
48 Refit the air cleaner hot air pick-up tube, element and cover. Run the engine to verify that the plug leads have been refitted correctly, then close the bonnet.

7 Clutch

Modified clutch thrust bearing and hub
1   GSA models produced from August of 1981 have been fitted with a redesigned clutch thrust bearing and hub. The bearing is of the self-centering type and the inner hub is plastic. A revised retaining clip is fitted to this bearing/hub assembly and it is essential, when assembling it, to ensure that its direction is correct as shown.
2   Lubricate the bearing and hub before fitting to the guide sleeve with 'Total Multis' or similar.
3   This latest bearing and hub assembly are fully interchangeable with earlier models using the previous type of unit. The clutch adjustment for clearance remains the same.

Fig. 13.40 Clutch thrust bearing and clip fitted to later models (Sec 7)

Fig. 13.41 Orientation of clip (a) relative to thrust bearing (Sec 7)

8 Manual gearbox

Four-speed gearbox – modifications from July 1978

With the introduction of the GS X3 models in July 1978 various modifications were made to the manual gearbox, although the ratios remained the same as those fitted to the 1220 gearbox.

The modifications made are as follows:

Gearbox housing

1 To improve the thrust faces for the ball bearings the slots in the bearing seats of the primary and secondary shafts on the cover face were suppressed, see Fig. 13.42. The boss height shown was also increased so that a plug could be fitted to improve the tightness.

Primary shaft

2 This had a new rear ball bearing fitted (SKF 44 40 79A) and the torque wrench setting for the retaining nut was changed – see Specifications in this Chapter.

Secondary shaft

3 An alternative rear ball bearing was fitted in some instances and this is identified by its reference number of SKF 44 40 80C (or SNR GB 10865 on later models). Where this bearing type is fitted, the shaft diameter at the bearing location is reduced to suit being 24.5 mm (0.96 in). The adjustment washer diameter will have correspondingly changed also. The torque wrench setting for the nut with this bearing type differs and is given in the Specifications in this Chapter.

Synchromesh

4 New synchro rings with 6° cones are fitted (the previous types having 7° cones). Also modified were the pinions and sliding rings for the 1st, 2nd, 3rd and 4th gears, the profiles of the synchro rings and contact faces of 3rd and 4th gears.

5 The modified items mentioned above are not interchangeable with the corresponding components on previous gearbox types and it is therefore essential to double check and compare any new parts being fitted against those they replace to ensure correct replacement.

Gearchange lever

6 The gearchange lever was modified in December of 1978, the ball joint diameter being increased (to 35 mm from 32 mm). This in turn entailed the ball casing, seats and rubber joints being changed to suit. The early and late type gearchange assemblies or their components are not interchangeable. When fitting the later type gearchange ensure that the tie-rod is coupled snugly to the levers.

Secondary pinion

7 Later models have been fitted with retarding dowels incorporating a wear compensation provision for 3rd and 4th gear location. With these fitted the dowels of 1st and 2nd gear fitted to earlier gearbox types are eliminated.

Fig. 13.42 Later type gearbox housing (Sec 8)

1 Bearing seat slots   *2 Increased boss height*

Fig. 13.43 Identification of later pattern synchro rings (Sec 8)

Fig. 13.44 Sectional views of early type (A) and later type (B) gearchange lever assembly (Sec 8)

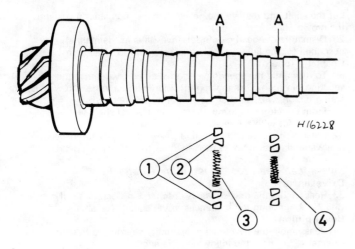

Fig. 13.45 Secondary pinion retarding dowels on later models (Sec 8)

1   Outer dowels   4   Spring – 4th gear
2   Inner dowels   A   Oil holes
3   Spring – 3rd gear

Fig. 13.46 5-speed gearbox rear cover (13), showing half the retaining bolts (14 and 12). Clutch housing and bolts are arrowed on right (Sec 8)

Five-speed gearbox – removal and refitting

8   As with the four-speed gearbox, the five-speed gearbox cannot be removed from the vehicle as a separate unit but has to be lifted out together with the engine.

9   The removal and refitting of the engine and gearbox is described in Chapter 1. This procedure should therefore be used in conjunction with the updated information for later models in Section 4 of this Chapter.

10   To dismantle and overhaul the five-speed gearbox proceed as follows.

Five-speed gearbox – dismantling procedure (stage 1)

11   Proceed as described in Section 10 of Chapter 4, paragraphs 1 to 3 inclusive.

12   Unscrew and remove the rear cover securing bolts and pull the cover away. Note that the cover is also secured by two smaller bolts on its lower edge which are removed from the front.

13   Unscrew and remove the clutch housing securing bolts and withdraw the housing forwards from the gearbox.

14   Using a suitable punch, drive out the roll pin securing the 5th gear selector onto its shaft. Support the shaft during pin removal to prevent damage or distortion to the shaft.

15   Relieve the nut lock staking on the rear end of the bevel pinion shaft and unscrew and remove the nut. To prevent the shaft from turning with the nut, select 3rd gear by pushing on the shaft fork to engage 3rd gear and also move the 5th gear sliding gear into mesh so that the two gears are simultaneously engaged.

16   The 5th gear synchromesh hub gear and fork assembly can now be removed.

17   Temporarily refit the 5th gear synchromesh unit and hand tighten the retaining nut. Engage 3rd and 5th gears simultaneously to lock the shafts (see paragraph 15). Now relieve the nut lock staking on the rear end of the primary shaft and unscrew and remove the nut. Remove the synchromesh hub and 5th gear drive pinion, the drive pinion and its spacer.

18   Unscrew the bearing thrust plate bolts and remove the plate.

19   At the differential housing end, pull free and remove the speedometer drive pinion connector.

20   Position a finger over the plug and then withdraw the split pin and remove the plug, disc, spring and ball (photo).

21   Now proceed as given in paragraphs 5 to 8 inclusive in Section 10 of Chapter 4.

Five-speed gearbox – dismantling procedure (stage 2)

22   Proceed as given in paragraph 1, sub paragraphs a, b and c in Section 11 of Chapter 4. If fitted it will also be necessary to remove the circlip and seal. Extract the cylindrical pin.

Fig. 13.47 5-speed gearbox with rear cover removed (Sec 8)

18   Sliding 5th gear   21   5th gear selector fork
19   Pinion shaft nut   22   Roll pin
20   Synchro hub

8.20 Remove the plug, split pin, disc, spring and ball

23 The 5th gear safeguard must now be disengaged. Slide the safeguard along the shaft (prising it with a screwdriver) so that it is clear of the shaft (A in Fig. 13.48). As the safeguard clears the end of shaft A the plunger and spring will eject so be prepared to catch them.

24 Move the shaft rearwards, placing a finger over the lock ball recess to prevent the ball and spring ejecting once the shaft is clear of their recess. When the shaft is clear remove the ball and spring. Now drive out the roll pin securing the shaft and withdraw the shaft. *Do not remove shaft A.*

25 Dismantle the right-hand half casing as described in paragraph 2 of Section 11 in Chapter 4.

26 Separate the control shaft from the primary shaft by extracting the circlip and remove the needle roller bearing.

27 Dismantle the bevel pinion assembly in the manner described for the four-speed gearbox (Chapter 4, Section 11, paragraph 4) but ignore the reference to the speedometer drive nut in sub-paragraph (a).

28 To dismantle the differential unit use a universal puller and remove the bearing. Extract the satellite gear shaft securing clip, drift out the shaft and remove the gears. Remove the planet gears and the crownwheel.

29 Dismantle the gearbox output driveshafts in the manner described for the later type given in paragraph 6 of Section 11, Chapter 4 (photo).

30 To dismantle the speedometer drive assembly, remove the securing pin (compress the spring), then withdraw the cup washer, spring pinion, washer, shaft, spacer and seal (photos).

31 From the clutch housing, remove the control shaft seal by levering it out with a screwdriver.

32 Clean and prepare all parts and assemblies ready for inspection, renewal and reassembly as described for the four-speed gearbox.

Five-speed gearbox – reassembly (Stage 1)
Driveshafts

33 Reassemble the driveshafts as described in Section 13 of Chapter 4, ignoring the references to the earlier type shafts.

Bevel pinion

34 Reassemble the bevel pinion assembly referring to Section 14 of Chapter 4, but note the following differences:

(a) *Paragraph 2: When fitting the 1st gear synchro unit the selector fork groove must face away from the 1st gear pinion. No retarding dowels are fitted to 1st and 2nd gear pinions*

Fig. 13.48 5th gear safeguard removal (Sec 8)

1   Shaft location pin
2   Reverse gear
3   Reverse gear shaft
4   Spacer
6   Lever
7   Lever pivot shaft
8   Selector shaft
9   Safeguard
A   Shaft (do not remove)

8.29 Output driveshaft assembly

8.30A Speedometer driveshaft unit

8.30B Speedometer driven gear showing cup, spring and retainer pin

Fig. 13.49 Bevel pinion assembly (Sec 8)

20 1st/2nd synchro hub   22 1st gear pinion
21 Synchro ring   b   Groove

(b) *Paragraphs 6 and 7: Fit the 3rd gear pinion with the lock pins and spring, then locate the synchromesh ring, hub and sliding gear assembly. To adjust the end clearance of the 3rd and 4th gears, select a stop ring of suitable thickness to give a maximum clearance at J3 (Fig. 13.50) of 0.05 mm (0.002 in). Stop rings are available in thicknesses of 1.42 to 1.58 mm (0.056 to 0.062 in) in increments of 0.4 mm (0.015 in). When selected fit the stop ring*

(c) *Paragraph 8: Refit the spring and retarding dowels, the 4th gear pinion and synchro ring followed by the adjustment washer, the thickness of which must be measured and noted, then the bearing*

(d) *Now locate the thrust plate, 5th gear pinion spacer, the synchromesh hub and sliding gear unit and the stop washer. Fit and tighten the retaining nut to 2.2 to 2.5 kgf m (16 to 18 lbf ft). Do not lock the nut by peening it at this stage. To hold the bevel pinion shaft whilst tightening the nut, clamp the 1st gear pinion interlocked with the bevel pinion by the slider of 1st/2nd gears in a vice fitted with light alloy grips*

Control (drive) shaft and primary shaft
35 Locate the needle roller bearing unit into position with face 'a' (Fig. 13.52) to the control shaft.
36 Fit the control shaft and pinion shafts together slightly opening the circlip to engage the two (photo).
37 Fit the ball bearing to the primary shaft with the shoulder pointed towards the rear (photo).

Clutch housing
38 Reassemble as described in Section 16 of Chapter 4.

Half casings
39 Assemble the right-hand half casing in the manner described in paragraphs 2 and 3 of Section 17 in Chapter 4.
40 To assemble the left-hand casing proceed as follows:

(a) *Lubricate the reverse pinion shaft with oil then slide it into position with its stop slot towards the front. Assemble the pinion with its groove to the front and spacer if fitted, as the shaft is passed through. With the shaft fully fitted insert the lockpin. When in position the lockpin must protrude slightly since it also acts as a stop for the primary shaft bearing (photos).*

Fig. 13.50 3rd/4th gear end clearance is adjusted by stop ring J3 (Sec 8)

Fig. 13.51 Bevel pinion shaft reassembly (Sec 8)

8   Drive plate   11 Stop washer
9   5th gear pinion spacer   12 Nut
10 Synchro hub

Fig. 13.52 Primary shaft needle roller bearing (15). For 'a' see text (Sec 8)

8.36 Control shaft, pinion shaft and circlip

8.37 Fit primary shaft bearing with shoulder to rear

8.40A (1) Refit reverse gear and shaft ...

8.40A (2) ... and insert lock pin

(b) Lubricate the selector driveshaft with oil and smear its detent slots with grease, then slide it through the rear bearing with its detent (lock) slots to the front. Locate the 5th gear safeguard onto the shaft as it is passed through then drive the lockpin into position so that it protrudes by 3 to 5 mm (0.118 to 0.196 in) (photo).

(c) Lubricate the spring and ball with grease and insert them into their recess and compress them with a 5 mm diameter rod to enable the shaft to pass through and retain them (photo).

(d) Now locate the plunger and spring into the 5th gear safeguard, tap the safeguard recess pin fully home, then compress the plunger into the safeguard and simultaneously slide the safeguard along to engage with the locking shaft (photos).

(e) Locate the reverse lever into position and tighten its retaining/pivot bolt from the outside (photos).

(f) Refit and tighten the reversing light switch.

Differential unit

41 Proceed as described in Section 18 of Chapter 4, but secure the satellite shaft with circlip instead of the pin used on earlier models and note location of speedometer drivegear (photo).

Bevel pinion/crownwheel – adjustment (general)

42 Refer to Section 19 in Chapter 4.

8.40B Fit selector shaft, drive roll pin into position and grease detent slots

8.40C Insert spring and ball

8.40D (1) Fit spring and plunger into safeguard

8.40D (2) Slide safeguard along its shaft to engage it with the locking shaft

8.40E (1) Refit the reverse lever ...

8.40E (2) ... and tighten its pivot bolt

8.41 Differential unit showing circlip retaining the satellite shaft. Also note the speedometer drive pinion under the bearing

Bevel pinion adjustment

43 Bevel pinion adjustment is made in a similar manner to that described for the four-speed gearbox type in Section 20 of Chapter 4, but the following differences concerning the five-speed type should be noted in paragraphs 1 and 6:

(a) *Paragraph 1: Locate the bevel pinion unit with the left half casing as previously sub-assembled with the thrust plate and 5th gear assembly – see paragraph 34, sub-paragraph (d). Secure the thrust plate with three bolts*

(b) *Paragraph 6: When the correct thickness shim has been fitted to give the correct bevel pinion adjustment, refit the bearing (photo)*

Crownwheel adjustment

44 Proceed as given in Section 21 of Chapter 4.

Five-speed gearbox – reassembly (stage 2)

45 Proceed as described in Section 22 of Chapter 4, but note the following differences (photos):

(a) *Paragraph 4: The springs in the holder plate only differ in the four-speed gearbox (photos)*

(b) *Paragraph 7: On the five-speed gearbox, coat the seal surface for the lockplate with a sealing compound, locate the lockplate and hand tighten the retaining bolts only at this stage (photo). Now tighten the half casing assembly bolts fully to the specified torque wrench setting and in the sequence shown in Fig. 13.53. The thrust plate securing bolts can then be tightened to a torque wrench setting of 2.5 to 3.0 kgf m (18 to 21 lbf ft)*

(c) *Proceed up to and including paragraph 9 (Section 22 –*

8.43 Bevel pinion (secondary) shaft assembly with rear bearing fitted together with selective washer for pinion adjustment

8.45 (1) Lower crownwheel and differential unit into position ...

8.45 (2) ... then fit the bevel pinion (secondary) shaft ...

8.45 (3) ... followed by the primary shaft assembly

8.45 (4) Insert interlock plunger of 1st/2nd gear and reverse gear selector shafts

8.45A (1) Locate holder plate (identical springs) ...

8.45A (2) ... and balljoint

8.45A (3) Locate balljoint guide and spring into right-hand casing. Grease well to retain in position when fitting case

8.45A (4) Carefully lower right-hand case into position

Fig. 13.53 Tighten the half casing bolts in alphabetical order (Sec 8)

Fig. 13.54 Sectional view of 5th gear components (Sec 8)

13 5th gear drive pinion
14 Pinion nut
15 Driven pinion bush
16 Driven pinion
17 Spacer
18 Nut
19 Synchro hub assembly
20 Stop plate
21 5th gear sliding gear

8.45B Refit the lockplate

8.45C (1) Relocate the speedometer driveshaft unit ...

8.45C (2) ... and check mesh of pinions

Chapter 4), then continue as follows for the five-speed gearbox (photos)

(d)   Locate the 5th gear drive pinion and nut (photos)

(e)   Fit the 5th gear driven pinion with its spacer followed by the hub/syncromesh sliding gear unit and bush and retain them with the stop plate washer and nut (photos)

(f)   The 5th gear drive pinion nut can now be tightened to the specified torque wrench setting of 6.0 to 7.0 kgf m (44 to 51 lbf ft). To prevent the shaft from turning select 3rd and 5th gears as described during dismantling. When the nut is tightened, lock it by peening and then disengage the gears (photos)

(g)   Now remove the nut and 5th gear hub/synchromesh assembly and the lock plate

(h)   Assemble and simultaneously refit the 5th gear selector fork, the ring and synchromesh unit ensuring that the identification groove on the sliding gear is positioned rearwards. Locate the stop plate washer and nut. Insert the stop pin to secure the selector fork on its shaft. Reselect 3rd and 5th gears as described previously and tighten the driven gear assembly nut to 22 to 25 kgf m (159 to 189 lbf ft) (photos)

(i)   Smear the rear cover mating face with sealant, then locate the cover, insert and tighten the securing bolts to the specified torque wrench settings (photo)

(j)   Adjust the reverse gear stop by first selecting reverse gear, then locate the adjuster screw (smeared with sealant) and tighten so that it is just touching the fork shaft, then

8.45D (1) Fit the 5th gear driven pinion and spacer ...

8.45D (2) ... and retaining nut

8.45E (1) Locate the 5th gear driven pinion spacer ...

8.45E (2) ... hub and sliding gear unit ...

8.45E (3) ... and nut with stop plate washer

8.45F (1) Select 3rd and 5th gears to lock assemblies for tightening ...

8.45F (2) ... the drive pinion nut

8.45H (1) Refit 5th gear selector fork ...

8.45H (2) ... then the stop plate washer and nut

8.45H (3) Drive lock pin into position to secure selector fork on shaft ...

8.45H (4) ... then tighten 5th gear synchro hub nut to specified torque

8.45I Fit the rear cover

8.45J Adjusting the reverse gear stop

8.45K Refitting a differential output shaft

unscrew it a quarter of a turn and tighten the locknut to secure (photo)

(k) Refit the differential output shafts as described in paragraph 10 of Section 22 in Chapter 4 (photo)

(l) Refit the drain plug and filler/level plug using a new copper washer for each. Tighten the plugs to the specified torque wrench setting

All gearboxes – modification from July 1983

46 From the above date, the bearing at the engine end of the gearbox primary shaft was modified. The old and new arrangements are shown in Figs. 13.55 to 13.57.

47 The primary shaft is also modified to accept the new bearing. The new type bearing and shaft can be fitted together to old type gearboxes. The old type bearing is still available for repairs.

48 When fitting the new type bearing and shaft, make sure that the locating pin in the gearbox casing enters the bearing groove (Fig. 13.58).

Fig. 13.55 Old type primary shaft bearing – sectional view (Sec 8)

Fig. 13.56 New type primary shaft bearing – sectional view (Sec 8)

1   Sleeve

Fig. 13.57 New type primary shaft bearing – note circumferential groove (Sec 8)

Fig. 13.58 Locating pin (1) must enter groove in bearing (Sec 8)

All gearboxes – oil filler plug
49 When a reversing light switch is fitted, oil may be added to the gearbox via the reversing light switch hole (after removing the switch). This hole is more accessible than the level plug hole. Refit the switch on completion, applying a little sealant to its threads.

9 Semi-automatic gearbox

Parking lock – from March 1980
1 From March 1980 the semi-automatic transmission fitted to GSA models was equipped with a parking lock. Other differences incorporated into the gearbox at this time were:

    (a) *Converter oil pump gasket had microturbine on contact surface*
    (b) *Another fork pivot pin (for 'park' function)*
    (c) *Locking pin which enables gearbox to be locked via the 1st/reverse sliding pinion*

2 When using a semi-automatic transmission with a parking lock, it is essential to ensure that the vehicle has fully stopped before moving the shift lever into the P position.

Synchromesh
3 New synchromesh assemblies were fitted with 6° cones, the modifications being similar to those made to the manual gearbox type in July 1978 (see paragraphs 4 and 5 in Section 8).

Primary shaft bearing
4 From July 1983 the primary shaft bearing was modified. See paragraphs 46 to 48 in Section 8.

10 Hydraulic system

1 From September 1976 a safety valve unit is incorporated into the hydraulic system circuit, its position being shown (A) in Fig. 13.59. Some models are also fitted with a bleed screw for the front suspension circuit (B).
2 On models produced from February 1982 the safety valve mounting position was changed and the polyamide four-way union was replaced with a rubber return pipe assembly. The revised system layout is shown in Fig. 13.60. The associated pipe fittings of this revised system are not interchangeable with the earlier type.

3 The internal construction of the safety valve was altered in April 1983. Old and new valves are interchangeable, but the electrical connector will have to be changed as well.

Depressurising (later models)
Models produced up to 1976 without safety valve
4 Position the manual height control to the 'normal' setting position, then loosen off the pressure regulator release screw. Now position the height control to its upper setting to lower the car height setting completely. If it is found that the front of the vehicle does not lower fully, adjust the height corrector accordingly.
Models produced from 1976 with safety valve
5 Position the manual height control to the 'upper' setting position, then when raised support the vehicle at this height with safety stands. Loosen off the pressure regulator release screw and then move the manual height control to the 'normal' setting position.
Models produced from 1976 with safety valve and a bleed screw on the front suspension
6 Position the manual height control to the 'normal' setting position, then loosen off the pressure release screw on the regulator. Referring to Fig. 13.64, loosen the front suspension circuit union screw (2) located on the right-hand side of the scuttle. To lower the pressure in the rear circuit of the system extract the plug from the floor cover flap and insert a short screwdriver through the exposed hole in the flap, engage it with the corrector control and push it towards the front of the vehicle.

Suspension spheres (all models) – renewal
7 Suspension spheres can be renewed independently of the suspension cylinders. The rear cylinder must be removed for access to the spheres, but the front spheres can be removed *in situ* (after depressurising). Refer to Chapter 6, Section 22 or 23.
8 Several firms offer a reconditioning or exchange service for suspension spheres. Consult the advertisements in a DIY-orientated motoring magazine to locate such firms.
9 Always use a new sealing ring between the suspension sphere and cylinder. Check for leaks on completion.

Suspension cylinder (all models) – overhaul
10 Individual components are available for suspension cylinders and in theory at least it is possible to overhaul them.
11 Hydraulic test gear is needed to check the success of cylinder overhaul, which should therefore be left to a Citroën dealer or other competent specialist.
12 Reference to the accompanying illustrations will assist the enthusiastic owner who is prepared to renew the cylinder seals on a speculative basis.

A : Safety valve
B : Union with bleed screw

—— High pressure
—·—·— Suspension pressure
—··—··— Rear brake pressure
– – – – Return
———— Overflow return

Fig. 13.59 Revised hydraulic system circuit with safety valve (Sec 10)

Fig. 13.60 Hydraulic system circuit from February 1982
(Sec 10)

1   Safety valve   4   Front height corrector
2   Rear height corrector   5   Revised return pipe assembly
3   Pressure regulator

Fig. 13.61 Safety valve (B) located on pressure regulator (Sec 10)

Fig. 13.62 Sectional view of early type safety valve (1) (Sec 10)

A High pressure feed
B To front height corrector
C To rear height corrector
D To brake control valve
E Overflow return

Fig. 13.63 Sectional view of later type safety valve (2). For A to E see Fig. 13.62 (Sec 10)

P Plunger   T Slide valve
R Spring

Fig. 13.64 Front suspension circuit union (1) and bleed screw (2) (Sec 10)

Fig. 13.65 Lowering the pressure in the rear suspension circuit using a screwdriver (arrowed) to engage the height control (Sec 10)

3   Floor cover flap

Fig. 13.66 Suspension cylinder components (Sec 10)

4   PTFE seal   7   O-ring seal
5   O-ring seal   10 Piston
6   Felt seal

Fig. 13.67 Sectional view of a suspension cylinder (Sec 10)

4   PTFE seal   6   Felt seal
5   O-ring seal   7   O-ring seal

11 Front axle and suspension

Driveshaft rubber gaiters – renewal

1   Removal and refitting of the gaiter on the outboard driveshaft joint is described in paragraphs 14 to 26 as a necessary part in the overhaul procedure.
2   Renewal of the gaiter on the inboard driveshaft joint is carried out in the following way.
3   Jack up the car and support it on axle stands. Remove the roadwheel.
4   Release the pressure from the hydraulic system, as described in this Chapter (Section 10).
5   Unscrew and remove the nuts which secure the inboard end of the driveshaft to the differential output shaft.
6   Disconnect the suspension lower arms and the steering linkage from the stub axle carrier.
7   Gently pull the driveshaft/hub assembly outwards to disengage its inboard end; then support the driveshaft on axle stands or blocks.
8   Remove the gaiter clips and withdraw the drive housing.
9   Extract the balls without damaging the needles, and remove the gaiter.
10 Clean all the components and fit the new gaiter. To do this, grease the joint trunnions and gaiter, and lever the gaiter over one joint trunnion at a time using the fingers to manipulate it.
11 Apply multi-purpose grease to the balls and needles (28 needles per joint) and locate them on the three joint trunnions.
12 Divide 7 oz (200 g) of multi-purpose grease between the interior of the drive housing and the gaiter.
13 Fit the drive housing, connect the gaiter to it, making sure that it is not twisted, then fit and tighten the two gaiter clips.

Driveshaft outboard joint – overhaul

14 It is recommended that when wear occurs in an outboard driveshaft joint, a complete or factory-reconditioned driveshaft assembly is fitted. Where parts are available, however, overhaul of the original shaft can be carried out in the following way. It should be noted that on all later models, the diameter of the balljoint stub axle component has been increased to incorporate 25 splines instead of the earlier type with 22 splines. New balljoints are only supplied as spares with 25 splines, and overhaul using one of these new assemblies will necessitate buying a new hub as well.
15 Remove the driveshaft, as described in Chapter 7, Section 10.
16 Grip the driveshaft in a vice fitted with jaw protectors.
17 Remove the clips from the outboard joint gaiter and slide the gaiter from the joint.
18 Using a flat tool as a lever, insert it between the claw and the shaft, and give the tool a sharp blow to free the joint. Do not strike

Fig. 13.68 Sectional view of driveshaft (Sec 11)

| 1 | Venting ring | 2 | Snap-ring | 3 | Yoke | 4 | Inboard balljoint |

the ball cage or the stub axle housing during this operation.

19 The ball cage cannot be dismantled.

20 Extract the ring from the end of the driveshaft, and pull off the gaiter.

21 Clean all components thoroughly. If a new joint is being fitted, apply grease to it and pack the inside of the stub axle housing with grease as well.

22 Slide the flexible gaiter onto the driveshaft and locate the venting ring as shown (Fig. 13.68).

23 Fit the snap ring to the driveshaft so that it is located 0.65 in

(16.5 mm) from the shoulder. Unless this is carried out accurately, the groove on the claw will not engage with the ring when the joint is refitted.

24 Engage the claw with the shaft so that the ring is inside the claw. Tap the end of the driveshaft with a soft-faced hammer to fully engage the joint assembly with the driveshaft.

25 Pack the interior of the flexible gaiter with 2.8 oz (80 g) of multi-purpose grease, slide the gaiter into position, and fit and tighten the clips.

26 Install the driveshaft after reference to Chapter 7, Section 10.

Fig. 13.69 Driveshaft, showing inboard components (Sec 11)

| 1 | Drive housing | 2 | Gaiter clip | 3 | Gaiter clip |

Fig. 13.70 Driveshaft, showing outboard components (Sec 11)

3   Driveshaft   4   Gaiter clip   5   Gaiter clip

Fig. 13.71 Driveshaft outboard joint exposed (Sec 11)

1   Claw   6   Cage
3   Driveshaft   7   Stub axle housing

Fig. 13.72 Sectional view of a driveshaft outboard joint (Sec 11)

1   Claw   c   0.65 in (16.5 mm)
2   Snap-ring

Driveshaft modifications – 1978 on

27 In 1978 the driveshaft diameter was increased from 22 mm to 27 mm. The vibration damper was also modified accordingly.
28 Large diameter driveshafts can be fitted in place of small ones provided that both shafts are changed at the same time. On 1977 and earlier models it will also be necessary to enlarge the driveshaft groove in the suspension upper arm (Fig. 13.73).
29 From 1979 the driveshaft mounting flanges were circular instead of three-legged.
30 From 1983 the driveshaft nut is plain and is secured with a locking collar and spring clip. These components can be used in place of the castellated nut and split pin fitted to earlier models. The tightening torque is the same.

Front hub bearings

31 As from July 1981 the hub bearing was increased in diameter being 82 mm instead of 80 mm. The associated swivel and ring nut was changed accordingly.

Lower arm joint

32 A revised fluid bloc bush and arm spindle have been fitted from November 1981 and where fitted can be identified by the marking 10-9 on the head of the spindle. This marking indicates the torque wrench setting of 9 to 10 kgf m (65 to 72 lbf ft) which is increased from 8 to 9 kgf m (58 to 65 lbf ft) of the previous type. This new type bush and spindle are interchangeable with the earlier fitting, but only as a pair, and the increase in torque wrench setting to the spindle nut must be observed.

Link rods

33 GS models from March 1979 were produced with a revised link rod between the anti-roll bar and the upper arms. This modification was necessary owing to the new type balljoint conical stem fitting on the anti-roll bar.

Suspension balls (later models) – lubrication

34 From around 1979 model year, the suspension cylinder ball and socket is sealed. Greasing as described in Chapter 7, Section 3, is no longer possible.

21 mm (0.826 in) approx.

26 mm (1.023 in) approx.

Fig. 13.73 Suspension upper arm, showing dimension of early (left) and late (right) driveshaft grooves (Sec 11)

Fig. 13.74 Later type driveshaft nut (1), locking collar (3) and spring clip (4) (Sec 11)

Fig. 13.75 Later type hub bearing ring nut with chamfer (a) (Sec 11)

Fig. 13.76 Later type lower arm joint (Sec 11)

35 Lubrication of the later type ball and socket is by LHM.
Approximately 7 cc of LHM should be introduced into the dust boot
of a new suspension cylinder. If the joint becomes dry, further LHM
can be injected via the boot vent pipe.

12 Braking system

Rear disc brake squeal – rectification

1   With a consistently lightly-loaded vehicle (driver only) the
retarding effect of the rear brakes is very slight when the foot pedal
is applied, and squeal can occur due to the lack of movement in the
caliper pistons and pads which permit dust and corrosion to build
up.
2   When the vehicle is occasionally heavily loaded, this condition is
not so likely to occur provided applications of the brake are made
several times during the journey.
3   Where squeal persists, remove one brake pad at a time and insert
a worn-out pad or backing plate only, then depress the brake pedal.
This action will have the effect of ejecting the caliper piston slightly
for it to be cleaned and smeared with LHM hydraulic fluid. When
refitting the pads smear their backing plates with a little
copper-based brake pad grease.
4   Push the piston well back into its caliper cylinder in order to
accommodate the unworn pad again. Finally, when both pads have
been refitted, apply the foot pedal two or three times to position
them against the disc.

Handbrake adjuster lubrication (GSA)

5   When adjusting the handbrake it may be found that the
eccentric adjuster screw threads have corroded and seized. In this
event, remove the two screws and lubricate the areas indicated in
Fig. 13.77 with high-melting point brake grease. Refit the screws
and adjust the handbrake.

Handbrake adjustment (GSA)

6   Raise and support the front of the vehicle on stands.
7   Remove the spare wheel and fully release the handbrake.
8   On each brake unit, release the handbrake cable adjusting
locknuts until the lever arms are in contact with the brake unit.
9   Turn each eccentric adjuster screw, in a clockwise direction until
both brake pads are just touching the disc. Continue adjustment
until the brake pads are the minimum distance from the disc without
the corresponding roadwheel binding when rotated.
10 Check for correct location of the handbrake cable and tighten
the cable adjustment nut until it touches the lever arm. Pulling on
the cable will ease this task. Tighten the locknuts.
11 Check the end of each cable adjuster to ensure that the number
of threads showing is the same (within 5 mm/0.2 in) for each brake
unit.
12 Test the handbrake for correct operation, refit the spare wheel
and lower the vehicle.

**Fig. 13.77 Later type handbrake adjuster screws. Lubricate
length L as described in text (Sec 12)**

L = 55 mm (2.2 in)

Front brake discs – from April 1979

13 Although the front brake discs remained dimensionally
unchanged, the discs fitted from this date have a circular groove in
their periphery. The wear limit of this disc type is 7 mm (0.28 in)
and the runout must not exceed 0.2 mm (0.007 in). The new type
disc must only be fitted as a pair on models previously fitted with
the earlier type disc.

Brake control valve – from July 1981

14 A revised brake control valve was fitted to all models from the
above date. The new valve has a slide valve which is reduced in
diameter to 7.5 mm (previously 8.5 mm). When fitting this control
valve type (replacement part number 95 556 217) it is essential also
to renew the brake pads at the same time, using either Textar T292
or Ferodo F578 type pads. Renew both the front brake and rear
brake pad sets. The late type control valve can be identified by a
blue marking on its body.

Front brake unit – from 1981

15 New type brake units were fitted from the above date. Although
similar in design to the previous type, the two types are not
interchangeable.

Circular groove

Fig. 13.78 Later type brake disc with circular groove (Sec 12)

Fig. 13.79 Later type front brake unit (Sec 12)

1 Caliper   3 Retaining spring
2 Pad

Fig. 13.80 Rear brake unit modifications – anti-rattle pad (2)
is no longer fitted (Sec 12)

1 Spring

FRONT OF VEHICLE

Fig. 13.81 Orientation of later type rear brake anti-rattle
pad (Sec 12)

Rear brake unit – from March 1982
16 The rear brake units on GSA models produced from the above
date were modified in having an anti-rattle plate fitted. This plate is
located between the brake pads and the pistons, while the
anti-rattle pad previously used is no longer fitted. When assembling
the pads on this latter type it is most important to ensure that the
anti-rattle plate is correctly positioned and the pad retainer spring is
located so that it rests on the rear part of the pads.

Rear brake spiral pipe – removal and refitting
17 Raise and support the rear of the vehicle. Depressurise the
hydraulic system and remove the rear roadwheel.
18 Undo the hydraulic unions at each end of the pipe. Unscrew the
three brackets and release the pipe from the brackets and metal clip.
19 Pull the outboard section of the pipe away from the suspension
arm, then rotate the pipe to wind out the spiral section. Assuming
the pipe is to be renewed, either cut off or fold up the union on the
end of the spiral to prevent it fouling.
20 When fitting the new pipe, leave the end caps in place until
after the spiral section has been wound into position. Secure the
union nut at the spiral end with sticky tape so that it does not run
back up the coils. It may be necessary to bend the end of the pipe
into the coils for fitting, then carefully unbend it afterwards, Do not
bend the spiral part.
21 Secure the hydraulic unions, using new seals moistened with
LHM. Do not overtighten the unions.
22 Secure the pipe brackets and clip. Make sure that the rubber
protectors are in place and in good condition – renew them if
necessary.
23 Check that the spiral part of the pipe does not touch the arm at
any point – there should be a clearance of at least 2 mm (0.08 in).
Carefully bend the pipe if necessary to achieve this. When the pipe

is not touching, it will 'ring' when tapped. If the pipe touches the
arm, it will eventually chafe through.
24 Bleed the hydraulic system, refit the roadwheel and lower the
vehicle. Tighten the wheel nuts to the specified torque.

Brake pad wear warning system – checking
25 If it is wished to check the function of the front brake pad wear
warning system, proceed as follows.
26 Open the bonnet and remove the spare wheel.
27 Disconnect a pad wear warning connector. Insert a metal object
such as a paper clip into the harness connector.
28 Have an assistant switch on the ignition and observe the
instrument panel warning lights. Touch the paper clip to earth
(vehicle metal) (photo). The 'pads worn' warning light should
illuminate.
29 Repeat for the other three wires, then remake the original
connections.
30 It is emphasised that even when the wear warning system is
known to be functioning, the brake pads should still be inspected
periodically.

Fig. 13.82 Rear brake spiral pipe rotation (Sec 12)

F1   Direction of removal   *F2   Direction of fitting*

12.28 Earthing a brake pad wear warning wire

13 Steering, wheels and tyres

Steering rack and pinion assembly – overhaul

1   With the steering gear removed from the vehicle as described in Chapter 9, grip the rack housing carefully in a vice fitted with soft jaws.
2   Pull the flexible bellows away from the rack housing and release the tabs on the lockwashers.
3   Hold the rack steady and unscrew the track and balljoints. Withdraw the plastic sheaths.
4   Extract the pin and unscrew the slotted threaded plug.
5   Withdraw the spring and the plunger.

6   Unbolt and remove the coverplate and withdraw the pinion, together with its bearing.
7   Pull the rack from the steering housing and then remove the rubber bush.
8   Drive out the needle bearing using a piece of 13 mm diameter tubing as a drift.
9   Clean and renew all components; renew the seal in the coverplate and the rubber bush after separating it from its support sleeve.
10   Commence reassembly by fitting the needle bearing into the pinion housing so that it is 0.04 in (1.0 mm) below the machined face of the housing. When installed, stake the bearing by using a pin punch at three equidistant points round the inner edge of the rim of the pinion housing.
11   Fit the new rubber bush complete with support sleeve.
12   Apply multi-purpose grease liberally to the needle bearing, the rack and the pinion. Slide the rack into the steering housing then fit the pinion.
13   Fit the new seal to the coverplate, and bolt the plate to the housing. Make sure that the seal lip is facing outwards and tighten the cover set bolts to the specified torque.
14   Fit the plunger and spring, having liberally applied multi-purpose grease to all components.
15   Screw in the slotted plug until it seats, then unscrew it between $1/8$ and $1/6$th of a turn.
16   Turn the pinion slowly and fully in both directions. If any binding is felt or the meshing of the teeth feels 'notchy', further release the slotted plug by the minimum required to smooth the action.
17   Fit the locking pin into the slots of the threaded plug.

Steering column lock (GSA) – removal and refitting

18   Disconnect the battery earth lead.
19   Remove the steering column lower cover, which is retained by four screws.
20   Disconnect the steering column from the universal joint on the Cardan shaft. Withdraw the steering wheel and column.
21   Remove the instrument panel, as described in Section 14.
22   Remove the two screws which secure the lower part of the dashboard on the driver's side.
23   Unbolt the column tube bracket and move it aside.
24   When a keyhole light is fitted, remove its securing screw and pivot the light out of the way.

Fig. 13.83 Sectional view of rack-and-pinion steering gear (Sec 13)

1   Plunger   3   Slotted screwed plug   5   Cover plate   7   Needle bearing
2   Spring   4   Seal   6   Pinion

Fig. 13.84 Pinion housing components (Sec 13)

7   Cover plate and seal   9   Needle bearing
8   Pinion

Fig. 13.85 Rack housing (b) and rubber bush (10) (Sec 13)

Fig. 13.86 Pinion housing slotted plug (4), spring (5) and plunger (6) (Sec 13)

25 Unplug the ignition/starter switch connector from the base of the switch. (The switch is secured to the lock by a circlip).
26 Remove the four screws which secure the column tube. Withdraw the tube, bending the lower part of the dashboard as necessary.
27 Remove the lock from the column tube by sawing a slot in the head of the securing bolt, then undoing the bolt with a screwdriver in the slot. A new shear head bolt will be needed for reassembly.
28 Fit the lock into the column tube and secure it with a new shear

Fig. 13.87 Steering column lock access – first stage (Sec 13)

1 Speaker grille	4 Dashboard lower securing screw	6 Steering column lower cover
2 Instrument panel upper screw	5 Steering column lower cover screws	7 Dashboard lower securing screw
3 Instrument panel lower screws		

Fig. 13.88 Steering column lock access – second stage (Sec 13)

a Access to speedometer cable	8 Column tube bracket	9 Ignition/starter switch connector

head bolt. Just nip up the bolt at first. Use the key to check that the lock will turn to all positions. When satisfied, tighten the bolt until its head breaks off.

29 The remainder of refitting is a reversal of the removal procedure.

Wheels and tyres – general

30 Wheels and tyres should give no real problem in use provided that a close eye is kept on them with regard to excessive wear or damage. To this end, the following points should be noted.

31 Ensure that tyre pressures are checked regularly and maintained correctly. Checking should be carried out with the tyres cold and not immediately after the vehicle has been in use. If the pressures are checked with the tyres hot, an apparently high reading will be obtained owing to heat expansion. Under no circumstances should an attempt be made to reduce the pressures to the quoted cold reading in this instance, or effective underinflation will result.

32 Underinflation will cause overheating of the tyre owing to excessive flexing of the casing, and the tread will not sit correctly on the road surface. This will cause a consequent loss of adhesion and excessive wear, not to mention the danger of sudden tyre failure due to heat build-up.

33 Overinflation will cause rapid wear of the centre part of the tyre tread coupled with reduced adhesion, harsher ride, and the danger of shock damage occurring in the tyre casing.

34 Regularly check the tyres for damage in the form of cuts or bulges, especially in the sidewalls. Remove any nails or stones embedded in the tread before they penetrate the tyre to cause deflation. If removal of a nail *does* reveal that the tyre has been punctured, refit the nail so that its point of penetration is marked. Then immediately change the wheel and have the tyre repaired by a tyre dealer. Do *not* drive on a tyre in such a condition. In many cases a puncture can be simply repaired by the use of an inner tube of the correct size and type. If in any doubt as to the possible consequences of any damage found, consult your local tyre dealer for advice.

35 Periodically remove the wheels and clean any dirt or mud from the inside and outside surfaces. Examine the wheel rims for signs of rusting, corrosion or other damage. Light alloy wheels are easily damaged by 'kerbing' whilst parking, and similarly steel wheels may become dented or buckled. Renewal of the wheel is very often the only course of remedial action possible.

36 The balance of each wheel and tyre assembly should be maintained to avoid excessive wear, not only to the tyres but also to the steering and suspension components. Wheel imbalance is normally signified by vibration through the vehicle's bodyshell, although in many cases it is particularly noticeable through the steering wheel. Conversely, it should be noted that wear or damage in suspension or steering components may cause excessive tyre wear, Out-of-round or out-of-true tyres, damaged wheels and wheel bearing wear/maladjustment also fall into this category. Balancing will not usually cure vibration caused by such wear.

37 Wheel balancing may be carried out with the wheel either on or off the vehicle. If balanced on the vehicle, ensure that the wheel-to-hub relationship is marked in some way prior to subsequent wheel removal so that it may be refitted in its original position.

38 General tyre wear is influenced to a large degree by driving style – harsh braking and acceleration or fast cornering will all produce more rapid tyre wear. Interchanging of tyres may result in more even wear, but this should only be carried out where there is no mix of tyre types on the vehicle. However, it is worth bearing in mind that if this is completely effective, the added expense of replacing a complete set of tyres simultaneously is incurred, which may prove financially restrictive for many owners.

39 Front tyres may wear unevenly as a result of wheel misalignment. The front wheels should always be correctly aligned according to the settings specified by the vehicle manufacturer.

40 Legal restrictions apply to the mixing of tyre types on a vehicle. Basically this means that a vehicle must not have tyres of differing construction on the same axle. Although it is not recommended to mix tyre types between front axle and rear axle, the only legally permissible combination is crossply at the front and radial at the rear. When mixing radial ply tyres, textile braced radials must always go on to the front axle, with steel braced radials at the rear. An obvious disadvantage of such mixing is the necessity to carry two spare tyres to avoid contravening the law in the event of a puncture.

41 In the UK, the Motor Vehicles Construction and Use Regulations apply to many aspects of tyre fitting and usage. It is suggested that a copy of these regulations is obtained from your local police if in doubt as to the current legal requirements with regard to tyre condition, minimum tread depth, etc.

Light alloy wheels (GSA)

42 Light alloy wheels are fitted to some GSA models. Inner tubes must not be fitted to this type of wheel.

43 Note that the wheel nut tightening torque is higher (and more critical) when light alloy wheels are fitted (see Specifications). Do not grease the threads of the wheel nuts or studs when light alloy wheels are fitted.

Front wheel adjustment

44 It is important that the toe-in is set with the steering and the front roadwheels in the 'straight-ahead' position.

45 To centre the steering, raise the front of the vehicle and turn the steering to full lock on one side. Mark the steering wheel rim with a piece of masking tape and then stick another piece on the instrument panel in alignment with the first piece. Now turn the steering to full opposite lock counting the number of turns as one piece of tape passes the other. Divide the total number of turns by two, then turn the steering back from the full lock position by this (half) number of turns. The steering will now be centred.

46 The front roadwheels must now be checked to see that they are in the 'straight-ahead' position. The best way to do this is to place a length of wood or steel tubing along the side of the vehicle so that it touches both sidewalls of the front and rear tyres. If it does or the roadwheel toe-in (or toe-out) is equal on both sides of the vehicle, this is satisfactory. If not, release the track-rod lock nuts and turn the track-rods in or out as necessary to achieve the basic setting without moving the previously set position of the steering wheel. This setting can be confirmed if the number of exposed threads on one track-rod is exactly equal in length to that on the opposite one.

47 Using a suitable gauge, check and adjust the toe-in by turning the track-rods equally.

48 When measuring toe-in, check the distance between the inside or the outside of the wheels rims at the rear of the wheel first and then roll the vehicle through 180° before taking the measurement between the wheels at the front part of the rim.

49 Remember that front wheel alignment can only be checked if the following conditions are complied with:

Engine running.
Body height correct (lever in 'Normal' position).
Tyres correctly inflated.
Vehicle standing on level ground.

50 Castor and camber angles are set in production and cannot be adjusted.

14 Electrical system and instruments

Speedometer drive cable

1 Some models develop a noisy speedometer drive cable after a certain period of operation.

2 If this occurs, first check that the cable routing is correct without sharp bends or any sign of pinching between body panels or components.

3 The inner cable should be greased periodically and this can be done if the complete cable assembly is first disconnected from the gearbox and speedometer ends.

4 On models where there is a join in the speedometer outer cable under the protective sleeve, part the cable by unscrewing the sleeve nut at this point.

5 Either pour thick oil down the inner cable, or charge the outer cable using a grease gun and cable lubricator fitting. A suitable fitting can be made up using the male and female end fittings from an old cable into which a grease nipple has been screwed. These old end fittings are then simply fitted temporarily to the ends of the noisy cable for the greasing operation. Take care not to get oil or grease into the speedometer itself.

Instrument panel (GSA) – removal and refitting

6 Disconnect the battery earth lead.

7 Remove the speaker grille and (when fitted) the loudspeaker on the driver's side (photos).

14.7A Remove the speaker grille by unsnapping the lugs (arrowed)

14.7B Removing the loudspeaker

14.9A Removing the instrument panel upper securing screw

14.9B Removing one of the instrument panel lower securing screws. Other screw is to right (arrowed)

14.9C Unplugging one of the instrument panel wiring connectors

Fig. 13.89 Alternator fuse – Ducellier type shown (Sec 14)

8 Disconnect the speedometer cable by tugging it sharply from under the bonnet.

9 Remove the three screws which secure the instrument panel. Working through the loudspeaker hole, release the panel and tip it away from the dashboard at the top. Unplug the electrical connectors and withdraw the panel (photos).

10 Before refitting, feed the speedometer cable into the vehicle to provide enough slack for reconnection. It may be necessary to release the cable from its bulkhead grommet when doing this. Connect the cable to the speedometer by reaching through the loudspeaker hole.

11 The remainder of refitting is a reversal of the removal procedure.

Alternator fuse (GS) – renewal

12 Some Ducellier and Paris-Rhone alternators with separate regulator have a built-in fuse. If alternator output fails and the drivebelt is OK, check the fuse as follows.

13 Disconnect the battery earth lead.

14 Disconnect the output (heavy) lead from the rear of the alternator. Remove the black plastic cover, freeing its spring clip if necessary.

15 The fuse should now be accessible. It takes the form of a copper strip printed on a plastic rectangle. Remove the central nut and the screw at each side and extract the fuse.

16 If the copper strip is broken or burnt, the fuse must be renewed. Check for burning around the securing holes. In an emergency the fuse can be 'repaired' by refitting it and winding 15 amp domestic fuse wire around the central stud and under the heads of the side screws.

17 Fit the new fuse and secure it with the nut and screws. Make sure the fuse fastenings are secure: loose fastenings will lead to poor contact and rapid burning.

18 Refit the plastic cover and reconnect the alternator output lead.

19 Reconnect the battery, run the engine and check that the alternator output is satisfactory.

20 If the alternator fuse persistently blows for no apparent reason, have the charging circuit checked by an auto-electrician.

Alternator – later models

21 On later models an alternator with a built-in voltage regulator is fitted. Removal and refitting procedures are unchanged.

Starter motor – later models

22 Although later type starter motors have been fitted, their basic construction and operation is the same as the earlier types described in Chapter 10.

23 On the Ducellier starter motor the pinion adjustment is set in the same manner, but the clearance between the sleeve and bolt head must be set to 1.5 to 1.0 mm.

24 On the Paris-Rhone starter motor the pinion adjustment is made by turning the eccentric sleeve in the desired direction after removing the shaft and partially withdrawing the sleeve from the bore splines.

25 On both types the starter pinion adjustment should be as given below:

    Solenoid – not energised 46.8 mm (minimum)
    Solenoid – energised 37.3 mm (maximum)

Left column switch block (satellite type) – warning light bulb renewal

26 Prise free and pull the switch cover to the left and remove it. The bulb can now be withdrawn for inspection/renewal. Refit the cover to complete.

Right column keyboard switch (satellite type) – warning light bulb renewal

27 Use a suitable small screwdriver with a fine blade and inserting it each side of the pushbutton to be removed, disengage the anchor pins. The button can then be pulled free and the bulb extracted using a small hooked implement to aid its removal.

Fig. 13.90 Pinion adjustment – Ducellier starter motor (Sec 14)

1 Bolt   *2 Sleeve*

Fig. 13.91 Pinion adjustment – Paris-Rhone starter motor (Sec 14)

3 Eccentric sleeve   *4 Shaft*

Fig. 13.92 Starter pinion adjustment dimensions (Sec 14)

A Not energised   *B Energised*

28 Refit the pushbutton unit by simply pushing it back into position until it is felt to engage with the anchor pins.

Right column keyboard switch (satellite type) – adding a new function switch
29 Pull free the end covers, prising from the bottom. Then using a couple of small screwdrivers, detach the end faces by levering them outwards and push the cover free.
30 Now remove the dummy pushbutton by inserting the screwdrivers to release the pushbutton retaining stubs (in the middle line of the button). The pushbutton will spring free when released and the lock ring can then be removed.
31 The backing plate must now be slid backwards from the unit. So align the wiring then unscrew and remove the two backplate retaining screws and withdraw the plate along the wires, (taking care not to disconnect them).
32 If the new function switch has an indicator light, fit the two blades into the cross-shaped hole (A in Fig. 13.97). Fit the blades so that they are positioned in the same manner as those for the heated rear window switch. The blades must be fully inserted without bending or deforming them.
33 If the switch has a latch pushbutton fit the catch into its aperture on the backplate side and locate the spring.
34 Fit the bulb into position then locate the pushbutton, pushing it down to engage with the retaining pins. It is important not to deform the pushbutton contact strips during the above operations.
35 Relocate the backplate and insert the retaining screws turning them about a half turn and hold the backplate against the screw heads.
36 The wiring for the new switch(es) is now located. Insert the wiring contacts, as indicated by the lead and backplate markings, onto the housing, then fit the backplate and fully tighten its retaining screws. Check when tightened that the backplate corners and housing are touching (B in Fig. 13.98), also that the leads are securely positioned.
37 For front foglamp function the yellow lead is engaged with the vacant space in the yellow connector.
38 Refit the switch unit and faces and covers.

Rear wiper motor – removal and refitting
39 Disconnect the battery earth lead.
40 Remove the wiper blade, arm and gland nut.
41 From inside the tailgate remove the screws which secure the wiper motor. There are two screws on Estate models and four screws on Saloons. Withdraw the motor and unplug its wiring connector.
42 Refit in the reverse order to removal.

Fig. 13.93 Later type switches and instrument panel (Sec 14)

2 Left-hand satellite switch   3 Instrument panel   4 Right-hand satellite switch   5 Warning light access cover

Fig. 13.94 Prising free the switch and faces (Sec 14)

Fig. 13.95 Removing the dummy button (Sec 14)

Fig. 13.96 Slide the backplate away from the switches
(Sec 14)

Rear light bulb renewal – GSA Estate
43 Access to the light bulbs is gained from inside the vehicle after
unclipping an access hatch (photo).
44 Carefully free the bulbholder unit from the lens/reflector
assembly and withdraw it through the hatch (photo).
45 Renew the bulb(s) and check for correct operation, then refit
the bulb holder unit and the access hatch.

Direction indicator flasher (GSA) – removal and refitting
46 Disconnect the battery earth lead.
47 Remove the instrument panel, as described earlier in this
Section.
48 Undo the securing screw, disconnect the wiring plug and
remove the flasher unit (photo).
49 Refit by reversing the removal operations.

Fig. 13.98 Backplate (1) is first located against screw heads (A), finally against housing (2) at corners (B) (Sec 14)

Fig. 13.97 Function switch detail (Sec 14)

1	Catch	3	Blade
2	Spring	A	Indicator light blades hole

Fig. 13.99 Rear wiper motor (E) and retaining bolts (6) – Estate. Also shown is aperture (B) for trim screw (5) (Sec 14)

14.43 Rear light bulb access hatch (GSA Estate)

14.44 Rear light bulb holder unit (GSA Estate)

14.48 Flasher unit location – securing screw arrowed

Colour code

Bc	White
Bl	Blue
Gr	Grey
J	Yellow
Ve	Green
Mr	Brown
Mv	Mauve
N	Black
R	Red

F + symbol =
Insulation colour
Fv = Flying lead

Legend

1015 and 1220 ———
1220 - - - - - -
Options + + + +

18

1 — R, Bl

2 — Mr, Ve, F.Gr

3 — Gr

4 — Bc

5 — Bc

6 — Gr

7 — Mr, Ve, F.Gr

8 — Bl, R

9 — Exc, +, M, J

10 — Bl, Gr

11 — Gr, Gr

12

13 — Mr

14 — N, R

15 — Bl

16 — Bat, Rup, Bl

17 — J J, Bl Bl, R R, Ve Ve

19 — Gr

20

21 — Ve

22 — Mv

23 — F.Gr, F.J, F.Bl

24

25 — Mr

26 — N

27 — R, N

28 — Mr 8, Bc 7, Mv 6, Ve 5, F.J 4, F.N 3, F.Gr 2, R 1

29 — Mr

68

F.V, Mv

R, N, Bc, Bl

R, Bc, F.Ve, B, N

F.Gr, R, J, V, F.Mr, M, Bc

Mr, R

Gr, Bl, Bc, Mv, Ve, R, J, N, Mr

Fig. 13.100 Wiring diagram for GSX and GS X2 models. For key see page 190

Fig. 13.100 Wiring diagram for GSX and GS X2 models. For key see page 190 (continued)

Key to Fig. 13.100. Not all items are fitted to all models

1 Front lamp cluster (RH)	35 Battery condition meter and lighting
2 Front headlamp (RH)	36 Tachometer and lighting
3 Supplementary headlamp (RH)	37 Speedometer and lighting
4 1st horn	38 Fuel gauge sender unit and lighting
5 2nd horn	39 Clock and lighting
6 Supplementary headlamp (LH)	40 Direction indicators, horn and headlamps flasher switch
7 Front headlamp (LH)	41 Main beam headlamp relay
8 Front lamp cluster (LH)	42 Warning lamp for hazard warning
9 Alternator	43 Engine oil temperature and brake pad wear warning lamp
10 Engine oil temperature switch	44 Engine oil pressure warning lamp
11 Brake unit (RH)	45 Hydraulic pressure warning lamp
12 Brake unit (LH)	46 Flasher unit
13 Engine oil pressure switch	47 Cigar lighter (1220)
14 Starter motor	48 Lighting switch
15 Distributor	49 Windscreen wiper and washer switch
16 Ignition coil	50 Fuel gauge rheostat
17 Fusebox	51 Interior lamp
18 Screenwasher pump	52 Fresh air blower switch
19 Hydraulic pressure switch	53 Warm air blower switch
20 Windscreen wiper motor	54 Heater rear window switch
21 Warm air blower	55 Hazard warning switch
22 Reversing lamp switch (1220)	56 Heated rear window
23 Voltage regulator	57 Rear direction indicator (RH)
24 Battery	58 Stoplamp (RH)
25 Door pillar switch (RH)	59 Tail lamp (RH)
26 Accessory terminal	60 Reversing lamp (RH) (1220)
27 Stoplamp switch	61 Boot lamp
28 Anti-theft switch	62 Number plate lamp
29 Door pillar switch (LH)	63 Boot lamp switch
30 Direction indicator warning lamp	64 Rear direction indicator (LH)
31 Dashboard lighting rheostat	65 Stoplamp (LH)
32 Main beam warning lamp	66 Tail lamp (LH)
33 Sidelamp warning lamp	67 Reversing lamp (LH) (1220)
34 Heater rear window warning lamp (optional)	68 Fresh air blower

Fuse rating
1   10 amp
2   16 amp
3   16 amp
4   10 amp

Key to Fig. 13.101. Not all items are fitted to all models

1 Front sidelight (RH) Direction indicator (RH)
2 Headlamp, main and dipped beams (RH)
3 Horn
4 Front fog lamp (RH) (X3)
5 Electrovalve for compensated idling (converter)
6 Front fog lamp (LH)
7 Headlamp, main and dipped beams (LH)
8 Front sidelight (LH) Direction indicator (LH)
9 Alternator with regulator
10 Suppressor capacitor
11 Idling damper
12 Engine oil temperature switch
13 Front brake unit (RH)
14 Front brake unit (LH)
15 Socket for diagnosis (12-contact)
16 Relay for torque converter (optional)
17 Relay for front fog lamps (X3)
18 Reversing lamp cut-off relay (X3)
19 Engine oil pressure switch
20 Windscreen washer pump
21 Hydraulic fluid pressure switch
22 Starter
23 Distributor
24 Suppressor capacitor
25 Ignition coil
26 TDC sensor
27 Battery
28 Contact for hydraulic fluid level
29 Windscreen wiper motor
30 Declutching solenoid (converter)
31 Oil temperature switch (converter)
32 Reversing lamp switch
33 Switch unit on gearbox (converter)
34 Air blower
35 Fusebox
36 Door pillar switch (RH)
37 Ignition switch (RH)
38 Anti-theft ignition switch
39 Windscreen wiper timer
40 Flasher unit
41 Braking light switch
42 Choke knob
43 Blower and lighting switch
44 Door pillar switch (LH)
45 Switches on keyboard:
       Rear-window heating
       Hazard warning lamp
       Front fog lamps (X3)
       Rear fog lamps
       Rear window wiper, intermittent
       Rear window washer/wiper, timed
46 Speedometer unit:
       Battery charge warning lamp
       Front brake wear warning lamp
       Converter oil temperature warning lamp (option)
       Engine oil temperature warning lamp
       Petrol level low warning lamp

Engine oil pressure warning lamp
Emergency STOP indicator lamp
Hydraulic fluid level warning light
Petrol gauge receiver
Clock and light
Tachometer
Silhouette light
Drum light
Odometer light
Petrol gauge receiver light
Choke warning lamp
47 Drum and silhouette lighting rheostat
48 Switching unit (satellite):
       Front windscreen/washer/wiper control
       Horn control
       Flasher control and indicator
       Lighting and headlamp flasher control
       Headlamp/dipped/sidelight indicators
49 Connector for radio power supply
50 Cigarette lighter
51 Door sill light
52 Fuel gauge rheostat
53 Rear window heating
54 Dome light
55 Rear window wiper timer
56 Rear window wiper motor
57 Rear lamp cluster (RH):
       Stoplights and sidelights
       Direction indicator
       Reversing light
       Fog lamp
58 Boot light switch
59 License-plate lights
60 Rear lamp cluster (LH):
       Stoplights and sidelights
       Direction light
       Reversing light
       Fog light
61 Rear window washer pump
62 Boot light
63 Choke indicator unit

Cable harness key
No identification mark: Front
C Converter (optional)
D Diagnosis
AR Rear
P Dome light
VS Choke indicator
DP Rear door (RH)
GP Rear door (LH)
MR Earths, rear
EC Boot light
EC Boot light
IEG Intermediate, rear window wiper
... X3 only

Colour codes

Bc White	Mr Brown
Bl Blue	Mv Mauve
Gr Grey	N Black
J Yellow	R Red
Ve Green	

F. + colour code = insulation colour

GSA 7/80 →

Fig. 13.101 Wiring diagram for GSA models – 1980/1981. For key see page 191

Fig. 13.102 Wiring diagram for GSA models – 1981/1982. For key see page 196

Fig. 13.103 Wiring digram for GSA models – 1983/1984. For key see page 196

Fig. 13.103 Wiring diagram for GSA models – **1983/1984** (continued). For key see page 196

Key to Figs. 13.102 and 13.103. Not all items are fitted to all models

1 Front sidelight (RH) Direction indicator (RH)
2 Headlamp, main and dipped beam (RH)
3 Front fog lamp (RH) (X3)
4 Electrovalve for compensated idling (converter)
5 Front fog lamp (LH) (X3)
6 Headlamp, main and dipped beams (LH)
7 Front sidelamp (LH) Direction indicator (LH)
8 Horn
9 Alternator with regulator
10 Suppressor capacitor
11 Idling damper
12 Engine oil temperature switch (60°C) (converter)
13 Fast idle relay (converter)
14 Relay for torque converter (optional)
15 Front brake unit (RH)
16 Front brake unit (LH)
17 Socket for diaphragm (12-contact)
18 Ignition module unit (1300)
19 Relay for front fog lamps (X3)
20 Rear fog lamps cut-off relay (X3)
21 Engine oil pressure switch
22 Starter motor
23 Distributor
24 TDC sensor
25 Ignition coil
26 Suppressor capacitor
27 Econoscope sensor
28 Windscreen washer pump
29 Hydraulic fluid pressure switch.
30 Engine oil thermal switch
31 Switch for hydraulic fluid level
32 Windscreen wiper motor
33 Declutching solenoid (converter)
34 Switch for reversing lamps
35 Oil temperature switch (converter)
36 Air blower
37 Switch unit on gearbox (converter)
38 Battery
39 Fusebox
40 Door pillar switch (RH)
41 Ignition keyhole lamp
42 Ignition switch
43 Rheostat for drum and silhouette lighting
44 Sockets for radio supply (optional)
45 Windscreen wiper timer
46 Flasher unit
47 Stoplamp switch
48 Choke lamp unit
49 Choke knob
50 Blower control and lighting
51 Door pillar switch (LH)
52 Switches on satellite:
    Heated rear window
    Hazard warning lamp
    Front fog lamps (X3)
    Rear fog lamps
    Rear window wiper, intermittent
    Rear window washer/wiper, timed
    Econoscope switch

53 Rheostat for fuel-gauge unit
54 Speedometer unit:
    Battery charge warning lamp
    Front brake pad warning lamp
    Converter oil temperature warning lamp (optional)
    Engine oil temperature warning lamp
    Low fuel level warning lamp
    Engine oil pressure warning lamp
    Emergency STOP indicator lamp
    Hydraulic fluid level warning lamp
    Petrol gauge receiver
    Clock and lamp
    Tachometer
    Silhouette lamp
    Drum lamp
    Odometer lamp
    Petrol gauge receiver lamp
    Choke knob lamp
    Econoscope lamps
55 Switching unit (satellite):
    Windscreen washer/wiper control
    Horn control
    Direction indicator control and warning lamp
    Headlamp lighting and flasher control
    Warning lamps for main beam/dipped side-lamp
56 Cigar lighter
57 Door sill lamp
58 Heated rear window
59 Interior lamp
60 Rear window wiper timer
61 Rear window wiper motor
62 Rear lamp cluster (RH):
    Stoplamp and tail lamp
    Direction indicator
    Reversing lamp
    Fog lamp
63 Boot lamp switch
64 Number plate lamp
65 Boot lamp
66 Rear lamp cluster (LH):
    Stoplamp and tail lamp
    Direction indicator
    Reversing lamp
    Fog lamp
67 Rear window washer pump

Cable harness key
No identification mark: Front
C Converter
D Diagnostic
E Econoscope
AR Rear
P Interior lamp
GP Rear door (LH)
DP Rear door (RH)
AT Transistorized ignition system
EC Boot lamp
MR Rear earthing points

Colour codes

Bc	White	Mr	Brown
Bl	Blue	Mv	Mauve
Gr	Grey	N	Black
J	Yellow	R	Red
Ve	Green		

F. + colour code = insulation colour

Key to Fig. 13.104. Not all items are fitted to all models

1 Front sidelamp and direction indicator (RH)
2 Headlamp (RH)
3 Horn
4 Front fog lamp (RH)
6 Front fog lamp (LH)
7 Headlamp (LH)
8 Front sidelamp and direction indicator (LH)
9 Alternator with voltage regulator
10 Radio interference suppressor
11 Idle cut-off solenoid
12 Oil temperature switch (engine)
13 Front brake caliper (RH)
14 Front brake caliper (LH)
15 Diagnostic socket
17 Front fog lamp relay
18 Rear fog lamp relay
19 Oil pressure switch
20 Starter motor
21 Distributor
22 TDC sensor
23 Choke indicator lamp flasher
24 Radio interference suppressor
25 Ignition coil
26 Econoscope sensor
27 Fusebox
28 Windscreen washer pump
29 Hydraulic system pressure switch
31 Hydraulic fluid level switch
32 Windscreen wiper motor
33 Air blower
34 Reversing lamp switch
37 Battery
38 Door pillar switch (RH)
39 Door sill lamp
40 Air blower control
41 Windscreen wiper delay unit
42 Stop-lamp switch
43 Door pillar switch (LH)
44 Cigarette lighter

45 Radio connector
46 Satellite switches (RH)
47 Instrument panel
48 Instrument illumination rheostat
49 Flasher unit
50 Satellite switches (LH)
51 Ignition keyhole lamp
52 Ignition/starter switch
53 Choke control
54 Fuel gauge sender unit
55 Interior lamp
56 Heated rear window
57 Rear wiper delay unit
58 Rear lamp cluster (RH)
59 Luggage area lamp switch
60 Rear wiper motor
61 Number plate lamps
62 Luggage area lamp
63 Rear lamp cluster (LH)
64 Rear washer pump
67 Ignition module

Earthing points
m1 Alternator
m2 Bonnet hinge (RH)
m3 Bonnet hinge (LH)
m5 Luggage area lamp switch
m6 Inside luggage area (RH)
m7 Inside luggage area (LH)

Harness identification
AR Rear
AT Ignition system
AV Front
DP Tailgate (RH side)
EC Luggage area lamp
GP Tailgate (LH side)
P Interior lamp

Colour codes

Bc White	Mr Brown
Bl Blue	Mv Mauve
Gr Grey	N Black
J Yellow	R Red
Ve Green	

F. + colour code = insulation colour

Fig. 13.104 Wiring digram for GSA models – 1985. For key see page 197

Fig. 13.104 Wiring diagram for GSA models – 1985 (continued). For key see page 197

Fig. 13.105 Wiring and circuit diagrams – Decel system. For colour code see main wiring diagrams

1	Idle cut-off solenoid	3	Ignition coil	5	Clutch switch
2	Throttle switch	4	RPM sensor	F.AV	Front harness

C	Decel harness
m3	Earth (bonnet LH hinge)

Fig. 13.106 Heater/ventilation unit, showing air passages
(Sec 15)

Fig. 13.107 Heater blower unit (Sec 15)

Flaps :
V1 : Floor/windscreen distributor
(LH control)
V2 : Hot cold selector (RH control)
V3 : Air intake flap and blower
control (centre control)

Fig. 13.108 Schematic layout of heater and ventilation circuits (Sec 15)

15 Heating and ventilating system

General

1   The fresh air system relies upon air being drawn in through the grille at the base of the windscreen.
2   Fresh air ducts are located at both ends of the facia panel; two sets of controls are provided, one for air distribution and one for temperature.
3   The heater assembly consists of ducts with detachable covers which surround the exhaust front pipes (refer to Figs. 1.16 and 1.17 in Chapter 1). Air warmed by conduction is then lead through a distribution box and flexible hoses to the vehicle interior.
4   The heater control lever knobs are removed simply by pulling them off. The control cable to the heater distribution box can then be disconnected by releasing its swivel clamp from the flap lever.

16 Rear axle and suspension

Suspension arm support tube – removal and refitting (GSA)

A Citroën tool set, number 2074-T, is required to remove and refit the suspension arm support tube on GSA models.
1   Remove the suspension arm as described in Section 3 of Chapter 11, but to depressurise the hydraulic system refer to Section

10 in this Chapter and use Citroën special extractor tool number 4036-T to disengage the axle arm from the anti-roll bar.
2   Remove the inspection plate in the boot floor, then referring to Figure 13.110, unscrew the automatic height control attachment screw, then withdraw the anti-roll bar from the left side of the vehicle. Remove the locknut and detach the automatic height control rod.
3   Measure the amount the support tube protrudes beyond the axle unit and make a note of it. Now locate the stem A of special tool 2074-T together with parts B, C, D and E. When fitted check that their positions are correct and if required the spring pressure C can be adjusted to provide a satisfactory lock for items F and G. Locate the assembly into the support tube up to the automatic control access aperture (a) and hold the control unit up.
4   Now screw hook H onto item F and engage this assembly to aperture (a). Lock F into groove (b) and remove the hook.
5   Move the stem A in arrowed direction (Fig. 13.113), engage assembly with support tube and locate items I, J, K and L.
6   With the support tube removed the special tool can be dismantled, but leave items B, C, D and E in position.
7   To refit, reassemble the stem to the support tube location in the axle unit up to the automatic control access aperture (a). The automatic height control unit must be supported as during removal.

Fig. 13.109 Citroën tool 403GT used for detaching rear axle arm from anti-roll bar (Sec 16)

Fig. 13.110 Automatic height control attachments (Sec 16)

1   Rod   4   Attachment screw
2   Nut   a   Aperture
3   Control

Fig. 13.111 Citroën tool 2074-T components. For key see text (Sec 16)

Fig. 13.112 Measuring the suspension arm tube protrusion (Sec 16)

Tie a suitable length of thin string to item G so that it can be retrieved should it accidentally fall into the unit during assembly. Fit the hook H to item G, then engage the assembly through aperture (a) and slot G into the location groove and check that it is correctly positioned before removing the hook H.

8   Locate the stem into the support tube and assemble parts J, K and L as shown (Fig. 13.114). Supporting the stem, insert the support tube into the axle unit. Hand tighten the nut L to contact part J, then retaining the stem in the horizontal position further tighten the nut to fully position the support tube. The tightening torque of the tool nut is high during the whole operation of fitting the support tube and very high when the tube is fully positioned.

9   Check that the tube protrudes approximately the same distance from the suspension unit as noted during removal.

10 Special tool 2074-T can now be removed.

11 Relocate the anti-roll bar and the suspension arms. Refer to Section 4 of Chapter 11 for suspension arm refitting and check/adjust their lateral play as described in Section 5 of that Chapter.

Rear hub (all models) – removal and refitting without bearing renewal

12 If it is wished to remove the rear hub without disturbing the bearing – for instance to renew a brake disc – proceed as follows.

13 Raise and support the rear of the vehicle and remove the roadwheel.

Fig. 13.113 Suspension arm support tube removal. Letters refer to parts of tool 2074-T (Sec 16)

Fig. 13.114 Suspension arm support tube refitting. Letters refer to parts of tool 2074-T (Sec 16)

14 Remove the brake caliper on the side concerned.
15 Remove the ring nut sealing cap with a hammer and chisel. A new sealing cap must be obtained for reassembly.
16 Relieve the stacking and undo the hub nut. This nut is very tight. Obtain a new nut for reassembly.
17 Remove the hub/brake disc assembly, using a puller if necessary.
18 When refitting, use a new hub nut and tighten it to the specified torque, then stake it into the spindle groove. Smear the sealing cap and the ring nut with sealant, then tap the cap into place. If available use Citroën tools OUT 30 4071-T and 5601-T to seat the cap, as direct hammer blows may distort the cap and impair its sealing properties.
19 The remainder of refitting is a reversal of the removal procedure. Bleed the brake hydraulic system on completion.

17 Bodywork and fittings

Door trim panel (later models) – removal and refitting

1   To remove the door trim panel on later models first carefully peel back the armrest trim which is secured by a self-adhesive strip. Prise free the blanking plugs for access to the armrest securing screws.
2   Door trim panel removal procedures are now as described in Section 14 of Chapter 12.
3   Refitting is the reversal of the removal procedure but when relocating the armrest trim, clean the contact area with methylated spirit and then apply a new self-adhesive strip to stick the trim back into position.

Rear view mirror (later models) – removal and refitting

4   To remove the door rear view mirror prise free the protector shield from the baseplate to gain access to the two retaining screws. Unscrew and remove the screws and partially withdraw the mirror. You will now need to unscrew and remove the baseplate retaining screw which is recessed within the plate. If available, use Citroën special tool number MR 630-12/49 to remove this screw.
5   From inside the vehicle remove the control retaining nut and extract the retaining pin to disconnect the control cable and allow full removal of the mirror.
6   Refit in the reverse order to removal and check the operation of the adjustment control on completion.

Hatchback door – removal and refitting

7   Raise the hatchback door then remove the cover from the aperture on the right-hand inner wing panel at the rear. Detach the three wires of the wiring harness and tie a length of string to the harness then pull the harness through the body pillar. The string can then be untied from the harness but left in position in the pillar.
8   On models fitted with a rear window wiper detach the wire to the motor and pull it through in a similar manner to that described above.
9   If the hatchback door is being renewed then detach the wires from the accessories and extract the harness from the door.

Fig. 13.115 Rear hub bearing sealing cap (1) and ring nut (Sec 16)

Fig. 13.116 Fitting a new sealing cap using tools 4071-T, 5601-T and a hammer (Sec 16)

Fig. 13.117 Door mirror retaining screws (arrowed) (Sec 17)

Fig. 13.118 Removing the mirror baseplate screw with tool MR.630-12/49 (Sec 17)

Fig. 13.119 Extract the pin from the mirror adjustment control (G) in the direction arrowed (Sec 17)

10 Partly detach the rubber seal strip from the top edge and then disconnect the earth wire.

11 Prise free the retaining clip, remove the washer and detach the stay rod each side. An assistant will be required to support the door once the stay rods are detached.

12 Remove the hinge screws and lift the hatchback door clear of the vehicle.

13 Refitting is a reversal of the removal procedure. Before fully tightening the hinge screws, align the door to give a clearance of 6 mm (0.23 in) between the door edge and the roof and quarter cant panels.

14 Pull the wiring harness back through the body pillar by reattaching the string left in position during removal.

15 On completion check the operation of the hatchback door and its accessories.

Hatchback door – dismantling and reassembly

16 To remove the lock control first remove the two securing screws on the underside, then prise free the two small trim panels each side of the lock to allow access to the lock control retaining nuts and washers.

17 To remove the number plate lights, detach the wiring connectors in the right-hand side aperture then remove the light unit fasteners and withdraw the light unit(s).

18 Wiper motor removal is covered in Section 14.

19 Refitting of the components to the hatchback door is a reversal of the removal procedure. Check the operation of the number plate lights and rear window wiper on completion.

Tailgate (GSA Estate) – general

20 Removal of the tailgate on GSA models is similar to that described for earlier models in Section 10 of Chapter 12, but in addition to detaching the main feed wiring harness connections also detach the feed wires from the heated rear window at each side.

21 To remove the tailgate lock first remove the catch which is secured by three screws to the inside face of the tailgate, then disconnect the water outlet pipe and prise free the lock unit retaining clip. The lock unit can then be withdrawn.

22 Wiper motor removal is covered in Section 14.

Fig. 13.120 Hatchback door attachments (Sec 17)

2 Hinge screws	4 Hinge screws	C Earth wire
3 Earth wire screw	B Light wiring harness	D Wiper wiring harness

Fig. 13.121 Hatchback door components (Sec 17)

3	Earth wire screw	5	Stop screw	D	Stop
4	Lock screws	C	Stop	E	Embellisher retaining lugs

Fig. 13.122 GSA Estate tailgate details (Sec 17)

3	Stay clip	B	Seal	D	Heated rear window connector
A	Main wiring harness	C	Heated rear window connector		

**Fig. 13.123 Tailgate lock (GSA) with catch removed
(Sec 17)**

7   Clip   G   Locknut
F   Water outlet pipe

23 The refitting of the tailgate and its associated components is a
reversal of the removal procedure. On completion check the
operation of the number plate lights, and also the bumpers for
satisfactory alignment.

Rear bumpers (GSA) – removal and refitting

24 To remove the corner section bumpers, remove the two securing
bolts at the bumper leading edge along the side and the two bolts
from the end face at the rear.
25 The bumper centre section is removed by detaching the number
plate light wires, then unscrewing the four retaining bolts (two each
side).
26 Refitting of the rear corner and central bumper sections is a
reversal of the removal procedure. On completion check the
operation of the number plate lights, and also the bumpers for
satisfactory alignment.

Sunroof (GSA) – adjustment

27 Should any problems occur which necessitate the removal and
refitting of the sunroof, it is a task to be entrusted to your Citroën
dealer, but adjustments to the sunroof can be made as follows.
28 Loosen off the three runner screws each side just enough to
allow the runners to be moved for adjustment.
29 Adjust the runners so that there is a clearance of 11 mm (0.43
in) between the edge of the roof and the sliding panel. Alignment
must be within 1.5 mm (0.06 in) and the panel, when closed, must
be level with the roof line.
30 Adjust the sliding panel in a similiar manner.

Dashboard (GSA) – removal and refitting

31 Disconnect the battery earth lead connection.
32 Detach the carburettor choke cable.
33 Disconnect the speedometer cable and withdraw it through the
engine compartment.
34 Detach the handbrake control (on the engine compartment
side).
35 Remove the instrument panel as described in Section 14 of this
Chapter.
36 Detach and remove the ventilation and loudspeaker grilles each
side and also remove the ashtray.
37 Disconnect and remove the ventilation and heating controls and
the heating ventilation control grille.
38 On the passenger side remove the door tower light.
39 Detach and remove the control ventilation grille unit.
40 Withdraw the choke control, then remove the steering column
lower cover retaining screws and lower the cover.
41 Remove the steering wheel and column.

**Fig. 13.124 Sunroof adjustment tolerances. Dimensions in
mm (Sec 17)**

A   Front edge   C   Side
B   Rear edge   H   = 1 mm (max)

Fig. 13.125 GSA dashboard removal – first stage. LHD shown, RHD similar (Sec 17)

1 Instrument panel screw
3 Dashboard screw
4 Lower cover screw
5 Instrument panel screws
6 Lower cover screws
7 Lower cover screw
8 Dashboard screw
J Steering column lower cover

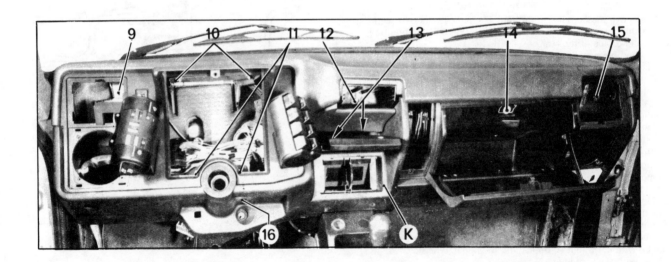

Fig. 13.126 GSA dashboard removal – second stage. LHD shown, RHD similar (Sec 17)

9   Dashboard screw
10 Dashboard screws
11 Dashboard screws
12 Dashboard screw
13 Handbrake handle screws
14 Dashboard screw
15 Dashboard screw
16 Ignition key light screw
K   Centre vent

42 Remove the ignition key illumination light unit.
43 Unscrew the handle retaining screws and remove the handbrake handle.
44 Referring to Figs. 13.125 and 13.126 remove screws 3, 8, 9, 10, 11, 12, 14 and 15.
45 Detach the wiring harness connectors to the dashboard and then carefully withdraw and remove the dashboard.
46 Refit the dashboard in the reverse order to removal, ensuring that the various wiring connections are securely made. Reconnect the speedometer cable by inserting your hand through the loudspeaker grille panel aperture.
47 On completion check the satisfactory operation of the various instruments and controls, the choke control and the handbrake.

Bonnet – removal and refitting

48 Raise the bonnet and get an assistant to support it by hand, then disconnect the strut rod.
49 Pencil mark an outline of the hinge positions on the bonnet to assist realignment during refitting.
50 Disconnect the screen washer hoses at the nozzles then unscrew and remove the bonnet hinge retaining bolts. Lift the bonnet clear.
51 Refit in reverse order of removal. Semi-tighten the hinge bolts at first, then check that the bonnet is correctly aligned before finally tightening them fully. On completion check that the bonnet closes and locks correctly and that the release and safety catch operation is satisfactory. Also check that the screen washers operate satisfactorily and check the supply hoses for any signs of leaks.

Fault diagnosis

Introduction

The vehicle owner who does his or her own maintenance according to the recommended schedules should not have to use this section of the manual very often. Modern component reliability is such that, provided those items subject to wear or deterioration are inspected or renewed at the specified intervals, sudden failure is comparatively rare. Faults do not usually just happen as a result of sudden failure, but develop over a period of time. Major mechanical failures in particular are usually preceded by characteristic symptoms over hundreds or even thousands of miles. Those components which do occasionally fail without warning are often small and easily carried in the vehicle.

With any fault finding, the first step is to decide where to begin investigations. Sometimes this is obvious, but on other occasions a little detective work will be necessary. The owner who makes half a dozen haphazard adjustments or replacements may be successful in curing a fault (or its symptoms), but he will be none the wiser if the fault recurs and he may well have spent more time and money than was necessary. A calm and logical approach will be found to be more satisfactory in the long run. Always take into account any warning signs or abnormalities that may have been noticed in the period preceding the fault – power loss, high or low gauge readings, unusual noises or smells, etc – and remember that failure of components such as fuses or spark plugs may only be pointers to some underlying fault.

The pages which follow here are intended to help in cases of failure to start or breakdown on the road. There is also a Fault Diagnosis Section at the end of each Chapter which should be consulted if the preliminary checks prove unfruitful. Whatever the fault, certain basic principles apply. These are as follows:

Verify the fault. This is simply a matter of being sure that you know what the symptoms are before starting work. This is particularly important if you are investigating a fault for someone else who may not have described it very accurately.

Don't overlook the obvious. For example, if the vehicle won't start, is there petrol in the tank? (Don't take anyone else's word on this particular point, and don't trust the fuel gauge either!) If an electrical fault is indicated, look for loose or broken wires before digging out the test gear.

Cure the disease, not the symptom. Substituting a flat battery with a fully charged one will get you off the hard shoulder, but if the underlying cause is not attended to, the new battery will go the same way. Similarly, changing oil-fouled spark plugs for a new set will get you moving again, but remember that the reason for the fouling (if it wasn't simply an incorrect grade of plug) will have to be established and corrected.

Don't take anything for granted. Particularly, don't forget that a 'new' component may itself be defective (especially if it's been rattling round in the boot for months), and don't leave components out of a fault diagnosis sequence just because they are new or recently fitted. When you do finally diagnose a difficult fault, you'll probably realise that all the evidence was there from the start.

Electrical faults

Electrical faults can be more puzzling than straightforward mechanical failures, but they are no less susceptible to logical analysis if the basic principles of operation are understood. Vehicle electrical wiring exists in extremely unfavourable conditions – heat, vibration and

A few spares carried in the car can save you a long walk!

chemical attack – and the first things to look for are loose or corroded connections and broken or chafed wires, especially where the wires pass through holes in the bodywork or are subject to vibration.

All metal-bodied vehicles in current production have one pole of the battery 'earthed', ie connected to the vehicle bodywork, and in nearly all modern vehicles it is the negative (–) terminal. The various electrical components – motors, bulb holders etc – are also connected to earth, either by means of a lead or directly by their mountings. Electric current flows through the component and then back to the battery via the bodywork. If the component mounting is loose or corroded, or if a good path back to the battery is not available, the circuit will be incomplete and malfunction will result. The engine and/or gearbox are also earthed by means of flexible metal straps to the body or subframe; if these straps are loose or missing, starter motor, generator and ignition trouble may result.

Assuming the earth return to be satisfactory, electrical faults will be due either to component malfunction or to defects in the current supply. Individual components are dealt with in Chapter 10. If supply wires are broken or cracked internally this results in an open-circuit, and the easiest way to check for this is to bypass the suspect wire temporarily with a length of wire having a crocodile clip or suitable connector at each end. Alternatively, a 12V test lamp can be used to verify the presence of supply voltage at various points along the wire and the break can be thus isolated.

If a bare portion of a live wire touches the bodywork or other earthed metal part, the electricity will take the low-resistance path thus formed back to the battery: this is known as a short-circuit. Hopefully a short-circuit will blow a fuse, but otherwise it may cause burning of the insulation (and possibly further short-circuits) or even a fire. This is why it is inadvisable to bypass persistently blowing fuses with silver foil or wire.

Spares and tool kit

Most vehicles are supplied only with sufficient tools for wheel changing; the *Maintenance and minor repair* tool kit detailed in *Tools and working facilities,* with the addition of a hammer, is probably sufficient for those repairs that most motorists would consider attempting at the roadside. In addition a few items which can be fitted without too much trouble in the event of a breakdown should be carried. Experience and available space will modify the list below, but the following may save having to call on professional assistance:

Spark plugs, clean and correctly gapped
HT lead and plug cap – long enough to reach the plug furthest from the distributor
Distributor rotor, condenser and contact breaker points
Drivebelt(s) – emergency type may suffice
Spare fuses
Set of principal light bulbs
Exhaust bandage
Roll of insulating tape
Length of soft iron wire
Length of electrical flex
Torch or inspection lamp (can double as test lamp)
Battery jump leads
Tow-rope
Ignition waterproofing aerosol
Litre of engine oil
Sealed can of hydraulic fluid
Emergency windscreen
'Jubilee' clips
Tube of filler paste

If spare fuel is carried, a can designed for the purpose should be used to minimise risks of leakage and collision damage. A first aid kit and a warning triangle, whilst not at present compulsory in the UK, are obviously sensible items to carry in addition to the above.

When touring abroad it may be advisable to carry additional spares which, even if you cannot fit them yourself, could save having to wait while parts are obtained. The items below may be worth considering:

Clutch and throttle cables
Alternator brushes
Tyre valve core

One of the motoring organisations will be able to advise on availability of fuel etc in foreign countries.

A simple test lamp is useful for tracing electrical faults

Jump start lead connections for negative earth vehicles – connect leads in order shown

Engine will not start

Engine fails to turn when starter operated
Flat battery (recharge, use jump leads, or push start)
Battery terminals loose or corroded
Battery earth to body defective
Engine earth strap loose or broken
Starter motor (or solenoid) wiring loose or broken
Automatic transmission selector in wrong position, or inhibitor switch faulty
Ignition/starter switch faulty
Major mechanical failure (seizure)
Starter or solenoid internal fault (see Chapter 10)

Starter motor turns engine slowly
Partially discharged battery (recharge, use jump leads, starting handle, or push start)
Battery terminals loose or corroded
Battery earth to body defective
Engine earth strap loose
Starter motor (or solenoid) wiring loose
Starter motor internal fault (see Chapter 10)

Starter motor spins without turning engine
Flat battery
Starter motor pinion sticking on sleeve

Flywheel gear teeth damaged or worn
Starter motor mounting bolts loose

Engine turns normally but fails to start

Damp or dirty HT leads and distributor cap (crank engine and check for spark)
Dirty or incorrectly gapped distributor points (if applicable)
No fuel in tank (check for delivery at carburettor)
Excessive choke (hot engine) or insufficient choke (cold engine)
Fouled or incorrectly gapped spark plugs (remove, clean and regap)
Other ignition system fault (see Chapter 3)
Other fuel system fault (see Chapter 2)
Poor compression (see Chapter 1)
Major mechanical failure (eg camshaft drive)

Engine fires but will not run

Insufficient choke (cold engine)
Air leaks at carburettor or inlet manifold
Fuel starvation (see Chapter 2)
Ballast resistor defective, or other ignition fault (see Chapter 3)

Engine cuts out and will not restart

Engine cuts out suddenly – ignition fault

Loose or disconnected LT wires
Wet HT leads or distributor cap (after traversing water splash)
Coil or condenser failure (check for spark)
Other ignition fault (see Chapter 3)

Engine misfires before cutting out – fuel fault

Fuel tank empty
Fuel pump defective or filter blocked (check for delivery)
Fuel tank filler vent blocked (suction will be evident on releasing cap)
Carburettor needle valve sticking
Carburettor jets blocked (fuel contaminated)
Other fuel system fault (see Chapter 2)

Engine cuts out – other causes

Serious overheating
Major mechanical failure (eg camshaft drive)

Engine overheats

Low oil level
Oil cooler blocked
Engine cowling loose
Fan damaged

Brakes binding
Ignition timing incorrect or automatic advance malfunctioning
Mixture too weak

Low engine oil pressure

Warning light illuminated with engine running

Oil level low or incorrect grade
Defective gauge or sender unit
Wire to sender unit earthed
Engine overheating
Oil filter clogged or bypass valve defective
Oil pressure relief valve defective
Oil pick-up strainer clogged
Oil pump worn or mountings loose
Worn main or big-end bearings

Note: *Low oil pressure in a high-mileage engine at tickover is not necessarily a cause for concern. Sudden pressure loss at speed is far more significant. In any event, check the gauge or warning light sender before condemning the engine.*

Engine noises

Pre-ignition (pinking) on acceleration

Incorrect grade of fuel
Ignition timing incorrect
Distributor faulty or worn
Worn or maladjusted carburettor
Excessive carbon build-up in engine

Whistling or wheezing noises

Leaking vacuum hose
Leaking carburettor or manifold gasket
Blowing head gasket

Tapping or rattling

Incorrect valve clearances
Worn valve gear
Broken piston ring (ticking noise)

Knocking or thumping

Unintentional mechanical contact (eg fan blades)
Worn fanbelt
Peripheral component fault (generator, etc)
Worn big-end bearings (regular heavy knocking, perhaps less under load)
Worn main bearings (rumbling and knocking, perhaps worsening under load)
Piston slap (most noticeable when cold)

Jacking and Towing

Jacking

The jack supplied with the car when new is intended for roadside wheel changing only. The jack is located in the spare wheel and its handle on the right-hand wheel arch. When jacking up to change a roadwheel first apply the handbrake which, it should be noted, operates on the front wheels. Run the engine at its idle speed and move the ground clearance adjustment lever to its maximum height setting position (rearmost notch). Once the car has risen to its maximum height the jack can then be engaged with its location slot at the rear of the central pillar and extended so that it just touches the ground. Now loosen off the wheel nuts (without removing them completely), raise the jack so that the wheel to be changed is clear of the ground, then remove the nuts and the wheel.

Whenever the roadwheels are being changed, it is advisable to chock the wheel diagonally opposite the one being removed, particularly on uneven ground.

Fit the replacement wheel, tighten the nuts so that the wheel is secured in position then lower and remove the jack. Fully tighten the roadwheel nuts to complete and lower the suspension height setting to its normal position.

To raise the car for maintenance or overhaul, use a trolley or pillar jack and supplement with safety stands positioned just to the rear of the front wheel arch and/or just forwards of the rear wheel arch as applicable. Whenever working underneath the vehicle it is most important that these points are observed. Do not rely solely on the maximum height setting of the manually adjustable integral ride height control.

Towing

Towing another vehicle is not recommended at all. The rear 'towing' hook is in fact a lashing eye for use during transportation on a vehicle carrier.

If your car must be towed in an emergency, use a proper towing rope attached to the front towing eye. Unlock the steering column before moving and remember that after the first few brake applications, the servo assistance will not be available and harder than normal foot pedal pressures will be required.

Do not remove the ignition key when being towed - this will automatically lock the steering.

On models fitted with semi-automatic (C-matic) transmission the vehicle should not be towed in excess of 20 mph and the maximum towing distance must not exceed 12 miles. Position the gearchange lever in the neutral setting. Citroen recommend 'wheel-up' towing for models with this transmission wherever possible.

Jacking points:

A — Lift points for trolley jack or support point for hoist rails
B — Lift point for vehicle jack or axle stand (after raising vehicle)

Safety first!

Professional motor mechanics are trained in safe working procedures. However enthusiastic you may be about getting on with the job in hand, do take the time to ensure that your safety is not put at risk. A moment's lack of attention can result in an accident, as can failure to observe certain elementary precautions.

There will always be new ways of having accidents, and the following points do not pretend to be a comprehensive list of all dangers; they are intended rather to make you aware of the risks and to encourage a safety-conscious approach to all work you carry out on your vehicle.

Essential DOs and DON'Ts

DON'T rely on a single jack when working underneath the vehicle. Always use reliable additional means of support, such as axle stands, securely placed under a part of the vehicle that you know will not give way.

DON'T attempt to loosen or tighten high-torque nuts (e.g. wheel hub nuts) while the vehicle is on a jack; it may be pulled off.

DON'T start the engine without first ascertaining that the transmission is in neutral (or 'Park' where applicable) and the parking brake applied.

DON'T suddenly remove the filler cap from a hot cooling system – cover it with a cloth and release the pressure gradually first, or you may get scalded by escaping coolant.

DON'T attempt to drain oil until you are sure it has cooled sufficiently to avoid scalding you.

DON'T grasp any part of the engine, exhaust or catalytic converter without first ascertaining that it is sufficiently cool to avoid burning you.

DON'T allow brake fluid or antifreeze to contact vehicle paintwork.

DON'T syphon toxic liquids such as fuel, brake fluid or antifreeze by mouth, or allow them to remain on your skin.

DON'T inhale dust – it may be injurious to health (see *Asbestos* below).

DON'T allow any spilt oil or grease to remain on the floor – wipe it up straight away, before someone slips on it.

DON'T use ill-fitting spanners or other tools which may slip and cause injury.

DON'T attempt to lift a heavy component which may be beyond your capability – get assistance.

DON'T rush to finish a job, or take unverified short cuts.

DON'T allow children or animals in or around an unattended vehicle.

DO wear eye protection when using power tools such as drill, sander, bench grinder etc, and when working under the vehicle.

DO use a barrier cream on your hands prior to undertaking dirty jobs – it will protect your skin from infection as well as making the dirt easier to remove afterwards; but make sure your hands aren't left slippery.

DO keep loose clothing (cuffs, tie etc) and long hair well out of the way of moving mechanical parts.

DO remove rings, wristwatch etc, before working on the vehicle – especially the electrical system.

DO ensure that any lifting tackle used has a safe working load rating adequate for the job.

DO keep your work area tidy – it is only too easy to fall over articles left lying around.

DO get someone to check periodically that all is well, when working alone on the vehicle.

DO carry out work in a logical sequence and check that everything is correctly assembled and tightened afterwards.

DO remember that your vehicle's safety affects that of yourself and others. If in doubt on any point, get specialist advice.

IF, in spite of following these precautions, you are unfortunate enough to injure yourself, seek medical attention as soon as possible.

Asbestos

Certain friction, insulating, sealing, and other products – such as brake linings, brake bands, clutch linings, torque converters, gaskets, etc – contain asbestos. *Extreme care must be taken to avoid inhalation of dust from such products since it is hazardous to health.* If in doubt, assume that they *do* contain asbestos.

Fire

Remember at all times that petrol (gasoline) is highly flammable. Never smoke, or have any kind of naked flame around, when working on the vehicle. But the risk does not end there – a spark caused by an electrical short-circuit, by two metal surfaces contacting each other, by careless use of tools, or even by static electricity built up in your body under certain conditions, can ignite petrol vapour, which in a confined space is highly explosive.

Always disconnect the battery earth (ground) terminal before working on any part of the fuel or electrical system, and never risk spilling fuel on to a hot engine or exhaust.

It is recommended that a fire extinguisher of a type suitable for fuel and electrical fires is kept handy in the garage or workplace at all times. Never try to extinguish a fuel or electrical fire with water.

Fumes

Certain fumes are highly toxic and can quickly cause unconsciousness and even death if inhaled to any extent. Petrol (gasoline) vapour comes into this category, as do the vapours from certain solvents such as trichloroethylene. Any draining or pouring of such volatile fluids should be done in a well ventilated area.

When using cleaning fluids and solvents, read the instructions carefully. Never use materials from unmarked containers – they may give off poisonous vapours.

Never run the engine of a motor vehicle in an enclosed space such as a garage. Exhaust fumes contain carbon monoxide which is extremely poisonous; if you need to run the engine, always do so in the open air or at least have the rear of the vehicle outside the workplace.

If you are fortunate enough to have the use of an inspection pit, never drain or pour petrol, and never run the engine, while the vehicle is standing over it; the fumes, being heavier than air, will concentrate in the pit with possibly lethal results.

The battery

Never cause a spark, or allow a naked light, near the vehicle's battery. It will normally be giving off a certain amount of hydrogen gas, which is highly explosive.

Always disconnect the battery earth (ground) terminal before working on the fuel or electrical systems.

If possible, loosen the filler plugs or cover when charging the battery from an external source. Do not charge at an excessive rate or the battery may burst.

Take care when topping up and when carrying the battery. The acid electrolyte, even when diluted, is very corrosive and should not be allowed to contact the eyes or skin.

If you ever need to prepare electrolyte yourself, always add the acid slowly to the water, and never the other way round. Protect against splashes by wearing rubber gloves and goggles.

When jump starting a car using a booster battery, for negative earth (ground) vehicles, connect the jump leads in the following sequence: First connect one jump lead between the positive (+) terminals of the two batteries. Then connect the other jump lead first to the negative (–) terminal of the booster battery, and then to a good earthing (ground) point on the vehicle to be started, at least 18 in (45 cm) from the battery if possible. Ensure that hands and jump leads are clear of any moving parts, and that the two vehicles do not touch. Disconnect the leads in the reverse order.

Mains electricity

When using an electric power tool, inspection light etc, which works from the mains, always ensure that the appliance is correctly connected to its plug and that, where necessary, it is properly earthed (grounded). Do not use such appliances in damp conditions and, again, beware of creating a spark or applying excessive heat in the vicinity of fuel or fuel vapour.

Ignition HT voltage

A severe electric shock can result from touching certain parts of the ignition system, such as the HT leads, when the engine is running or being cranked, particularly if components are damp or the insulation is defective. Where an electronic ignition system is fitted, the HT voltage is much higher and could prove fatal.

General repair procedures

Whenever servicing, repair or overhaul work is carried out on the car or its components, it is necessary to observe the following procedures and instructions. This will assist in carrying out the operation efficiently and to a professional standard of workmanship.

Joint mating faces and gaskets

Where a gasket is used between the mating faces of two components, ensure that it is renewed on reassembly, and fit it dry unless otherwise stated in the repair procedure. Make sure that the mating faces are clean and dry with all traces of old gasket removed. When cleaning a joint face, use a tool which is not likely to score or damage the face, and remove any burrs or nicks with an oilstone or fine file.

Make sure that tapped holes are cleaned with a pipe cleaner, and keep them free of jointing compound if this is being used unless specifically instructed otherwise.

Ensure that all orifices, channels or pipes are clear and blow through them, preferably using compressed air.

Oil seals

Whenever an oil seal is removed from its working location, either individually or as part of an assembly, it should be renewed.

The very fine sealing lip of the seal is easily damaged and will not seal if the surface it contacts is not completely clean and free from scratches, nicks or grooves. If the original sealing surface of the component cannot be restored, the component should be renewed.

Protect the lips of the seal from any surface which may damage them in the course of fitting. Use tape or a conical sleeve where possible. Lubricate the seal lips with oil before fitting and, on dual lipped seals, fill the space between the lips with grease.

Unless otherwise stated, oil seals must be fitted with their sealing lips toward the lubricant to be sealed.

Use a tubular drift or block of wood of the appropriate size to install the seal and, if the seal housing is shouldered, drive the seal down to the shoulder. If the seal housing is unshouldered, the seal should be fitted with its face flush with the housing top face.

Screw threads and fastenings

Always ensure that a blind tapped hole is completely free from oil, grease, water or other fluid before installing the bolt or stud. Failure to do this could cause the housing to crack due to the hydraulic action of the bolt or stud as it is screwed in.

When tightening a castellated nut to accept a split pin, tighten the nut to the specified torque, where applicable, and then tighten further to the next split pin hole. Never slacken the nut to align a split pin hole unless stated in the repair procedure.

When checking or retightening a nut or bolt to a specified torque setting, slacken the nut or bolt by a quarter of a turn, and then retighten to the specified setting.

Locknuts, locktabs and washers

Any fastening which will rotate against a component or housing in the course of tightening should always have a washer between it and the relevant component or housing.

Spring or split washers should always be renewed when they are used to lock a critical component such as a big-end bearing retaining nut or bolt.

Locktabs which are folded over to retain a nut or bolt should always be renewed.

Self-locking nuts can be reused in non-critical areas, providing resistance can be felt when the locking portion passes over the bolt or stud thread.

Split pins must always be replaced with new ones of the correct size for the hole.

Special tools

Some repair procedures in this manual entail the use of special tools such as a press, two or three-legged pullers, spring compressors etc. Wherever possible, suitable readily available alternatives to the manufacturer's special tools are described, and are shown in use. In some instances, where no alternative is possible, it has been necessary to resort to the use of a manufacturer's tool and this has been done for reasons of safety as well as the efficient completion of the repair operation. Unless you are highly skilled and have a thorough understanding of the procedure described, never attempt to bypass the use of any special tool when the procedure described specifies its use. Not only is there a very great risk of personal injury, but expensive damage could be caused to the components involved.

Conversion factors

Length (distance)

Inches (in)	X	25.4	= Millimetres (mm)	X	0.0394	= Inches (in)
Feet (ft)	X	0.305	= Metres (m)	X	3.281	= Feet (ft)
Miles	X	1.609	= Kilometres (km)	X	0.621	= Miles

Length (distance)
- Inches (in) X 25.4 = Millimetres (mm) — X 0.0394 = Inches (in)
- Feet (ft) X 0.305 = Metres (m) — X 3.281 = Feet (ft)
- Miles X 1.609 = Kilometres (km) — X 0.621 = Miles

Volume (capacity)
- Cubic inches (cu in; in^3) X 16.387 = Cubic centimetres (cc; cm^3) — X 0.061 = Cubic inches (cu in; in^3)
- Imperial pints (Imp pt) X 0.568 = Litres (l) — X 1.76 = Imperial pints (Imp pt)
- Imperial quarts (Imp qt) X 1.137 = Litres (l) — X 0.88 = Imperial quarts (Imp qt)
- Imperial quarts (Imp qt) X 1.201 = US quarts (US qt) — X 0.833 = Imperial quarts (Imp qt)
- US quarts (US qt) X 0.946 = Litres (l) — X 1.057 = US quarts (US qt)
- Imperial gallons (Imp gal) X 4.546 = Litres (l) — X 0.22 = Imperial gallons (Imp gal)
- Imperial gallons (Imp gal) X 1.201 = US gallons (US gal) — X 0.833 = Imperial gallons (Imp gal)
- US gallons (US gal) X 3.785 = Litres (l) — X 0.264 = US gallons (US gal)

Mass (weight)
- Ounces (oz) X 28.35 = Grams (g) — X 0.035 = Ounces (oz)
- Pounds (lb) X 0.454 = Kilograms (kg) — X 2.205 = Pounds (lb)

Force
- Ounces-force (ozf; oz) X 0.278 = Newtons (N) — X 3.6 = Ounces-force (ozf; oz)
- Pounds-force (lbf; lb) X 4.448 = Newtons (N) — X 0.225 = Pounds-force (lbf; lb)
- Newtons (N) X 0.1 = Kilograms-force (kgf; kg) — X 9.81 = Newtons (N)

Pressure
- Pounds-force per square inch (psi; lbf/in^2; lb/in^2) X 0.070 = Kilograms-force per square centimetre (kgf/cm^2; kg/cm^2) — X 14.223 = Pounds-force per square inch (psi; lbf/in^2; lb/in^2)
- Pounds-force per square inch (psi; lbf/in^2; lb/in^2) X 0.068 = Atmospheres (atm) — X 14.696 = Pounds-force per square inch (psi; lbf/in^2; lb/in^2)
- Pounds-force per square inch (psi; lbf/in^2; lb/in^2) X 0.069 = Bars — X 14.5 = Pounds-force per square inch (psi; lbf/in^2; lb/in^2)
- Pounds-force per square inch (psi; lbf/in^2; lb/in^2) X 6.895 = Kilopascals (kPa) — X 0.145 = Pounds-force per square inch (psi; lbf/in^2; lb/in^2)
- Kilopascals (kPa) X 0.01 = Kilograms-force per square centimetre (kgf/cm^2; kg/cm^2) — X 98.1 = Kilopascals (kPa)

Torque (moment of force)
- Pounds-force inches (lbf in; lb in) X 1.152 = Kilograms-force centimetre (kgf cm; kg cm) — X 0.868 = Pounds-force inches (lbf in; lb in)
- Pounds-force inches (lbf in; lb in) X 0.113 = Newton metres (Nm) — X 8.85 = Pounds-force inches (lbf in; lb in)
- Pounds-force inches (lbf in; lb in) X 0.083 = Pounds-force feet (lbf ft; lb ft) — X 12 = Pounds-force inches (lbf in; lb in)
- Pounds-force feet (lbf ft; lb ft) X 0.138 = Kilograms-force metres (kgf m; kg m) — X 7.233 = Pounds-force feet (lbf ft; lb ft)
- Pounds-force feet (lbf ft; lb ft) X 1.356 = Newton metres (Nm) — X 0.738 = Pounds-force feet (lbf ft; lb ft)
- Newton metres (Nm) X 0.102 = Kilograms-force metres (kgf m; kg m) — X 9.804 = Newton metres (Nm)

Power
- Horsepower (hp) X 745.7 = Watts (W) — X 0.0013 = Horsepower (hp)

Velocity (speed)
- Miles per hour (miles/hr; mph) X 1.609 = Kilometres per hour (km/hr; kph) — X 0.621 = Miles per hour (miles/hr; mph)

Fuel consumption*
- Miles per gallon, Imperial (mpg) X 0.354 = Kilometres per litre (km/l) — X 2.825 = Miles per gallon, Imperial (mpg)
- Miles per gallon, US (mpg) X 0.425 = Kilometres per litre (km/l) — X 2.352 = Miles per gallon, US (mpg)

Temperature
Degrees Fahrenheit = (°C x 1.8) + 32   Degrees Celsius (Degrees Centigrade; °C) = (°F - 32) x 0.56

*It is common practice to convert from miles per gallon (mpg) to litres/100 kilometres (l/100km), where mpg (Imperial) x l/100 km = 282 and mpg (US) x l/100 km = 235

Index